'FOR EVERY SAILOR AFLOAT, EVERY SOLDIER AT THE FRONT'

'FOR EVERY SAILOR AFLOAT, EVERY SOLDIER AT THE FRONT'

Princess Mary's Christmas Gift, 1914

PETER DOYLE

UNIFORM

Note on currency and weights:–

Throughout the text, the original pre-decimal currency values and weights are retained.

British Currency at the time was pounds (£) shillings (s) and pence (d). There were twelve pennies in a shilling, twenty shillings in a pound, and 240 pennies in a pound. A guinea was a pound and one shilling.

British Weights were given in tons (t), hundredweights (cwt), quarters (qtr), pounds (lb) and ounces (oz). There were sixteen ounces in a pound, twenty-eight pounds in a quarter, four quarters in a hundredweight, and twenty hundredweights in a ton.

Contents

'I want you all now to help me send a Christmas present from the whole nation to every sailor afloat and every soldier at the front… Please will you help me?'

HRH Princess Mary, 15 October 1914

'Please, will you help me?'

PRINCESS MARY WAS BORN at York Cottage, Sandringham on 25 April 1897. Quiet, dutiful and shy, Mary would grow to become one of the most respected senior members of the Royal Family – yet, despite her selfless devotion to significant causes – one of its least known.

The Princess in some ways remains an enigma, a royal whose biographies were written a hundred years apart. Though anyone with an interest in the Great War will surely have heard of her – and of the brass box that carries her image – so very few will know anything more about her life, and her dedication to duty. And all too often Mary will be confused with her mother and namesake, a Queen who had such a direct influence on her children, her husband and her country. Nevertheless, there are signs that Princess Mary is starting to emerge from behind the huge reputation of her mother.

Mary was the third child and only daughter of the couple who were destined to become King George V and his consort, Queen Mary. Ascending to the throne on the death of King Edward VII in 1910, George became king in a decade that would be overshadowed by war. Less glamorous and more stolid than his father, the King's serious demeanour was nevertheless in keeping with a war that would touch the lives of most of his subjects, the Royal Family itself not immune from its effects. Only too aware of the enormity of the conflict, and perhaps seeking community with the troops that served in his name, King George V became a frequent visitor to the Western Front, his steel-helmeted figure familiar to the men of his army, his devotion to duty self-evident.[1]

The royal couple were blessed with their only daughter in the jubilee year of her great grandmother, and, accordingly, she was named Princess Victoria Alexandra Alice Mary – a

YORK COTTAGE Sandringham, birthplace of Princess Mary

veritable compendium of royal names.[2] Famously, the Princess's birth was received with delight by the old Queen, who referred to her as: 'My dear little Diamond Jubilee baby' and the name 'Diamond' was at least entertained for the cherished new arrival, in remembrance of the event.[3] It is perhaps fortunate that this idea soon dissipated – especially for a girl who would become the serious and practical-minded young woman destined to be an inspiration to others. On the death of the royal matriarch in 1901, the young Victoria Mary reverted simply to Mary, named for her mother – an incredible role model for the young princess.

Mary's parents have often been labelled as taciturn, unfeeling and unemotional, but most biographers who have examined these reputations have largely rejected them. Instead, a more nuanced picture is painted of a deeply committed couple; committed to duty, yes, and to the citizens of the Empire, but also to the upbringing of their family. There is ample evidence that the Royal parents 'played more of a hands-on role with their children than most of their contemporaries', and it is clear

PRINCESS MARY AND HER SIBLINGS Prince Albert ('Bertie'), Prince Edward ('David') and Prince Henry

that the couple adopted a pattern of 'simple domesticity,' that had a positive impact on their family.[4] If further evidence was required, surviving letters provide an insight into the genuine love the Princess had for her parents, as one such letter from Mary to her mother, written in 1901, indicates: 'we shall be so pleased when you come home, we are going to hang our flags out of the house windows the day you come home. I send you and Papa a bear hug and a fat kiss.'[5]

King George V and Queen Mary

If she was shy with her father, the King, she became inseparable from her older brothers, David and Bertie, themselves destined to be kings, with Mary well capable of holding her own in sports and domestic arguments.[9]

Clearly there was a strong family bond, one that would be significant in the life of the young Princess:

No girl in the land has been brought up more carefully and lovingly than the Princess, and no girl loves her home more than she, and in the journey through life that stretches before her that love of home, her parents and brothers, is sure to remain a deep and abiding influence with her Royal Highness.[10]

There are indications that the King could indeed be harsh towards his children, but others suggest positive affection from Mary for her father while she was growing up.[6] For instance, writing in 1912, King George expressed satisfaction that he had 'invited her to come and sit in my room while I write, she is coming now, and seems pleased at the idea…'.[7] And by 1914, any reticence Mary might have felt towards her father had subsided, the young Princess taking time to ride with him.[8]

The King and Queen were steeped in the principles of honour and duty; principles that would be passed on, with varied success, to their children.[11] For example, it was reported that 'Queen Mary's dominant characteristics were patriotism, a love of order, an earnest desire to relieve distress and a concern about social conditions' – characteristics that her daughter would, in many ways, emulate.[12] There can be no doubt then, that this

PRINCESS MARY C.1913

close relationship with her parents – though perhaps at times somewhat cloying – was a positive influence on Mary's commitment to dutiful engagement in national service.[13] And from this background, Mary would rise as a reserved star, largely untainted by drama or acrimony.[14]

Mary was a bright young person. As a child she was described by Madame Poincaré, wife of the future President of France, as 'la belle rose anglaise', replete as she was with 'blue eyes, golden curls, and rosy cheeks'.[15] In these respects the young Princess was often compared with the Queen, described as 'the image of her mother in looks, kindness and her shyness'.[16] Nevertheless, perhaps to forge her own identity, Mary's long curls would soon be replaced by a fashionable bobbed style in the post-war era.[17]

The Princess was not one to play on her fresh, natural demeanour, and she applied her attention to her studies, practical, domestic and academic. The young Princess's curriculum was designed largely by her mother, in order to 'prepare her for every eventuality' and to allow her to develop a social conscience.[18] For instance, by the time she was eight, Mary 'could sew and knit [and] write a bold round hand'.[19] At this stage in her development she shared her beloved brothers' tutor. Later, she was schooled by a Governess, her chief lessons literature, geography and history.[20] Mary was educated for the new world she would soon inhabit; capable of typing and shorthand, fluent in French, and an able sportswoman.[21]

These practical studies set her in good stead – though perhaps at a cost. Writing in 1915, journalist W.T. Roberts commented: 'The whole training and upbringing of the Princess has tended to make her a rather serious-minded young person – a tendency that, has been perhaps accentuated by the fact that the Princess's intimate girl companions have been necessarily few, and these have been rather older than herself.'[22] Shyness and reticence remained with Mary throughout her life; perhaps evident in her marriage to an older husband, the Viscount Lascelles in 1922, and in her own dealings with her children, who grew up without over demonstrative emotions.[23] Despite this there is real joy in her eyes, quietly expressed, and self-evident in the official photographs reproduced as

DOWNING STREET, AUGUST 1914 – crowds wait in anticipation of war news.

postcards for a clamouring public following her children's arrival.

Mary developed an appreciation for aesthetics and the arts that would later become the focus of much of her attention during her married life.[24] One of her early biographers noted 'Her inherent love of the beautiful has given her a capacity for genuine artistic enjoyment', with a particular interest in old china.[25] It was recognised that, as with many aspects of her life, Queen Mary had influenced this, and particularly her 'remarkable

gifts for interior decoration'.[26] All of her artistic and creative endeavours no doubt had a bearing on the development and design of the Princess's Christmas Gift, one of her most enduring and significant achievements; her opinion must surely have been sought on its design.

When war came in 1914, it came right up to the gates of Buckingham Palace; and the Princess was there to record the occasion in her diary, in what was evidently her typical, no-nonsense style:

4 August 1914 Buckingham Palace, London. Fine day. There was a large crowd at 8pm in front of the Palace so Papa and Mama went out onto the balcony; the crowd was larger than the night before and they cheered tremendously. Another crowd collected at about 9:30pm, they sang, cheered and clapped incessantly and asked to see Papa, as they heard that Germany had declared war against England. At 11.15pm, Papa and Mama went on the balcony; the crowd was enormous and cheered enthusiastically.[27]

With the Great War darkening the world scene in 1914, Princess Mary was still just seventeen years old, an age which, 'in the ordinary course of events should have taken her place in the Royal Circle, on the occasion of her first Court after her eighteenth birthday in May 1915'.[28] This change of events no doubt had a significant effect on the young woman, who was suddenly propelled into a new world:

There has been nothing so striking since the beginning of the year than the sudden development of Princess Mary from a schoolgirl but little known outside her family circle, into a calm and dignified young woman. In the words of a prominent member of the household 'She has grown up in three months.'[29]

With war, there was no time for formality; instead, Princess Mary became heavily involved in war work. Her studies and practical nature had prepared her for this. Naturally, from the war's outset, the work of her mother and her dedication to needlework had a direct influence, and Mary was soon engaged with the London Needlework Guild, a focus of her activity with her mother.[30] This was particularly the case in despatching 'comforts' for the troops – knitted items, socks, mufflers, balaclavas and the like – which brought an appreciation of the needs of the men at the front and at sea. Mary was noted as having a 'tender heart', and sensitive to suffering, the deepening casualty lists making a deep impression upon her, despite her tender years.[31]

The combination of her interest and empathy undoubtedly led to her desire to develop her own gift for the Sailors and Soldiers of the Empire. Mary would become forever associated with the gift that has so much become part of the mythology of 1914. But her direct engagement with the war did not end there. In its last year, 1918, and on her twenty-first birthday, Mary 'ceased to be just a Royal sister and daughter', and 'entered with enthusiasm into hospital and nursing work with … thorough and conscientious energy'.[32] The young Princess asked her father if she could train as a nurse; she duly became the first daughter of a monarch to undertake the rigorous training required.[33] This training would stand her in good stead. Queen Mary visited Great Ormond Street on 10 August 1918, observing with great surprise her daughter carrying out her medical duties 'in the quietest, most composed manner'.[34]

PRINCESS MARY 1914

From 1914 to its end, Princess Mary had grown to take her part in this war, not just in the development of the Gift Fund that she is so often associated with, but also in numerous other activities that inspired a generation of young women; as a nurse, as a supporter of women's work, and as a role model for youth.

The remarkable story of the Princess's Christmas Gift started with a simple appeal to the nation.

On 16 October 1914, *The Daily Mirror* – a popular illustrated tabloid newspaper which, boldly, proclaimed its circulation of 'more than 1,000,000 copies – published the deliberations of a Committee set up to oversee a new public appeal that was to support the war effort.[35] This press notice, and others like it, announced to the world the germination of an idea based on a simple letter: a letter

full of genuine pathos, a letter penned by the youthful Princess herself. Carefully composed on a single sheet of Buckingham Palace headed notepaper, and dated 15 October 1914, this letter was destined to be distributed widely across the Empire.[36]

In it, with youthful sentiment, Princess Mary announced that there would be a Christmas gift for all those sailors and soldiers on active service in the war in the first year of its existence:

For many weeks we have all been greatly concerned for the welfare of the sailors and soldiers who are so gallantly fighting our battles by sea and land.

Our first consideration has been to meet their more pressing needs and I have delayed making known a wish that has long been in my heart for fear of encroaching on other funds, the claims of which have been more urgent.

I want you all now to help me to send a Christmas

present from the whole nation to every sailor afloat and every soldier at the front.

On Christmas Eve when, like the shepherds of old, they keep their watch, doubtless their thoughts will turn to home and to the loved ones left behind, and perhaps, too, they will recall the days when as children themselves they were wont to hang out their stockings, wondering what the morrow had in store.

I am sure that we should all be the happier to feel that we had helped to send our little token of love and sympathy on Christmas morning, something that would be useful and of permanent value, and the making of which may be the means of providing employment in trades adversely affected by the war.

Could there be anything more likely to hearten them in their struggle than a present received straight from home on Christmas Day?

Please, will you help me?

Mary[37]

The Princess's fresh voice and her genuine feelings of the importance of Christmas shone through in her letter, which was autographed in her distinctive style.

By the time the Princess's Gift Fund had been announced, there were already in existence many competing charitable schemes that clamoured for the public's attention in the autumn of 1914. But here was something a little different, a national fund to deliver a gift to men (and later, women) who were serving their country on Christmas Day itself. And the letter's words provided sincere access to its originator; it seemed to link directly to the young woman herself, particularly through its compelling plea, '*Please will you help me?*'

Mary's appeal was no doubt designed to provide some mark of recognition of the sacrifices being made by the armed forces, some way of providing comfort to them under challenging circumstances, and perhaps also to serve as a permanent souvenir of participation in a global event for all those who were on active service at Christmas 1914. And that reference was made to the provision of employment for artisans and workers was reflective of the uncertainty of the war, and that there were hard times to come.

The Princess's letter was carried by most major newspapers. Occupying much of a column on the second page of the *Daily Mirror*, this announcement sat alongside pictorial reports of action on land, at sea, and in the air. [38] These served to emphasise just how much of a gulf there was between those at home, and those who faced danger daily in the front line or at sea. They would also, perhaps, give pause for thought for those who had loved ones placed in danger. With the war very much in progress, with bitter fights on land and at sea, this was a national appeal to mark Christmas born of a sense of duty that was very much uppermost in the Royal Household. For the *Mirror's* million readers, both reports hinted at the nature of the war that would consume millions of armed men before it was done.

HEAVY SOILS IN FLANDERS, 1914

On the front page, for instance, a gun battery in action depicted the on-going battle the British Expeditionary Force was having on the Western Front.[39] Since its engagement at Mons in August 1914, the BEF had fought fierce rear-guard actions at Le Cateau and had helped turn the tide at the Aisne between 12–15 September 1914, leading to the fighting that would become known as the Race to the Sea. A month later and the battles had shifted to Flanders. In northern France, near Armentières, and surrounding the Mediaeval city of Ypres, the opposing forces fought to establish control and to break through the fragile and developing defensive lines. Illustrated on the same page in this edition was the Royal Navy's light cruiser HMS *Yarmouth*, fresh from its triumph in sinking

HEAVY SEAS ON PATROL, 1914

the German cargo steamer *Markomannia* on 12 October near Sumatra. This German vessel had reputedly accompanied the *Emden*, a ship that had been leading the Royal Navy a merry dance in eastern seas (before the daring vessel's final grounding near Sumatra a month later).

Newspaper editorials published in the days that followed the first announcement of the appeal took it up with gusto, examining Mary's motivations and painting pictures of life at war as the world lurched towards Christmas. Drawing on the youth of its originator as a powerful tool, they leaned heavily on the pathos of absent sons to promote the aims of the appeal:

PRINCESS SANTA CLAUS

Let us think of Christmas for a little while; it is not many weeks ahead. Christmas, that season of peace and good will; of happy firesides, of feasting and laughter, the season of giving and forgiving; what will it mean to the men in the trenches, the men the North Sea this year. What a horrible mockery it will be, what a day of bitter memories and terrible regrets. Think of Christmas Eve closing with a hell of rifle fire; Christmas Day dawning cold and wan over the sullen waves of an angry sea. Then think of the waits, the cheerful shops, the morning post rich with cards and presents, the family reunion, plum pudding, snapdragon, laughter, happiness. Think of the two Christmases and try to realise what it is going to mean this year to the men at the front. There is a little lady who has considered all this problem already; she is our only princess – Princess Mary. She is little more than a schoolgirl, but she has taken it upon herself to be Santa Claus to the men of the trenches and the fleet.[40]

Importantly, this was an appeal that ultimately transcended race and gender, an appeal sensitive to religious observances and to the growing diversity of Britain's Imperial forces – particularly so as the Indian Army, volunteers to a man, was already in France:

It was their good fortune to arrive just at the moment when they were most needed; just when our troops were using their last reserves and fighting against terrible odds, in fact when two extra divisions could help to stem the tide.[41]

Mary's appeal would try and cater for all who served. But, in truth, it was not the Princess alone who would deliver the gift. That was for others to initiate. As a seventeen-year-old, the Princess no doubt drew very heavily upon the sense of patriotic duty upheld by her parents, and particularly on Queen Mary, who in the opening days of the war busied herself in helping to deliver on 'various relief schemes'.[42] The Royal Family was rightly proud of the war work of their offspring, and notably George V, who 'was devoted to his duty, and expected the same of his family', and who kept a record and map of their engagements as a matter of pride.[43] To support them, networks of influential people were assembled to provide a backbone to the body of their endeavours, assemblies of experienced men and women gathered to make their wishes reality.

The first meeting of the General Committee of HRH The Princess Mary's Gift Fund – and of the smaller Executive Committee that would deliver the Princess's aspirations – had actually been held two days before the publication of the appeal (and the day before the letter was circulated), in the Ballroom of the Ritz Hotel in London, on the evening of 14 October 1914. The carefully prepared, freehand minutes (together with the publication of the final report of its activities, in 1920) of that committee are some of the most important documents that relate to the Princess Mary Gift Fund; it is fortunate that these were handed over in their entirety to the then fledgling Imperial War Museum following the winding up of the Gift Fund some years later.[44]

The General Committee itself was composed of thirty-eight people of note, men and women, with senior representation from across the Empire, the Government of the United Kingdom, and the services. Nominally it included the Prime Minister, Asquith; Lord Kitchener, the Secretary of State for War; and Winston Churchill, First Lord of the Admiralty, as well as the High Commissioners of Australia, Canada, New Zealand and South Africa, and the Private Secretary to Queen Mary, E.W. Wallington.[45] Chaired by the Duke of Devonshire, the Committee also included members with specific skills who were no doubt gathered

KING GEORGE V IN FRANCE, 1918

together to deliver on the Princess's promise that this gift would be sent out to all 'sailors afloat, all soldiers at the front' by Christmas. These men included Hedley Le Bas, of the Caxton Advertising Agency, and Sir William Lever of Sunlight Soap and Port Sunlight fame. In addition to the usual array of powerful men, there were thirteen women; and at least two of them, Lady Jellicoe and Lady French – influential wives of the Admiral of the Grand Fleet and Field Marshal commanding the British Expeditionary Force in France respectively – would have major roles to play in shaping the fortunes of the Gift Fund.

In the fine Louis XIV-inspired surroundings of the grand hotel in Piccadilly, at the heart of the Empire, the business of the General Committee commenced at 17.00 sharp. HRH The Princess Mary was present. The fresh-faced seventeen-year-old princess must no doubt have been nervous, despite being accompanied by Queen Mary's most senior 'Woman-of-the-Bedchamber', the seventy-nine-year-old Lady-in-Waiting Lady Katherine Coke.[46] Lady Katherine

remained a member of the General Committee throughout, and was undoubtedly a close observer of developments – reporting back to the Queen herself.[47]

It was the first time Mary had attended a meeting *on her own* – and though presumably daunted by all the senior figures present, the Princess recorded this momentous event in her diary with typically understated simplicity:

14 October 1914. I went with Lady Katty and Mr Wallington to the Ritz Hotel, where there was a meeting of the General Committee of the 'Princess Mary's Sailors and Soldiers Christmas Fund'. The Duke of Devonshire is the chairman of the Committee. It was the first time I had been to a meeting alone. It went off very well…[48]

Lord Cavendish, Ninth Duke of Devonshire and a skilled politician, took the chair when invited to do so. He would ensure the proceedings would run smoothly over the next two years of the Fund's operation, until he took the role of Governor-General

THE ELEGANCE OF THE RITZ HOTEL, c. 1914

THE DUKE OF DEVONSHIRE

General, an office he held until 1921.[50] Taking up his senior position in 1916 meant that the Duke passed on the Chairmanship of the Gift Fund to Sir Edward Wallington; nevertheless, it is perhaps difficult to predict whether he knew what he was letting himself in for in Chairing the Princess's Gift Fund.[51]

John Baring, Second Baron Revelstoke, a director of the Bank of England and a partner in the city bank Baring Brothers Co. Ltd, was duly appointed, appropriately, as treasurer. Baring held several significant wartime roles, including as a negotiator with Imperial Russia to help shore up their war effort.[52] He would steer the financial aspects of the Fund. And as Secretary, there was Rowland Berkeley of Cotheridge, Worcestershire, a member of a venerable family and a descendant of many who bore the same name.[53] It is Berkeley's steady hand that mostly allows us to be confident about the working of the Committee in its opening meetings.

of Canada in 1916. Cavendish had been elected Liberal-Unionist member for West Derbyshire at the age of twenty-three in 1891, and had inherited his title on the death of his father in 1908. After Eton and Cambridge, Lord Cavendish studied both as an accountant and a lawyer, and this education provided him 'practical insight into the financial and legal sides of business' that would prepare him for his life ahead, and the 'administration of the vast estates that he was destined to inherit.'[49] Not surprisingly, the Duke held a number of public offices, including Civil Lord of the Admiralty (1915–1916), before becoming Governor-

In taking the Chair in the grand apartment of the Ritz ballroom, Devonshire wasted no time in announcing the intention of the Gift Fund, a well-formulated objective that had clearly been prepared well in advance of the meeting, which became the watchword of the Fund:

> The Chairman explained Her Royal Highness's wish to send a Christmas present to the sailors and soldiers at the front. The gift to take the form, should the funds permit it, of an embossed brass tobacco box, pipe, tinder lighter, tobacco, cigarettes and a Christmas Card.[54]

With the passage of time, it is difficult to determine the absolute moment of germination of the idea, and how the gift, so clearly defined in the Duke's announcement, had been so exactly formulated. Nevertheless, it is clear that Princess Mary's wishes had been listened to well in advance of this announcement in the Ritz Hotel, and guidance had been given to her, as a seventeen-year-old, to determine what would be possible and achievable.

But what is less clear is the detail of this guidance and the players involved. Where had it come from, and what had inspired her? There was a hint in her appeal letter, with its reference to other appeals: 'Our first consideration has been to meet their more pressing needs and I

LORD REVELSTOKE

have been delayed making known a wish that has long been in my heart for fear of encroaching on other funds, the claims of which have been more urgent.'[55]

Could the atmosphere in the Royal Household have increasingly been one of duty to the nation in its hour of need? And could this have helped initiate and strengthen the Princess's resolve, while still a child, to do something that would make a difference? It is important to examine the evidence.

Charity, Comforts and a Queen's Chocolate Box

ON 6 AUGUST 1914, just two days after the outbreak of war (and two months before the Princess would announce her own appeal) the Prince of Wales' National Relief Fund was launched. The Fund was devised as a means of gathering monies through public subscription and direct donation and, according to its own publicity, it had two objectives 'of equal importance', namely: to 'aid the wives, families and dependants of Soldiers, Sailors, Reservists and Territorials' who were fighting the war or who had died while on active service; and, to 'prevent and alleviate distress among the civil population arising out of the War.'[56]

The Fund was required as it was apparent from its outset that the conflict would have a huge

PLAYING CARDS
To promote the Prince of Wales' National Relief Fund, 1914

disruption on families; not only would men leave to serve in the army and navy, but also the national refocus on war-like materials and on cost saving in non-essential industries might cause job losses. This was particularly apparent amongst women, as, it was claimed, 'within one month of the opening of hostilities, nearly two hundred thousand women were already out of work'.[57] The National Relief Fund was intended to provide assistance – at a time when there was little in the way of national support for the destitute.

The headquarters of the Fund was set up in a familiar place, York House, a wing of St James Palace in London that traditionally forms the home of the Prince of Wales. Naturally, it was a focus of attention for the young royals, and Princess Mary recorded her impressions of her first meeting with individuals who would play their part in her own war fund, yet to come:

9 August 1914. In the afternoon I walked with David to York House, which had been converted into offices for the Prince of Wales's National Relief Fund. Mr Wedgwood Benn MP, Mr C.A. Pearson, and Mr Hedley Le Bas and the Duke of Devonshire showed us round the rooms where clerks are busy opening letters and acknowledging cheques. It was most interesting.[58]

The National Relief Fund was headed nominally by the heir to the throne – although assisted by his mother and a committee of senior figures – and it reportedly 'netted a quarter of a million pounds' in its first twenty-four hours, a significant achievement for any fund-raising effort.[59] This success continued throughout 1914, raising some seven million pounds in the first year of its existence, with some sixty per cent of this going to support military families.[60] The campaign had clearly captured some of the mood of the country, associated as it was with its youthful and popular figurehead. The Fund was expanded as time went by in order to meet demand, taking in some of the work of the Queen Mother, Queen Alexandra, in supporting soldiers' and sailors' families, which was brought into the fold of the National Relief Fund in order to prevent duplication of royal effort.[61]

Much of the success of the Relief Fund may have been down to having the Prince of Wales as its champion, though there is evidence to suggest that he was displeased to be simply, in his eyes, a 'figurehead'.[62] Certainly, his father, King George V was insistent that this should be his role, thereby separating him from the running of the Fund in case of any be public criticism.[63] Nominally, the Prince of Wales was also the treasurer of this fund; but it boasted an Executive Committee with Wedgwood Benn MP as the Chairman, and included some names that will become familiar, particularly the Duke of Devonshire, and Walter Peacock, a barrister who served as Secretary to the Duchy of Cornwall and then the Prince's treasurer in 1914–15. (Peacock would reappear on the Executive Committee of the Princess's own fund in due course.) There can be no doubt that the Executive Committee carried out the bulk of the work relating to the Fund, as a similar committee would later do with that of the Princess.[64]

Nevertheless, behind its status in 1914, the origins of the Fund were

THE PRINCE OF WALES
Pictured in 1922 with his personal secretary A.F. Lascelles (left) and Sir Walter Peacock (right)

pre-war, as they had been devised by its chairman in the wake of a major London Dock strike in 1912, and was a scheme designed to assist the 'dependants of strikers'.[65] Benn took the idea to Lord Burnham of the *Daily Telegraph*, and an invitation for the Prince of Wales to serve as a figurehead followed. This had a dramatic effect on fundraising and was a means of giving the Prince a significant role in the developing war, fully in line with his parents' strongly developed sense of duty. Though Mary's brother was yearning for *active* military service overseas, this was not likely. The young prince was in direct line for the throne and as such the chance of him being killed, severely wounded or taken prisoner was not one that could be entertained.[66]

With the Prince of Wales so close to his sister, and in an atmosphere of dutiful engagement with their citizens promoted by their parents, it is not hard to see the germination of an idea that would inspire Princess Mary to develop her own form of direct public engagement with the war, and the creation of the idea of the Christmas Fund itself. With an imperative to serve the country in its hour of need, a strongly held theme within the Royal Family, it is also not hard to infer that there must have been discussions relating to roles in the developing conflict – and that influences from within the family would be strong. And this is not to under-emphasise the Princess's own determination to make a difference, and to prove to her parents that she was indeed capable of emerging from under the cloying constraints of her family to do so.

The Prince of Wales's fund was not the only engagement with wartime charitable matters that emanated from the royal household. At around the same time that the National Relief Fund was announced, the Queen launched her 'Queen Mary Needlework Guild' in a letter to the press, published on 10 August 1914. In existence already were a number of local and national needlework

THE PRINCE OF WALES equipped as a Lieutenant in the Grenadier Guards

The work of Queen Mary's Needlework Guild

'guilds', formed in late Victorian times in order to gather together like-minded individuals committed to the promotion of needlework skills, including embroidery, knitting and crocheting, and similar.[67] In the Boer War of 1899–1902, Queen Victoria herself had contributed to morale and the war effort by setting an example; she crocheted five khaki scarves, each marked with the monogram VRI, which were given to selected men of several regiments.[68] In the Great War that followed, Queen Mary was keen to harness the capabilities of the guilds on a much larger scale in order to furnish additional garments in wartime, not only for soldiers and sailors on active service, but also for those in need at home, collaborating with a large number of charitable organisations.[69] While there were initial concerns that this would lead to duplication of effort – providing clothes that had already been issued by the War Office or Admiralty – the Guild became highly effective, with, by the end of the war, over a million members distributed in 630 branches worldwide.[70]

Prominent amongst these was the London Needlework Guild, with a direct involvement in its activities of not only the Queen, but also her daughter.[71] Queen Mary wasted no time in introducing Mary to the workings of the Guild, and in her diary, the young Princess recorded her impressions of what was her very first attendance at a meeting. Coming the day after her visit to see the wheels in motion of the National Relief Fund at York House, it was no doubt hugely influential:

10 August 1914. At 12 I went with Mama to a meeting she had here with the ladies to do with the Queen Mary Needlework Guild, which is to get clothes for the soldiers and sailors and hospitals. It was the first time I had ever been to a meeting. It was quite interesting.[72]

Princess Mary was an able needleworker, and contributed directly to the Guild's outputs. Recorded in her diary for 1914 are many occasions when she 'worked for the sailors and soldiers' in producing garments; but more than that, she was active 'in supervising the despatch of comforts for the troops, and in assisting Queen Mary with her correspondence, now grown to huge dimensions'.[73]

The immediate challenge was the production of sufficient woollen goods for the army with winter approaching rapidly in Flanders, a challenge taken up by a number of Needlework Guild branches across the United Kingdom. The task to supply these essential winter goods was a huge one, and had been proposed by Britain's soldier war-lord himself:

The proposal to afford the women the Empire this opportunity to give immediate and highly practical expression to their gratitude for the gallant work of our

FIELD MARSHAL
LORD KITCHENER
Secretary of State for War
He was an icon of 1914–15

GOD DEFEND THE RIGHT!
Come the three corners of the world in arms
And we shall shock them; nought shall
make us rue
If England to itself do rest but true.

With Best Wishes
for a Happy Christmas
and a
Bright and Prosperous New Year

Field-Marshal EARL KITCHENER.   From

KNITTED GOODS from Queen Mary's Needlework Guild were sent out accompanied with a letter from the Queen, and the 'Women of the Empire'. This letter has come to be associated with the Princess Mary Gift, though it has no direct connection to it.

brave soldiers was made by the Queen at the instance of Lord Kitchener. The task of securing the 300,000 pairs of socks and the 300,000 body-belts which will be required – representing money value of about £50,000 – is being undertaken by an energetic body of ladies under the personal supervision of the Queen, who has delegated the general direction to one of her Ladies-in-Waiting. It is hoped that all the articles required will be obtained 1st November.[74]

Leaflets were produced to aid knitters in making their woollen belts, and others were printed under the title 'Gift to the Troops at the Front from the Queen and the Women of the Empire'.[75] Parcels of woollen goods started to arrive in November, and were distributed to the men, and to the base and clearing hospitals.[76] Each package of 'cholera belts' and socks was delivered with a personal message in the Queen's handwriting, reproduced on a piece of paper that bore the Imperial Crown and the

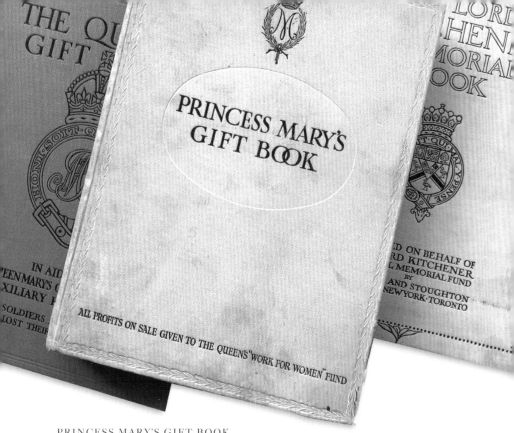

PRINCESS MARY'S GIFT BOOK
and other contemporary books to aid charitable donations in 1914–15.

imperious address, 'Buckingham Palace' simply reproduced in black. The paper bore the line: 'Gift from Mary R. and the Women of the Empire'. This letter would later become entangled in the post-war mythology of the contents of the 'Princess Mary Box'.[77] Though examples of the letter are often found with the gift box, they have no direct connection to it, as it was the 'needlewomen of Empire' who were being referred to – not donors to the Princess's Fund.[78]

Presumably these letters are found with some boxes as they formed part of a given individual's souvenirs of the conflict, kept together.

Ultimately, the Guild produced a staggering fifteen and a half million articles of clothing.[79] There is no doubt they were appreciated: Captain Arthur Ion Fraser with the 4th Cavalry (Hodson's Horse) described the glut of woollen goods he received in 1914 in a letter to his brother: 'I have now been inundated with presents for Xmas…I am in great risk of suffocation from the amount of warm things I now have.'[80]

Nevertheless, with so much feverish volunteer activity, the possibility that it could turn female textile workers out of their jobs had to be entertained, as 'the more fiercely the voluntary ladies worked, the more women were dismissed from clothing and other factories'.[81] And so, another charity, the 'Queen's Work for Women Fund' was founded, following consultation with 'industrial experts and working class women' on 20 August 1914, in an attempt to give aid to unemployed women workers.[82] Princess Mary would help fill the coffers of this fund herself by lending her name to a gift book aimed at the Christmas market, a volume of stories and illustrations produced by notable authors and artists, which sold widely across the Empire.[83]

The atmosphere of charitable giving to support the war effort from its outset in 1914 was pervasive. In addition to the National Relief Fund and the Needlework Guild described, there were immense efforts to support the influx of Belgian Refugees, as well as to assist with hospitals and the Red Cross.

An analysis of charities shows that it was the provision of 'comforts' to the troops that demanded most attention throughout the war, forming some twenty-eight per cent of all war charities.[84] In addition to the woollens provided by the needlework guild, a host of 'comforts' were eagerly sought by the men of the armed forces, and particularly so with the prospects of winter that followed on from the balmy summer weather that had ushered in the war. Rev. E.J. Kennedy, Chaplain Major to the British Expeditionary Force described the demands of 1914:

As the winter draws on apace, the heart of England will once more open in a response to the necessary comforts which her brave sons call for at her hands, and for which they will not call in vain. Let me give a few hints: Tobacco and cigarettes are, of course, always in demand, and under the peculiar circumstances of this nerve-racking campaign, are more or less of a necessity. Socks, too, are needed, for whether the weather is hot or cold, socks will wear out. The men dearly love sweets, such as toffee, chocolate, peppermints. Cardigan jackets – not too heavy – are largely called for; a packet containing writing paper, envelopes and an indelible pencil are acceptable; woollen sleeping helmets, and, of course, mittens will not be refused; boracic acid powder for sore feet; anything to do with a shaving outfit (especially safety razors) are gladly welcomed.[85]

The whole concept of 'comforts funds' – money gathered by subscription in order to provide troops at the front with items to improve their lives – was one that had come into focus in the harsh winter conditions experienced during the Crimean War of 1853–56. In this ill-fated campaign against the Russian Empire, failures and inadequacies of supply meant that soldiers were often left without adequate food and warm clothing. This was particularly trying during the harsh winter conditions so horribly endured in the trenches of Sebastopol and Balaklava in 1854–55, and efforts to relieve such inadequacies were reported almost daily in the press.[86] While the Government struggled to fulfil its duties to its soldiers,

the public responded with charitable funds to try and provide the troops with comforts to alleviate their suffering. And many of these were focused upon the Christmas period. As ever, tobacco was close to the top of the agenda:

There are those who say, 'far better send clothing, fuel, food, or books,' but I answer that all these things are being done, and that tobacco and pipes have been lamentably overlooked. It is perfectly idle to rail against the use of tobacco. You may as well attempt to stop the course of the Tyne at Shields; and all who have served on board a man of war or have bivouacked in the field know that, whilst on active service, and exposed to the dangers of battle and inclement weather, there is no greater comfort to the soldier and sailor than a pipe of good tobacco, which at once warms and cheers him.[87]

This attitude would prevail for at least another century.[88] As a result, many small funds were developed to supply such needs, funds that would no doubt find an echo some sixty years later, some

MEN OF THE 4TH DRAGOONS enjoy some comforts in the Crimea 1855

of them from perhaps surprising quarters:

THE SERVANTS' CHRISTMAS GIFT TO THE BRITISH SOLDIERS IN THE CRIMEA

Our readers… will be gratified at hearing that among other gifts recently sent out to the soldiers in the Crimea is one emanating from the household servants of London and the country. As compared with many other splendid donations this one may appear trifling, but the contributors have the satisfaction of knowing that by a careful administration of the fund, which amounted to upwards of £500, a quantity of tobacco has been sent out for the supply of the soldiers of the army before Sebastopol, with the addition of short pipes in tin cases, calculated to be serviceable for some time.[89]

Tobacco, woollen goods, small items of foodstuffs – all would be sent out to the battlefront in Crimea. This initiative was set to repeated in all subsequent wars – paid for by individuals and through charitable subscription – through to the present day. And such efforts would not just be the

Liebesgaben im Welt[

DISTRIBUTING 'LIEBESGABEN' IN 1914

preserve of the British military effort, for *Liebesgaben* – 'love gifts' – had become a feature of German military campaigns since at least 1870, and grew into a huge effort in 1914, derived from all corners of the Fatherland.[90]

The supply of comforts to the troops of the Boer War of 1899–1902 followed a similar pattern – though perhaps with differing needs. With the death of Queen Victoria in January 1901, the new king's consort, Queen Alexandra, took an active role in the organisation of comforts for the troops in South Africa. A year previously, three society ladies (the Countess of Airlie, Lady Charles Bentinck, and Lady Edward Cecil), had formed a Committee 'for the purpose of purchasing locally and distributing comforts for the use of the soldiers at the front', and specifically to supply them with 'tobacco, chocolate, cholera belts, socks, handkerchiefs, soap, matches, and writing materials'.[91] This became known as the 'Field Force Fund', and in October 1901 the new Queen became the fund's patron, suitably renamed 'Queen Alexandra's Field Force Fund'. Alexandra was 'a woman of intense, even exclusive, family affections,' who 'for ever retained the affections of the British people' and who was 'warm-hearted and generous'.[92] There can surely be little doubt that her commitments to good works would exert a future influence on her granddaughter.

With royal patronage, its originators no doubt hoped that the Field Force scheme would draw upon even greater support from public subscribers, and in October 1901, almost exactly fourteen years to the day before the announcement of Princess Mary's Gift Fund, the Queen Alexandra's Field Force Fund expressed the view to the press that 'readers will continue their generous support and contribute such sums as will enable every soldier of his Majesty to receive a gift at Christmas.'[93] Originally this was to give two shillings to each of the 200,000 men 'in the field' – but the idea grew in conception to the supply of a variety of objects, including tobacco, socks, handkerchiefs and 'housewives' (the traditional term for a soldier's sewing kit). This was finally crystallised into a gift to each man of a small parcel of uniform shape and contents, containing 'a pipe, a pound of tobacco, and a small plum pudding', purchased at a cost of two shillings: a 'Christmas present of the nation to the men now serving at the front.'[94] Some £30,000 was raised to pay for it, and the packages of 'Christmas puddings, pipes and tobacco, and other comforts' for 'the soldiers of the King', were delivered by the New Year.[95]

QUEEN ALEXANDRA
with Prince Olaf of Norway

It would be surprising if these precedents did not have a direct influence on Princess Mary in 1914. But perhaps one important event above all others must have influenced the princess in her choice of direct engagement with the war. In 1899, some fifteen years before the launch of her Christmas

FACING THE BOERS c.1900

On the 10th, at the remote railway junction of Stormberg, General Gatacre wandered into an ambush and his force melted away, leaving 600 men to their fate. A day after, at Magersfontein Hill, Lord Methuen's Highland Brigade, led by General Wauchope, assaulted the defences *en masse* and suffered heavily from the massed rifles of the skilled Boers. Many were killed or wounded in the first wave, and Wauchope himself fell. And then there was Colenso. Fought on 15th December, the battle was another disaster: 'Once again the British had walked into the arms of the Boers they could not see and whose strength or position was a total mystery to them'.[98] In the face of the two earlier defeats, General Buller had intended to cross the Tugela River and march on to Ladysmith. Once again superior Boer defensive tactics led to the defeat of the British. Buller would be relieved of his command. Though Christmas was around the corner, the mood – at home and in South Africa – was

Gift Fund at its inaugural meeting in the Ritz ballroom, and when Mary was just two years old, her great-grandmother, Queen Victoria determined that the troops then serving in South Africa should receive a present that would remind them of home – an example that Princess Mary would undoubtedly follow.[96]

In the first year of the conflict, the war against the Boers had not been going well. General Buller's campaign had been fraught with failure, so much so that in the so-called 'Black Week', 10–17 December 1899, the British forces succumbed to three major defeats.[97]

sombre; something was required that would lift the spirits of the average soldier.

Fortunate in this regard were the efforts from those at home to provide comforts to alleviate some of the hardships of the campaign, and serve to remind them of their people back in the homeland. Some were misjudged, but their purpose was evident: 'All along the fronts Christmas arrived in a cascade of gifts from home, including lovingly knitted balaclavas for men dripping with the sweat of midsummer. Messrs Lyons sent out 10,000 Christmas puddings…'.[99] There were also regimental gifts: for example, the Scottish Regiments' Gift Fund, chaired by the Anglican Archdeacon William MacDonald Sinclair, which sent out a handsome tin of 'Yankee plug' tobacco: 'Frae Scots, tae Scots' for the New Year 1900.[100] But perhaps paramount in this 'cascade', was a gift that was sent directly from the Queen herself, a New Year's present that would hopefully set a new course for the badly stuttering morale of the British in South Africa. Queen Victoria, suitably shocked by Black Week, was determined to make a difference.

The Queen's gift – of chocolate in a specially commissioned tin – was set to become one of the most treasured artefacts of the Boer War. On 19 November 1899, Sir Fleetwood Edwards, Keeper of the Queen's Privy Purse, wrote a letter to the Secretary of State for War, Lord Lansdowne; a letter reproduced in the press:

QUEEN VICTORIA IN 1882
pictured by Bassano

Windsor Castle,
November 19, 1899
Dear Lord Lansdowne, The Queen commands me to inform you of her anxiety to make some personal present as soon as possible to each of her soldiers serving in South Africa. Her Majesty has decided upon sending chocolate, which, she is given to understand, will be appropriate and acceptable. It will be packed for each man in a tin that has been specially designed for the occasion. The Queen hopes that you may be able to arrange for its conveyance and distribution.[101]

The gift was to be paid for by the Queen herself:

It is understood the Queen's order has been placed equally between Messrs. Fry and two other firms, and each one will contain one pound of chocolate. Seeing that something like 80,000 troops are concerned, the expenditure entailed by the Royal gift will be considerable; but apart from this, the gracious and thoughtful kindness of Her Majesty is what will most appeal to the whole nation, and the fortunate recipients, by whom the designed tins will doubtless be prized only less dearly than the war medals which will fall to their share.[102]

With such a gift being given directly from the Sovereign to every soldier serving in South Africa, it was likely to be highly prized; particularly so, given the fact that the tin, and its contents, were so carefully designed:

Her Majesty's Order for a Hundred Thousand Boxes of Chocolate for the troops has been divided among three firms. The chocolate, which will be suitable either as beverage or a sweetmeat, will be supplied in tin boxes, each containing half a pound, a quantity sufficient to make from twelve to sixteen cups. A special box has been designed. The lid will have a red ground with a large gilt, medallion of the Queen in

Top: QUEEN VICTORIA'S CHOCOLATE TIN, 1900.
Bottom: THE INTERIOR, showing the packing materials (the chocolate long gone)

the centre as well as the Royal monogram in red, white, and blue, and the inscription, 'South Africa, 1900.'[103]

The three companies committed to manufacturing the chocolate (which could be eaten or made into a warming drink) were Cadburys, Rowntree and Frys. All of them had Quaker connections, who though opposed to the war, were unlikely to refuse a direct request from the Queen herself.[104] Each was commissioned to design a suitable gift tin, and the final design, chosen from a field of three by the Queen herself, was that submitted by Frys. It was designed, produced and copyrighted by stationers and tin manufacturers Barclay and Fry of Southwark, and this formed the basis of the tins produced for all three chocolate firms.[105] One of these was the Mansfield manufacturer Barringer, Wallis & Manners, who 'put their best workmanship into everything they turned out', and who supplied 'a considerable portion of the chocolate boxes which the late Queen Victoria sent out to the South African troops.'[106]

The beautifully produced tin-plate boxes were distinctive, complex, and of high quality; each of them bore an unusually direct and personal message from the Queen herself, written in her own hand, and printed prominently upon its lid: 'I wish you a Happy New Year. Victoria R.I.'.

The first shipment of the chocolate boxes, suitably packed in wooden crates, was sent on 16 December 1899; by March 1900, they had been distributed.[107] Later, following Victoria's death and the accession of her son, King Edward VII, to the throne, Queen Alexandra was to issue a chocolate box for the troops in South Africa in Christmas 1901–02.[108] Though carrying the new Queen's image upon it, it had less impact – and, if the scarcity of surviving examples is anything to go by, it was less well known.

With such care and attention lavished on Queen Victoria's gift, it is perhaps not surprising that these gift tins would soon be treasured by their recipients. Perhaps more surprising was just how soon into the New Year the chocolate boxes began changing

CHRISTMAS 1902.
FROM
QUEEN
ALEXANDRA

hands for *real* money. Newspapers carried classified advertisements for the boxes, while, as early as March 1900, other papers carried reports of the likely prices obtained at auction:[109]

> Prices realised for the Queen's chocolate boxes vary very much, according to condition and the sympathetic interest to be found in the circumstances of each case. Prices accepted for full boxes in one lot have reached £12 13s but the average offers have been ten guineas. Empty boxes have fetched either five guineas or £5. A box partially full brought £6 10s.[110]

In some cases, the reason for such auctions was in order to provide for the families of soldiers who had died in the war, or were disabled by it:

> The Queen's box of chocolate, which was to have been given to the late Pvte. Wm. Tegg, was sold by auction, for the benefit of his mother, in Reading Corn Exchange... The auctioneer, Mr. Arthur Ayres, who conducted the sale gratuitously, explained the circumstances under which the box of chocolate, then exhibited, was to be sold. He pointed out that Pvte was a Reservist in the R.A.M.C., and that he had worked at the Biscuit Factory. He was called to go to South Africa and took part in the battles of Belmont, Graspan, Modder River, and Magersfontein, but was seized with enteric fever, and died in the Modder River Hospital on Jan. 20. He bore an exemplary character. The Queen's present was forwarded to his mother... who had largely depended upon her son for support.[111]

With an appreciation of growing intrinsic value, came inevitable reports of related criminal activity. John Mackay, labourer, of Shore, Dundee came up before Leith Police Court for the theft of a box from his sister's house. He was placed under '£2 caution for six months'. Elsewhere, Thomas Spreadbury of Lambeth was summoned for the 'unlawful detention of a soldier's chocolate box and a Boer belt'. Temptations clearly ran high.[112]

Despite the sales of some tins, there is ample evidence of what each one meant to its recipients, or to the families of those bereaved by the war, as this poem published in the *Falkirk Herald* and dedicated to the mother of Lance-Corpl Liddle, 'who fell in action in South Africa' reveals:

Only a little box of tin!
Why should move us so?
Arousing our sympathies,
Causing our tears to flow.

We noticed the old lady in black
As she slowly untied each string,
Then laid the box before us
As if 'twere a sacred thing.

She held it in her hand.
Shaking with grief, I ween;
While her quivering lips
said sadly,
"'Tis the chocolate box
of the Queen."[113]

It is hardly surprising that such tokens, sent directly to the soldier at the front, and signed by the Monarch at home, should be treasured, framed, and retained for future generations – a fact that was not lost on the Press in 1914:

One of the most cherished relics in thousands of homes today is the box in which Queen Victoria's gift of chocolate was made to the troops in the South African war. In many a country cottage the well-known tin reposes under a glass case. It was not the value of the gift. It was the kindly feeling that prompted it which made it precious.[114]

Princess Mary's own box, influenced by that of her Great Grandmother, and manufactured by the same firms, would evoke similar sensibilities just fifteen years later.[115]

H.R.H. Princess Mary's Gift Fund

WHEN PRINCESS MARY attended the inaugural meeting of the General Committee of the fund that would bear her name on 14 October 1914, the nature of the gift to be delivered on Christmas Day had already been decided. The purpose of the meeting was thus to launch the Committee that would carry out her wishes, and to source and fund the gift itself. All that was left was to determine how to pay for the gift, and how to gather the money to do so.

Though, as has been described, the absolute origins of the gift are hard to pin down, the context of duty and public service set by the example of her parents, no doubt influenced by the antecedents of her Grandmother and Great Grandmother, were of paramount importance. Yet evidence of such nascent conversations is slim. Nevertheless, Princess Mary's diary hints at the very day the idea for the scheme was crystallised, just six days before it was launched:

8 October 1914. Buckingham Palace, London. Fine Day. I worked in the morning. I had my music lesson with Mr Keene. I saw Mama, David and Mr Peacock about arranging a fund for sending pipes and tobacco to the sailors and soldiers at the Front...[116]

Such a matter-of-fact entry for what would become such a huge undertaking.

It is evident from this entry that, then as ever, the influence of Queen Mary on her children had been strong. This meeting, attended by her mother, her brother, and the treasurer of the Prince of Wales's National Relief Fund, was presumably to establish what was possible in finding a role for the Princess, and the provision of a Christmas gift to all on Active Service must have appealed. The Princess's engagement in many 'quite interesting meetings' in the preceding weeks must also have sown a seed that was beginning to germinate, a vital seed that was, again, propagated by her mother. Nevertheless, Mary's biographers have all identified the direct engagement of the young princess in the development of the idea, and her desire to deliver upon it herself:

So great was Princess Mary's interest in every phase of the War, and so heartfelt her sympathy with its sufferers... she expressed a desire to her mother to send a personal gift to the fighting forces out of her own private income. Although this scheme was impracticable, it was a clear indication of the deep desire of Princess Mary to take some personal part in the various understandings then in progress all over England for the welfare of the troops at the Front.[117]

In considering this, no doubt the Princess was influenced by the act of Queen Victoria (and Victoria's daughter-in-law, Queen Alexandra) to present a uniquely *personal* present, a New Year's gift funded from her own coffers.[118] But then the army in South Africa was much smaller than that which was fielded as the British Expeditionary Force in 1914; and there was the navy to support. There was clearly no possibility that Mary could fund her gift herself, and a call to the public was needed. This call would take the scheme from a purely personal act by a royal princess, to a fully public plan to recognise the efforts of the armed forces, in a year when there had been reverses on the battlefields, and losses on the high seas. In this, it was similar to Queen Victoria's morale-boosting gift after the challenges of 'Black Week' during the South African War.

If Mary herself was not to pay for the gift, then all that was left was finding a way of funding the scheme, and then delivering on its ideals – with barely more than two months to go. Directly following the meeting of the General Committee on 14 October 1914, and six days after Mary's initial meeting, the appeal was launched. The day after, the first meeting of the Executive Committee set up to deliver the gift was held at the Ritz, with twelve influential people determining the future direction of the fund.[119] At this meeting, chaired by the Duke of Devonshire, and attended by principal officers Walter Peacock, Hedley Le Bas, and Rowland Berkeley (together

THE ROYAL SANTA CLAUS : H.R.H. PRINCESS MARY—A NEW PORTRAIT.
Princess Mary is appealing for help to send a Christmas present from the Nation " to every sailor afloat and every soldier at the front." The gift is a brass tobacco or cigarette box, pipe, and tinder lighter. Remittances should be addressed to H.R.H. the Princess Mary, Buckingham Palace, S.W., the envelopes marked " Sailors' and Soldiers' Christmas Fund." — [*Photo. by Ernest Brooks.*]

PRINCESS MARY AS 'SANTA CLAUS'
How the press reacted to her appeal in 1914

with H.V. Higgins, Capt Foley Lambert RN, General S.S. Long, Lady Jellicoe and The Hon. W. Lawson) the initial number of recipients was determined, amounting to 145,000 sailors and 350,000 soldiers (inclusive of the 'Indian contingent'). It was Walter Peacock, treasurer to National Relief Fund, and one of four people who had attended that pivotal meeting of the 8 October 1914, who was left to sum up the fund-raising task that lay ahead:

Queen Victoria's chocolate box sent to the soldiers fighting in South Africa, 1900

Princess Mary's christmas box sent to the soldiers fighting in France and Belgium, 1914

COMPARISON OF PRINCESS MARY'S BOX WITH ITS ANCESTOR

Mr Walter Peacock informed the Committee that should the gift consist of a brass box, tinder-lighter, pipe, tobacco, and cigarettes, for 500,000 men, it would cost £55,000 to £60,000.[120]

Armed with the Princess's affecting letter of 15 October, the Fund was announced by the national press in the following day's newspapers.[121] In place of the estimated amount identified by Mr Peacock, the newspapers suggested that £100,000 was to be raised in order to deliver on the Princess's ideals, as 'memories of her own childhood seem to cling round the Princess's letter asking for funds'.[122]

Princess Mary's letter remained central to the ethos of the fund, and was one of the most important parts of the Princess's engagement with it, a real pull to drive fund raising. Requests to advertise the fund in Christmas 'trade catalogues' were also entertained – such as that published in the catalogue of Dundee store Draffen & Jarvie, of Nethergate Street.[123] But this was not the norm. It was instructed in all outlets and advertisements that remittances were to be addressed to 'HRH Princess Mary, Buckingham Palace, SW.' The idea of addressing a letter to the premier royal palace must have been an exciting, if not daunting prospect. To distinguish them, the envelopes were to be marked 'Sailors' and Soldiers' Christmas Fund.'[124]

Kick-starting the fund were subscriptions from prominent individuals who were listed out in the newspapers, the contribution by the Royal Family relatively modest, but naturally still significant. Amongst the early donors were members of the Committee that delivered the gift itself.[125]

Mary's appeal quickly went outside of the confines of the United Kingdom, even to the extent of being reported widely across the United States of America, appearing there on the same day as it appeared in the British press.[126] Perhaps with

PRINCESS MARY
APPEALS
FOR
SAILORS AND SOLDIERS.

For many weeks we have all been greatly concerned for the welfare of the sailors and soldiers who are so gallantly fighting our battles by sea and land. Our first consideration has been to meet their more pressing needs, and I have delayed making known a wish that has long been in my heart for fear of encroaching on other Funds, the claims of which have been more urgent.

I want you all now to help me to send a Christmas present from the whole nation to every sailor afloat and every soldier at the front. On Christmas Eve, when, like the shepherds of old, they keep their watch, doubtless their thoughts will turn to home and to the loved ones left behind, and perhaps, too, they will recall the days when, as children themselves, they were wont to hang out their stockings, wondering what the morrow had in store.

I am sure that we should all be the happier to feel that we had helped to send our little token of love and sympathy on Christmas morning, something that would be useful and of permanent value, and the making of which may be the means of providing employment in trades adversely affected by the war. Could there be anything more likely to hearten them in their struggle than a present received straight from home on Christmas Day?

Please, will you help me?

Mary.

FORM OF THE GIFT.
It is hoped that a sum of £100,000 will be forthcoming. The gift will take the form of an embossed brass tobacco or cigarette box, a pipe, and a tinder lighter. In the case of the Indian troops sweets will be supplied instead of tobacco or cigarettes.

HOW THE PRINCESS'S APPEAL APPEARED IN THE PRESS, 16 OCTOBER 1914

more direct relevance, Canadian newspapers also published the appeal, again surprisingly quickly after its first announcement. For example, the *Vancouver Daily World* reproduced the Princess's letter in full just a day after it had appeared in the British press. It was very specific in what could be expected: 'It is hoped that the appeal will result in the raising of $500,000 for the provision of gifts taking the form of an embossed brass tobacco or cigarette box, pipe and tinder lighter, and candies for the Indian troops.'[127] Elsewhere

in the Empire, in New Zealand, the *Auckland Star* put the case for the fund succinctly, again just days after the announcement: 'PIPES FOR TARS AND TOMMIES… Princess Mary is appealing for £100,000 to provide a Christmas gift of a pipe and tobacco for every soldier and sailor on active service.'[128]

By November, the Canadian Press was enthusiastically reporting on the progress of the fund, its coffers being enhanced by the patriotic citizens of the Dominion – which reported also on a playful wager between the Princess and her brother, Prince Albert:

HALF MILLION FOR CHRISTMAS FUND
Fund Started by Princess Mary Swells Rapidly
LONDON, Nov 26 – The Christmas fund raised for soldiers at the front and the sailors on duty at sea, today reached the sum of $500,000. So generous has been the response to the appeal of the princess to afford a Christmas

'HOORAH FOR THE KING!'
Patriotic Christmas Card designed by General Rawlinson to be sent home from Flanders, 1914

	£	s	d
The King	100	0	0
The Queen	50	0	0
The Prince of Wales	50	0	0
Princess Mary	25	0	0
Lord and Lady Rothermere	1000	0	0
Sir William H. Lever, Bart	500	0	0
Sir Sigismund Neumann, Bart	262	10	0
Mr H. Mallaby-Deely, MP	62	10	0
Harrods Ltd	262	10	0
Duke of Devonshire	250	0	0
Lord Ashton	250	0	0
Lord Portman	200	0	0
The Misses Kennedy Jones	105	0	0
Sir john Ellerman, Bart	105	0	0
Lord Revelstoke	100	0	0
Lord Rothschild	100	0	0
Mr Leopold de Rothschild	100	0	0
Mr Alfred de Rothschild	100	0	0

Early Donors to the Gift Fund

gift for the men in the service that the plan has now been extended to include all troops, including those at home. Princess Mary is elated at the success with which the fund she sponsored has met; incidentally she has won a pair of gloves from her brother, Prince Albert, who wagered she would not raise a half million dollars by December 1.[129]

At each meeting of the Executive Committee, the growing funds were reported, starting with the £12,058 gathered in time for that of 20 October.[130] This was reported in the press with an increasing emphasis on the shrinking time-frame: 'REMEMBER SCROOGE! Do you desire to wish the soldiers at the front a Merry Christmas? If so, you must hurry with your subscription to Princess Mary's Fund. One hundred thousand pounds are wanted and 12,000 has been subscribed to date.'[131]

This direct approach through the press and across the Empire was gathering dividends, but it was clear that there would need to be more effort in collecting money if the initial estimated minimum fund of £55,000 to £60,000 to deliver the gift was to be achieved. Nevertheless, and despite competition from the much larger fund being garnered by the Prince of Wales, the Princess's appeal was gathering momentum. By the end of the month, it was reported that Princess Mary's Gift Fund had reached £31,630, while '£870,000 has now been allocated for distribution from the National Relief Fund, which to-day reached the total of £3,546,000'.[132] That the Princess herself took part in working for the fund is demonstrated by contemporary newspaper reports:

[Princess] Mary is extremely pleased that half the £100,000 required for her scheme for Christmas presents to the men on service with the Fleet and

'FIGHTING FLEAS IN FLANDERS' 4th Division Christmas Card, 1914

the Army in the field has now been raised, and she hopes the whole sum required be available by the end of this month, since it will be necessary to begin despatching these presents early in December. Her Royal Highness passes several hours daily at Buckingham Palace to deal with the mass of correspondence that arrives in connection with the subject.[133]

It was obvious that the growing responsibility for the collection of the funds and the handling of the administration would require an office and a staff; a separate account to handle the day-to-day operations was opened to avoid complication.[134] The Secretary was to furnish that office with everything that was needed (including, if required, waste paper baskets from the Disabled Sailors' and Soldiers' Society), and was authorised to recruit staff with a total budget of £15 a week.[135] By the end of October, four typists were employed at 30 shillings a week, with a paid assistant in the 'collecting room' at £2/- a week – with three boy scouts retained at a cost of 2s a day each – an interesting counterpoint to the 1s

SIR HEDLEY LE BAS
Mastermind of the 'Your Country Needs You' recruiting campaign, and pivotal member of the Executive Committee.

a day earned by the average soldier on joining in 1914. All of these would draw down on the 'No2 Drawing Account'.[136]

An important figure in the raising of the Fund was Sir Hedley Le Bas, and he remained a pivotal member of the Executive Committee. Le Bas had been a soldier in the late nineteenth century before leaving the army to join the publishers Blackie & Son. Rejected for further service in the South African War, Le Bas instead invested £150 to build his own concern, the Caxton Publishing Company, evidently drawing upon his past experience with Blackies.[137] Le Bas was an influential person in 1914, for he has been credited, more than any other, in convincing the British Government 'of the advantage to be gained from domestic propaganda.'[138] His role in the recruitment campaign that built the New Army from August 1914 was of paramount importance, creating a brand with the main message, delivered by Lord Kitchener, 'Your Country Needs You'.[139] It was Le Bas who took a significant part in the development of the communications of the Princess Mary Gift Fund.

Perhaps taking the lead of Le Bas, there was often enthusiastic encouragement of people to provide money to the scheme – even if they could ill afford it. As an example, the *Perthshire Constitutional* set out six reasons why its readers should contribute to the Fund in late November 1914:

SIX REASONS why you should support H.R.H. The Princess Mary's Fund:
BECAUSE we owe a priceless debt to our Soldiers and Sailors for our security and comfort;
BECAUSE our Soldiers and Sailors are engaged in a righteous war for Peace, the reign of which Christmas foretells;
BECAUSE you will enjoy your Christmas more having remembered our Soldiers and Sailors;
BECAUSE you will never miss a small Contribution, and even if you do, what better sacrifice could you make?
BECAUSE when the War is over, you will remember with pleasure your gift to the Soldiers and Sailors;
BECAUSE there are men at the front who will be called on to lay down their lives for us before another Christmas comes round.[140]

Nevertheless, the Executive Committee were still very keen that the correct tone should be struck in approaching the public. Not for the Princess Mary Gift Fund the flag days that had proliferated, to become part of the fabric of charitable giving during the Great War.[141] For instance, the Borough of Croydon's Mayoress's 'Flag Day Committee' alone arranged twenty-eight separate

Your King and Country need you.

WILL you answer your Country's Call? Each day is fraught with the gravest possibilities, and at this very moment the Empire is on the brink of the greatest War in the history of the world.

In this crisis your Country calls all her young unmarried men to rally round the Flag and enlist in the ranks of her Army

If every patriotic young man answers her call, England and her Empire will emerge stronger and more united than ever

If you are unmarried and between 18 and 30 years old, will you answer your Country's Call, and go to the nearest Recruiter—whose address you can get at any Post Office, and—— ———

Join the Army To-day.

G. R.

To all Ex-N.C.O.'s

EX - NON - COMMISSIONED OFFICERS of any branch of His Majesty's Forces are required for the duration of the War, their assistance in training the new Army being urgently needed.

PARTICULARS.

Promotion to non - commissioned rank immediately after enlistment. Age no obstacle so long as competent. No liability for service abroad if over 45, or in special cases 40. Pensioners may draw their pensions in addition to pay of rank at Army rates.

Apply for information or enlistment at any recruiting office, or ask O.C. Depot to re-enlist you in <u>your old Corps.</u>

God Save the King.

THE WORK OF SIR HEDLEY LE BAS

Flag Days across the war period, raising some £318,160 9s 0d for several war charities.[142] With this amount of competition, and desiring, perhaps, to set a different tone, the Executive Committee created collecting cards and boxes for 'window collection' only. 'The Committee felt that it was very undesirable that collections should be made in the streets', and that anyone applying for the collecting boxes would have to be informed fully to that effect.[143] Despite this,

and relevant groups in order to get funds. This appeal was made using handsome reproductions of the Princess's letter of 15 October 1914. These were printed on imposing Buckingham Palace letterhead, capped by a red Imperial Crown and signed with Mary's facsimile signature, and bore the familiar touching message from the young Princess that had already been published in the press.[145] These letters were sent out widely, with, in addition to the stationery and other fees, a cost of £80–£100 to fund and address letters and envelopes.[146]

In the minutes of the Executive Committee for 27 October, the extent of the appeal, and the nature of those being appealed to, was presented. It was indicative of the solid Middle Classes of the nation, and therefore people with at least some disposable income:

some local organisers got around it by using the proceeds from other Flag Days to fund the scheme, with the 'street sale of flags' during Stirling's 'Navy Flag Day' of early December being used 'to swell Princess Mary's Soldiers' and Sailors' Christmas Fund.'[144]

Applications for money were made through a direct appeal to prominent citizens, landed gentry

> Mr Le Bas reported that he has had 39,200 appeals sent out at the cost of £6/- a thousand. Amongst these, 1,500 were sent to Social Clubs, 1,500 to Golf Clubs, 1,600 to Schools, 2,600 to Masonic Lodges and 7,000 to persons who kept more or five servants.[147]

Christmas Smokes

SAILORS & SOLDIERS
CHRISTMAS FUND

CHARITY FLAGS
Including 'unofficial' ones for the fund

CORRESPONDENCE FROM THE PALACE relating to the Princess's Gift Fund and others. P.R. Craft was a renowned painter.

The same largely middle-class audience was also engaged through the medium of a special 'Matinee' at Drury Lane, initiated by Harry Higgins in aid of the Princess Mary Gift Fund. The entertainment was organised for the afternoon of 4 December, and had a cast of Edwardian theatrical luminaries who engaged in a dozen or so presentations, excerpts from plays, humorous sketches and readings.[148] With Princess Mary and other members of the Royal Family in attendance, together with the Duke of Devonshire, the Prime Minister, Mr Asquith, Lord Lansdowne and Lord Kitchener, it was not surprising that, minus expenses, the event brought some £826 18s 4d into the fund.[149]

For each donation made, a receipt was issued, sent in a simple envelope that was franked with the oval cachet 'TREASURER. H.R.H. THE PRINCESS MARY

CHRISTMAS FUND'. Each pro-forma receipt – printed on water-marked paper of Harrison & Sons, 'Printers-in-Ordinary' to the King – carried a reproduction of the signature of Queen Mary's private secretary, E.W. Wallington, and carried the words 'I am desired by the Princess Mary to thank you very much for the kind donation of … which you have so generously given to Her Royal Highness's Sailors' and Soldiers' Christmas Fund.' It seems that no one was forgotten, as five-year-old Lily Parish from Upper Tooting, making a donation of one shilling and tuppence, was rewarded by one of the grand receipts that were headed in red with the Imperial Crown over the address, Buckingham Palace.[150]

Wallington had suggested that, during its collection phase at least, the fund should be run in a similar manner to that of the Prince of Wales' National Relief Fund, with the monies invested in the Treasury, which was approached with this in mind.[151] Certainly, the form of the receipts issued mirrored ones supplied for both the Prince of Wales's National Relief Fund, and the Women's War Work Fund.[152] By the end of October it was reported that

the number of receipts sent by the Christmas Fund per day was 596, with an average, including additional letters, of 650, a significant undertaking.[153]

With its emphasis on Christmas, and the youth of the Princess, it was expected that the Fund would have special resonance with young people, 'who knew the enjoyment of home, and who appreciated the happiness of Christmas gifts,' and who would no doubt 'show by kind reminders sent to them during their absence from home their sympathy with their brave soldiers and sailors.'[154] It is not surprising, then, that school children were especially targeted as providers of 'coppers' by local fund-raisers:

In connection with Princess Mary's Fund for providing Christmas presents for soldiers and sailors, opportunities are being afforded to the young folk of Liverpool, as well as their parents, to make sacrifices on behalf of the men at the front. Collecting boxes have been issued, and it is hoped that Liverpool's efforts will be commensurate with its past reputation for generosity. That her Royal Highness's spin

23rd October, 19

Madam,

I am desired by the Princess Mary
to thank you very much for the kind
donation of

S.

which you have so generously given to
Her Royal Highness's Sailors' and
Soldiers' Christmas Fund.

Your obedient Servant,

E. W. Wallington

D. 2.

Miss Lily Parish

P4578

has not been made in vain is shown by a letter written by a little fellow whose parents occupy a high position in the life of Liverpool. He expresses his feelings thus 'Dear Princess Mary, — 1 am sending you my present from daddy and mother. Daddy and mother said we could have our present for ourselves or for the soldiers. We chose the soldiers, daddy and mother gave each a pound for the soldiers' Christmas present. I am making a chest protector. Lora from Toddy.'[155]

As a result, schools featured prominently in the fund-raising efforts, and ultimately raised £6252 2s 2d for the fund.[156] Surviving school records show that this was not just the preserve of public schools; for example, at Gellidawel School in Tonyrefail in October 1914, 'the Headteacher recorded sending a £1 postal order to HRH Princess Mary for her fund to provide Christmas gifts for servicemen. The teachers had provided the prizes and there was a prize draw amongst the children,

who paid a penny for each ticket.'[157] At Montrose Academy, there was excitement as 'some of the young contributors insisted on changing their sixpences into pennies, and others their pennies into halfpennies for the pleasure of putting coins into collecting boxes.'[158] And 'the pupils of the Rochdale Secondary School and the teachers of the Central School' had decided to 'forego their annual Christmas party' in favour of sending the £17 10s to the Princess Mary Fund.[159]

Up and down the country there was evidence of poignant donations from children, in some cases in remembrance of siblings who were serving overseas, such as the efforts of two boys from the tiny Devon village of Loxhore:

Through the efforts of Masters Freddie Norman, of Lower Loxhore, and Freddie Pickard, of Loxhore Town, the sum of £2 11s 6d. has been… [gathered] in aid of Princess Mary's Fund for providing Christmas presents for the soldiers. The former has four brothers serving in the Forces and the latter two.[160]

Popular war periodicals carried 'specials', and gifts had a patriotic flavour.

Perhaps the most tragic notice of all – picked up in newspapers across North America – being the generosity of a 'dying crippled girl in Sheffield named Gertie Nelson' who 'sent her last shilling to Princess Mary's Sailors' and Soldiers' Christmas fund.'[161]

Soon, money flooded in from a variety of sources, as the scheme developed a significant momentum of its own. And away from the middle classes originally contacted, people less able to contribute also paid their way. Local Mayors also assisted by gathering money for the fund – perhaps engaging with a wider cross section of their constituents in the act – creating collecting houses for small donations that could be forwarded *en masse* to Buckingham Palace. For example, the Mayoress of Birkenhead, a northern town situated across the Mersey from Liverpool, published her appeal in the local newspaper on 24 October 1914:

> Dear Sir, – I have received a strong appeal for subscriptions to be invited to provide a Christmas present to our brave soldiers and sailors at the front.

Such an object must touch the heart of every soul in our town, which has sent so many of our relatives and friends to fight our country's battles, and therefore I ask those who desire to contribute to this fund to send their donations to me at the Town Hall, and I shall have infinite pleasure in forwarding them to the Central Fund.

Mary E. Moon, Mayoress, The Mayor's Parlour, Town Hall, Birkenhead[162]

This call to 'all classes' was a particular component of the success of the fund, a means of providing some 'Christmas cheer' to those on active service – for all would receive the gift. With this in mind, in November, the Honorary Secretary of the Executive Committee, Rowland Berkeley, wrote to editors up and down the country to assist those who wanted to send in their contribution, no matter how small: 'As Her Royal Highness the Princess Mary is anxious that all classes should be represented in the Fund that she is raising for presenting Christmas gifts to our sailors afloat and our soldiers at the front, my Committee would deem it a favour if you could find room in your paper for enclosed coupon.'[163] The results were widely reported:

RICH AND POOR HELP.
FINE RESPONSE TO
PRINCESS MARY'S
APPEAL

Princess Mary's appeal for providing our sailors and soldiers with a Christmas gift has met with a magnificent response. All classes are represented in the first day's subscription list. Workers have sent their coppers and sixpences, whilst the well-to-do have sent substantial cheques. Her Royal Highness is grateful for small contributions as well as large.[164]

The undistinguished money that arrived in envelopes, given by small children and adults of all social classes – was, sadly, a target for thieves, some within the Post Office itself. In November 1914, Auxiliary Postman Abraham Crick (22) of Nelson, Lancashire helped himself to a 'ten bob' note from a letter addressed to 'H.R.H. Princess Mary, Buckingham Palace, which contained Treasury note for 10s'. Crick admitted his crime and was duly remanded in custody.[165]

As already discussed, public generosity in giving to the Fund was not restricted to Great Britain, as it applied across the Empire, and particularly Canada. This prominent Dominion had despatched the first contingents of its Expeditionary Force to Europe in a flotilla of ships on 3 October 1914, which landed in England twelve days later, coincident with the announcement of the fund.[167] Though the CEF would not appear *en masse* in France and Belgium before the New Year, Canadians of the No2 Stationary Hospital arrived at Boulogne on 8 November, and a battalion of Princess Patricia's Light Infantry joined the British regular 27th Division as the first Canadian fighting troops in France on 21 December 1914.[168] (These troops would be eligible to receive the full gift on Christmas Day.) Perhaps in recognition of this event, in Winnipeg, Manitoba, a Mrs W.P. Fillmore,

Donor type	Receipts		
General donations	£ 135,714	7s	5d
Mayor's collections	£ 6,822	11s	4d
School collections	£ 6,252	2s	2d
Church collections	£ 4,399	10s	4d
'Employees of firms'	£ 1,333	0s	0d
Advertising cards	£ 1,748	10s	1d
'Flag Day' & Public Collections	£ 4,017	19s	3d
'Concerts & Entertainments'	£ 2,269	4s	11d
Box collections	£ 35	7s	11d
Total from donations	£ 162,592	13s	5d

Donations received by the Princess Mary Gift Fund [166]

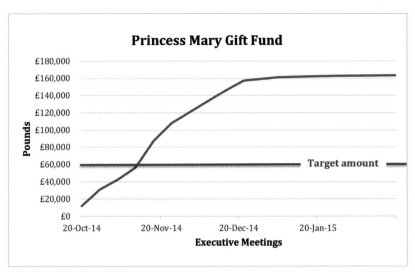

Princess Mary Gift Fund

Target amount

Funds accrued by the Princess Mary Gift Fund, 1914–15

assisted by Mrs Fred. J.C. Cox, 'gave a patriotic tea', the proceeds of which were to go to the Princess Mary fund. The local press reported the occasion as one to be remembered, 'The reception room and the dining room were aglow with red, white and blue lights. The tea table was centred with a battleship, around which were smaller ships, with tiny soldiers and flags surrounding them.'[169]

Raising sufficient funds to meet the immediate needs of the Gift Fund – and deliver its stated objects – was the principal concern of the Executive Committee in the first weeks of its operation. Aided by Sir Hedley Le Bas's advertising

acumen, and the energy of the office staff, the weekly rise in donations accrued by the Fund soon went beyond the expectations of the Executive Committee.

The rise in donations was steep and steady, exceeding its original minimum estimation of the requirement of the Fund, only tailing off as Christmas 1914 passed. This meant that by the end of November, the level and extent of support indicated that the scheme could be expanded, and announcements were made by the Chairman to this effect:

The Duke of Devonshire writes that the public are responding

PRINCESS MARY.

Christmas Fund Raised by King George's Daughter Now $500,000.

© 1914. by American Press Association.

The Christmas fund raised by Princess Mary of England for the soldiers at the front and the sailors on duty at sea has reached the sum of $500,-000.

So generous has been the response to the appeal of the princess to afford a Christmas for the men in the service that the plan has now been extended to include all troops, including those at home.

so generously to Princess Mary's Fund for sending Christmas gifts to all sailors afloat and all soldiers at the front that her Royal Highness has decided to extend it by sending a present to all the British, Colonial, and Indian troops serving outside the British Isles. Should the public still continue to support the Fund it may be possible further to extend its scope to include all his Majesty's troops in the British Isles, that every sailor and soldier of the King in whatever part of the world he may be shall receive a present from the Homeland.[170]

This would have major ramifications for the Executive Committee; but first, the priority was to deliver the original, full, gift to 'all sailors afloat, all soldiers at the front' – and this meant sourcing all the materials, from a diverse range of companies. Like all the activities of the Executive Committee – it was a significant undertaking in such a small amount of time.

REPORTING THE EXTENSION OF THE SCHEME
This was carried in newspapers as far afield as the United States. (*Bemidji Daily Pioneer*, Bemidji, Minnesota, 27 November 1914)

Gifts for Christmas Day, 1914

CHRISTMAS CARD, 1914
Aimed at the 'Senior Service',
'those who fight for the Glory
of the Empire'

PRINCESS MARY WANTS to send to every soldier and sailor a gift consisting of an embossed tobacco box, tinder lighter, pipe, tobacco and cigarettes. It is a modest enough little gift and everyone can be represented in the presents our gallant defenders are to receive Christmas morning.[171]

Princess Mary's Gift Fund was to provide a gift for all 'Sailors afloat and Soldiers at the front' on Christmas Day 1914. The significance of that day had been spelled out in Princess Mary's letter, a letter that provided such an impetus to the development of the Gift Fund. And in framing the name of the fund, there was surely never any doubt that, with the largest navy in the world, and with a father whose character had been so clearly shaped by his time with the 'Senior Service', sailors came first in any pecking order.[172] This principle remained inviolate throughout the existence of the fund.

Even so, with the first meeting of the Executive Committee, the idea of who would qualify to receive a gift became even more refined through association with the respective commanders of the armed forces, serving at sea and in the field. In this way, the gift was 'in the first instance…limited to sailors serving under Sir John

Sir David Graaf, South African High Commissioner and member of the General Committee, who met with Rowland Berkeley in order to put the case that the '30,000 troops fighting in South Africa' should also be supplied with the gift. This sparked a debate at the Committee meeting on 3 November 1914, particularly as Graaff proposed to raise funds to supply the gift to soldiers in Africa. Though the idea that 'each Colony and dependency' could raise their own funds in this way was mooted, it was rejected on the grounds that it would only serve to dilute the message that the gift came directly from 'Her Royal Highness, The Princess Mary's Soldiers' and Sailors' Christmas Fund'.[175] The matter as raised by Graaff was dropped, and the High Commissioner himself later confirmed that his hope to raise the additional funds had proven to be illusory.[176] Graaff had planted a seed of doubt, such that a possible extension to the fund had to be considered, and the Committee, as a precaution, 'decided to order a further 100,000 gifts' as soon as there was money to do so. Nevertheless, the expectation remained that the gift would be distributed to those

Jellicoe and soldiers serving under Sir John French'.[173] This proposal was made by committee member H.V. Higgins, a London solicitor, late of the 1st Life Guards, and it was seconded by the Duke of Devonshire himself. Higgins was well connected, having been Queen Alexandra's Aide de Camp – and he was also Chairman of the Ritz.[174] His suggestion was taken seriously, and this allowed the gift to be fully aligned with those who were on active service – leaving those serving in uniform, but at home, without consideration.

Nevertheless, the Committee was challenged by some – particularly

hardy warriors who were already committed to the North Sea or to France, and that this would amount to something approaching 500,000 recipients, including those soldiers from the Indian Army who were serving in Flanders.

Graaff's seed started to push up shoots. By late November, the success of the fund-raising effort meant that with just over a month's collection of funds from all sources, an extension to scheme could now be safely entertained. It appeared there was now sufficient money to allow the Executive Committee to enlarge the 'area of distribution of the gift', such that 'every soldier wearing the King's uniform at Christmas' would receive at least part of it. The soldiers in Africa would receive their gift after all, and many more besides:

After a long discussion it was decided that all the Soldiers under Sir John French and all the Sailors under Sir John Jellicoe at Christmas time should receive the full gift, and that the wounded, prisoners and men interned should receive, if possible the full gift, and should donations to the fund ultimately permit of it,

every soldier wearing the King's uniform at Christmas should receive a present consisting of a brass box, and what else was left for further discussion. [177]

The extension of the scheme was to take in the growing numbers of recruits, though with fewer men serving in the Royal Navy, only a small additional increase was required for them. But for the King's Armies, both at home and in the colonies, this was a considerable commitment. As such, at Executive Committee meeting of 24 November, it was determined

FIELD MARSHAL
SIR JOHN FRENCH

that an additional million boxes would be ordered – a momentous decision that effectively committed the Executive Committee to the continuance of its work for the whole duration of the war. And to ratify this decision, an emergency meeting of the General Committee held on the same day resolved that 'owing to the response that had been made' to the appeal 'it had been found possible to very much extend the area of distribution'.[178]

In the *Final Report* of the Fund, published in May 1920, the extension of the Gift Fund was neatly – and retrospectively – boxed into three 'classes' of recipients, then labelled A, B and C.[179] That this is a retrospective classification is evident from the fact that these 'classes' were not identified in the contemporary minutes of the Executive Committee. Nevertheless, most subsequent writers examining the fund have used this as a means of highlighting the subtly complex nature of the scheme, determining the differences between those, who, as originally defined, 'were serving under the command of Sir John Jellicoe at sea, and Sir John French on land', and those who were in the the army serving in the colonies (B), or at home (C).[180] It is clear

that this extension was far from the minds of the Executive Committee in the opening days of the Gift Fund – and to tidy them up in this way does not provide a clear picture of the way in which the plans were developing on an almost daily basis.

Nevertheless, 'Class A' would come, eventually, to include naval personnel at sea and serving as soldiers in France, nurses at the front, next of kin of those who had been killed, and men who were on furlough, had been wounded, or were taken prisoner. 'Class B' and 'C' included all those men serving in uniform, and all those who had enlisted in 1914 – a significant extension.[181] Despite this retrospective classification, the *Final Report* is a valuable document, as it permits us to understand the increasing complexity of the Gift Fund as it unfolded in the weeks following the original announcement, made after the initial meeting at the Ritz on 14 October 1914. However, it is important to remember that the starting point was always to supply the gift as intended, and as announced to the press the next day.[182] All modifications, additions to and substitutions from the scheme start at this point.

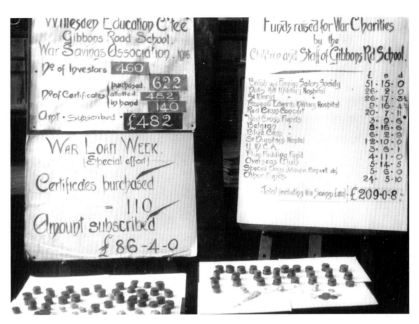

The text inside the photograph (signs):

Willesden Education C'tee
Gibbons Road School.
War Savings Association. 1916
Nº of Investors 460
Nº of Certificates { purchased. 622 / allotted. 482 / in hand 140 }
Amt · Subscribed · £482

War Loan Week.
(Special effort)
Certificates purchased
= 110
Amount subscribed
£86-4-0

Funds raised for War Charities
by the
Children and Staff of Gibbons Rd School.

	£	s	d
British and Foreign Sailors Society	51	15	0
Potts Hill Military Hospital	26	2	0
St Mary's	26	17	3½
Kings Edward's Military Hospital	8	16	4
Red Cross Concert	20	7	11
Red Cross Funds	3	9	6
Belgian	8	16	6
Blue Cross	6	2	9
St Dunstan's Hostel	12	10	0
U.M.C.A.	3	6	1
Plum Pudding Fund	4	11	0
Overseas Club	5	14	5
Special Days (Mayor, Cornwell &c)	5	6	0
Other Funds	24	5	10
Total (excluding War Songs Led)	£209-0-8		

PRESS PHOTOGRAPH OF THE EFFORTS OF THE 'GIBBONS ROAD WAR SAVINGS ASSOCIATION', WILLESDON IN 1916. Typical of patriotic demands on the children and staff to support an increasing number of charities. In 1914 the Princess Mary's Gift Fund would have loomed large.

The Princess's letter and the subsequent efforts of Sir Hedley Le Bas to publicise the Fund had paid dividends, and the Gift Fund was benefitting enormously. But the idea of 'comforts funds' for soldiers at the front had long been a concept familiar to the public, and in effect, the Princess's scheme was entering into competition with a wide variety of fund-raising activities. The charitable efforts of the British public, in many competing funds with Royal connections, were widely reported across the then neutral United States, these reports focusing on the remarkable commitments being made to supporting the health and well-being of those fighting for Britain and the Empire. It was certainly true that the range of funds, and choice for giving, was staggering:

BRITONS GIVE MILLIONS FOR PURPOSES OF WAR
Private subscriptions being raised in England for war

purposes have reached remarkable proportions. The National Relief Fund today totalled more than $16,930,000. *The Times'* fund for sick and wounded amounts to more than $2,500,000.

Queen Mary's fund for providing work for women has reached nearly $400,000. The *Daily Telegraph* raised nearly $200,000 for the Belgians in the few days since the fall of Antwerp, while The *Pall Mall Gazette* previously had turned over to the Belgian Minister in London $125,000. A fund for wounded and needy Indian soldiers started a few days ago by British people who formerly lived in India, now amounts to $275,000.

Princess Mary's appeal for Christmas gifts for men at the front has yielded nearly $900,000 and the readers of *The Daily News* have sent in $5,000 for Christmas puddings.

In response to Queen Mary's appeal to women for 300,000 belts and the same number of pairs of socks, 10,000 of each are being shipped to the front daily.[183]

In many cases, the efforts to supply funds for concurrent schemes must have been a challenge. Not least in this was the revival of the concept of the 'Field Force Fund', which had been so successful in the South African War in supplying some 235,500 parcels of comforts a year to those 'in the field'.[184] The Field Force Fund once more received a boost from the patronage of Princess Mary's Grandmother, Queen Alexandra, who again made direct appeals to the public.[185]

Others were more local in nature, in the Borough of Reigate, Surrey, for example. In early December 1914, it was recorded that the Mayoress had sent £34 to Princess Mary's Gift Fund, £50 to the Queen's Work for Women scheme, and that pupils at one school had collected the sum of £2 0s. 4d. for the *Daily News* Christmas Pudding Fund, as well as making 'garments' for 'different causes.' This was evidently a challenge as it 'meant quite a bit of self-sacrifice' though 'the children were quite delighted and eager to help in this way'.[186] A headteacher in Pen-y-bont School, Bridgend noted wearily in October 1914 that raising money was difficult 'due to the war and

the many calls ... upon the pockets of the people'; nevertheless, in the end, seven pounds was raised 'to purchase cigarettes, woollen mufflers and chocolates ... sent to Old Boys stationed in Scotland.'[187]

Looming large and rotund in most fund-raising efforts in the autumn of 1914 were Christmas puddings. Early in the life of the Princess Mary's Gift Fund campaign it seemed to some that an association with other schemes then in play might be beneficial, and particularly that being developed by *The Daily News*. This national newspaper proposed sending out a Christmas pudding to all men in the field, an echo of the Field Force Fund's efforts during the South African War. The matter of an association with the *Daily News* was discussed at the meeting of the Executive Committee on 15 October, having been raised by Lord Rothschild. In the event, the Executive decided that any extension of the scheme might lead to delays – and the editor of the newspaper was therefore not invited to join the scheme.[188]

Despite this, Christmas puddings still found their way to the front in 1914, as they would throughout the war, remaining a major effort for the *Daily News* and its readers. At the front, the matter of who was providing what 'comforts' was starting to blur – as indicated by the diary of Major Gerald Achilles Burgoyne of the 2nd Royal Irish Rifles, at Locre, Belgium:

December 20th 1914

Princess Mary is sending out a plum pudding for each officer and man here, and strict orders have been issued as to the method in which these puddings are to be distributed...It is really rather touching to think how the people at home think of us. I never thought England loved her soldiers so.[189]

In addition to this national scheme, there were many others devised to provide the pudding so sacred to the British soldier. Most of these were local arrangements, and one in particular was directly associated with its intended recipients, those serving with Rawlinson's IV Corps, who had suffered much in the First Battle of Ypres:

Lieut.-General Sir Henry Rawlinson, of whose Seventh Division is the bravest of the brave... must be artist as well as a soldier. Lady Rawlinson, who is organising a Christmas gift for each man with the Fourth Army Corps, 7th and 8th Divisions – has arranged to place with each gift a Christmas card designed by Sir Henry himself. I wonder whether he drew the card in the intervals of work at the front.[190]

LADY RAWLINSON PROVIDED CHRISTMAS CARDS (designed by her General-husband) and puddings for the men of the IV Corps in France, 1914

There was a great deal of effort put in to provide Christmas puddings for soldiers and sailors, both overseas, and at home.

The gift was, inevitably, a pudding, and contributions were invited from families of soldiers serving in battalions of the division to support them, such as the 2nd Warwickshires.[191] The Christmas card is commonly encountered, sent home by many who received it; and the General sent one to the Princess herself.[192] The card was prophetic; Rawlinson depicting a solitary sentry peering out over no man's land, while on the horizon, the year 1915 dawns. It would take three more such dawns for that sentry to stand down.[193]

There is evidence that recipients of the puddings themselves may well have become sick of the sight of them as Christmas dawned – certainly that was Major Burgoyne's experience with the 2nd Royal Irish Rifles in Flanders:

We return to our trenches tomorrow for Xmas... We don't get our plum puddings till we return of them. Some Battalions had theirs issued already, and my Sergeant Major tells me the place is littered with lumps of plum pudding simply chucked away. It's pearls before swine to try and treat some men as human beings; they don't appreciate anything that is done for them.[194]

Providing cigarettes and tobacco was a focus of many charitable schemes in 1914 and throughout the war, with some ninety-six per cent of men smokers at the time.

Evidently the flow of puddings was becoming all too much – though it may well have been simply a matter of taste, with Burgoyne noting: 'they weren't very nice. Some horrid flavouring'.[195]

If puddings were sought after as suitable Christmas 'comforts', then this was topped by the increased desire for yet more tobacco, and particularly the ubiquitous cigarette. Tobacco had figured in comforts funds from at least the Crimean War, and with the invention of the Bonsack machine in 1880 – which could make some 120,000 cigarettes a day – loose tobacco and pipes of all types would be supplanted by the humble paper cylinder packed with processed tobacco.[196] With an estimate of ninety-six per cent of all British soldiers in the early part of the war being smokers, it is not surprising then that alongside the *Daily News'* Christmas Pudding fund, there should be the *Weekly Dispatch* Tobacco Fund, devised by the newspaper of the same name.[197]

The *Weekly Dispatch* Tobacco Fund was set up to supply tobacco and cigarettes to soldiers and sailors, and produced prodigious efforts in fund raising: one local newspaper reported that by mid-December the tobacco fund had forwarded some '50,000,000 cigarettes and tons of tobacco to the sailors and soldiers at the Front'.[198] Like the *Daily News* Christmas Pudding Fund, the *Weekly Dispatch* Tobacco Fund was supported by local subscribers – such as the citizens of Cliburn, Penrith who, in December 1914, not only provided the sum of £3 18s for the *Daily News* Christmas pudding fund, but also £2 3s 1d for the *Weekly Dispatch* tobacco 'Christmas box', for 'the men at the front.'[199] Something like a

quarter of a million pounds was raised by the tobacco fund, which supplied smoking materials to all fronts.[200] Both schemes continued their work throughout the war – and would be supplemented by a myriad of local schemes designed to supply yet more puddings, and even more prodigious amounts of tobacco:

It is likely, however, that Santa's sack will contain more tobacco than anything else. Newspapers all over the country are running tobacco funds for the soldiers and in many towns Boy Scouts and little girls are collecting cigarettes. A number of cigar stores contain a box like an ordinary penny collecting box for the hospitals,

REPLY CARDS to thank donors to the 'Weekly Dispatch' Tobacco Fund

with an appeal to customers to drop one cigarette in before they leave.[201]

As an example, the Sunday newspaper *The People* had its own scheme under the title 'Bravest of the brave; send our "Tommies" the smokes they crave', with the extent of the gift being relative to the amount of money provided: 2/6 providing 280 cigarettes and 4oz tobacco (or 350 cigarettes); 5s giving 500 cigarettes and 5oz tobacco (or 700 cigarettes). As an alternative, two shillings gave ¼lb of United Service Tobacco, a briar pipe, and a tinder lighter – similar in some respects to Mary's own gift.[202]

One provincial scheme, provided by the City of Nottingham, was a

significant success – or at very least was a matter of great pride for the newspapers that organised it, the *Nottingham Guardian* and the *Nottingham Evening Post*. Unlike other funds, this one was designed to supply soldiers from Nottinghamshire regiments and Nottinghamshire sailors – including those serving on the light cruiser HMS *Nottingham*, launched just a year before the war commenced. The scheme was announced in November 1914, leaving just three weeks to gather sufficient funds for the 5,481 parcels that were sent out in time for Christmas day. The fundraising scheme was opened on the 16th, with subscribers being asked to give 'one shilling and upwards', and very quickly the donations flowed in. The comforts provided by the fund were despatched without delay.[203]

The generous parcels from the people of Nottingham contained much of value to the average man on active service (foreshadowing care parcels still sent out to the forces today) including the inevitable Christmas pudding: 'Plum pudding, 10,962 lb;

Chocolate, 5,481 lb; Woollen mittens, 5,481 pairs; Cigarettes 275,050; Booklets of greetings, 5,481; Plain postcards, 54,810; together with 5,481 pencils, tins of formeloids, tins of peppermints, tablets of soap, caramels, tins of boric ointment, laces, tins of dubbin, tins of Vaseline. Altogether, no fewer than 130,844 articles were packed and despatched 'as a token of appreciation of the services of those undertaking the hardships and risking the dangers of the great conflict.'[204] Each gift was provided with a specially produced 'Christmas booklet' that carried the message 'With most cordial Christmas Greetings from the people of Nottingham and Nottinghamshire.' The booklet included inspiring words quoted from Nottinghamshire dignitaries, together with portraits of the King and Queen, the Prince of Wales, and Princess Mary, and the words of the King's speech made on 18 September 1914: 'We are fighting for a worthy purpose, and we shall not lay down our arms until that purpose has been fully achieved.'[205]

There were very many gifts sent from other corners of Britain. For sailors and soldiers from Dunbar, a

THE CITY AND COUNTY OF NOTTINGHAM CHRISTMAS PRESENTS FUND 1914 was a high-profile Christmas fund scheme

Scottish town of fewer that 4,000 residents, the Dowager Duchess of Roxburghe organised a scheme that would send boxes 'of new tin', measuring '9 ins x 7 ins x 5 ins' and containing:– 'One or two knitted garments (according to bulk), a plum pudding, ½ lb, currant loaf, ¼ lb chocolate, 20 cigarettes, packet of stationery and pencil, cake of soap, and shaving stick. Khaki handkerchief, boracic powder, ointment, etc. copy of Dunbar Roll of Honour Gospel trust, view card with Christmas and New Year message, corners of boxes filled with walnuts, Brazil nuts, pandrops and peppermints'.[206] And at the other end of the country Bristolians made an appeal for Chocolate, for their sons at war:

The principle guiding the Bristol Chocolate Day is very simple. An appeal is made for gift – in the sustaining form of plain chocolate – to the troops at the front and to the sailors in the North Sea, and this will be timed to be distributed about Christmas. The public are asked to purchase chocolate tied up in varying sized packets at moderate price ranging from threepence to a shilling, and having made their purchase they may leave the packet with the confectioner to be forwarded to a collecting depot.[207]

For this gift, the local firm of J.S. Fry conveniently supplied their 'Royal Chocolate', 'made up in dainty cases, which can be used eventually for cigarettes.'[208] While Fry's factory was local to Bristol, Rowntrees, another one of the 'big three' chocolate manufacturers that also included Cadbury's, was associated with the City of York. From Rowntrees came a chocolate tin (in many ways reminiscent of the one they supplied in 1900), a gift commissioned by the City for its men on Active Service. Decorated with the flags of the Allies and the arms of York, it bears the words 'The Lord Mayor of York John Bowes Morrell and the Sheriff Oscar F. Rowntree send best wishes for a Happy Christmas and a bright New Year to all York men who are serving their King and Country, Christmas 1914'.[209] Both Morrell and Rowntree were directors of the chocolate company, and as a result, the tin contained two layers of Rowntree's chocolate, and was sent to all York men serving overseas – though who actually paid for the gift is still subject to debate.[210]

Amongst this seeming plethora of local gift funds, there was actually one further national scheme that was designed to supply gifts for Christmas 1914; locally run but coordinated nationwide – that of the British Grocer's Federation. How the money was raised is not apparent, but no doubt this relied on local grocers themselves:

> Prominent among the funds now being raised is that of the Grocers' Federation of the United Kingdom. This remarkable trade organisation, which is one of the most effective in the country, is unreservedly using all its machinery to raise a fund for sending a Christmas gift to every man the front the Army and Navy.
>
> After consultation with the authorities, and acting on their advice, the Federation has decided to send a parcel of toffee to each man in the fighting line and at sea. The tins, which are handy in size and shape and can be placed in a man's pocket, bear a portrait of the King on the Union Jack and khaki ground. They

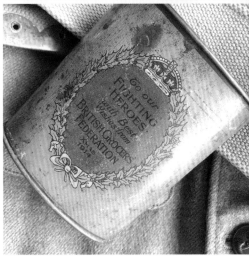

THE BRITISH GROCERS'
FEDERATION CHRISTMAS GIFT
The tin contained toffee and was designed to fit inside a soldier's tunic pocket. On the rear of the tin is a dedication 'To Our Fighting Heroes'

THE NAVY VERSION OF THE KING
AND QUEEN'S 1914 CHRISTMAS CARD
and its envelope with embossed royal arms.
Neither this, nor its Army version, had anything
directly to do with Princess Mary's Gift.

THE ARMY VERSION OF ,
THE KING AND QUEEN'S
1914 CHRISTMAS CARD
The card was protected with a layer of tissue.
Some soldiers, like Pte Kent of Edmonton, London,
addressed the envelope and sent their cards home.

each contain, half a pound of the finest British made toffee, and a slip bearing the heartiest Christmas greetings and thanks of the donors for the magnificent defence which has held up the enemy for so long. Needless to say this effort will cost some thousands of pounds.[211]

This specially designed tin was delivered with a small slip from the local donors, 'Be of Good Cheer. King, Country, Humanity are your cause. Victory. Honour. A safe return is the wish of [the name of the donor].'[212] In at least one case, the Grocer's Federation tin has been framed in perpetuity with that of the Princess Mary Gift – it was clearly valued.[213]

Undoubtedly though, even amongst all the local schemes and national gifts, it was the receipt of a Christmas Card from King George V and his wife Queen Mary – given to 'those on Active Service' – which, completely unconnected with their daughter's Gift Fund, nevertheless made a great impact on its recipients:[214]

The Christmas cards which King George and Queen Mary sent to every man made a cheery opening for the day and the Royal message: 'May God protect you and bring you home safe,' reproduced in facsimile from the King's handwriting, in conjunction with a Christmas greeting, roused lusty cheers which were repeated again and again in the long line of British trenches. The King's popularity with the Army he recently saw at work is a very real thing indeed, and the kindly thought which prompted the sending of the cards was acknowledged by the men in the warmest and most intimate of terms.[215]

The card was developed following the suggestion of Major-General Sir William Robertson, Quartermaster General of the British Expeditionary Force, and an Army Council Instruction of 12 December 1914 announced it would be delivered.[216] There were actually three types of card produced, each one deliberately depicting, in sepia tones, the bejewelled Queen next to her uniformed husband, the King's uniform either that of Admiral of the Fleet, or Field Marshal, as appropriate for the intended

The message on the rear of both the navy and the army's Christmas Card was the same: 'May God protect you and bring you home safe.'

recipient. Some 350,000 Army cards were delivered to the British and Indian troops then serving in France and Flanders; 250,000 Navy cards were sent to 'officers and men serving in ships flying the White Ensign, or serving on Hospital Ships', and 60,000 cards were sent to the sick and wounded 'who had served afloat or at the front.'[217] The card was delivered in an envelope, the flap of which bore the Royal Arms, embossed in red.[218]

It was especially well received on Christmas Day by hospital trains, busily carrying their broken cargo to the hospitals near the French coast:

Everyone on the train has had a card from the King and Queen in a special envelope with the Royal Arms in red on it. And this is the message (in writing hand) – '*With our best wishes*

for Christmas, 1914. May God protect you and bring you home safe. MARY R. GEORGE R.I. That is something to keep, isn't it?[219]

The message of the card was intimate; it connected each recipient with their sovereign, and was greatly appreciated.[220] The card was a success, a surprise, one kept secret from those who were to receive it, and was later reported widely across the Empire, especially in Australia:

LONDON December 24

Every officer and man in the army and navy will receive from King George and Queen Mary a Christmas card bearing the portraits of their majesties, and a reproduction of their autograph greetings. The gift was kept secret until today.[221]

In his diary, Staff Captain Billy Congreve recorded the reaction of men receiving it on Christmas Day, 1914:

At breakfast we received a card from the King and Queen, a very nice one too. The men are especially pleased. They had heard about the 'Princess Mary's' gift, but this Christmas card was kept very secret.[222]

Other soldiers receiving the cards were also actually depicted in an official photograph, evidently one of a series looking at soldiers of the Army Veterinary Corps at Christmas 1914. The image is an unusual one, looking rather as though it was staged. Nonetheless, outside a cottage, AVC men are pictured in mufflers, balaclavas and gloves (all no doubt supplied from home), their legs bound up with sandbags, examining and exchanging the cards and envelopes, adding them to 'a sort of Christmas tree hung with old boots and mess tins.'[223] This photograph was reproduced widely.

The cards proved so popular that a special 'Royal Christmas

MEN OF THE ARMY VETERINARY CORPS examine the King's Christmas Cards and use them (and their envelopes) to decorate a tree

RECONSTRUCTION OF
A TYPICAL DOMESTIC
'COMFORTS PACKAGE'
FOR A 'MAN AT THE
FRONT'

Card Wallet Frame' was produced commercially by The Ellbee Novelty Co. of London – seemingly for the navy alone. Finished in robust blue or dark green cardboard, it had provision for the recipient to place his name, number, squadron and ship, as appropriate – further evidence of its lasting significance.[224] In other cases, the card was carefully framed behind glass; its royal patrons – and their messages – visible for examination and preserved for posterity.[225]

In that first Christmas of the war, it must have seemed like there was a never-ending stream of 'comforts' for the troops; and depending upon their home-town, a soldier or sailor could expect to receive – in addition to the ubiquitous Christmas pudding – woollen goods, parcels of useful items, chocolate, tins of sweets, packets of cigarettes and tobacco. The flow of cards, letters, boxes and Christmas

pudding to men 'at the front' or at sea in December 1914 was staggering, and in the days before Christmas, *The Daily Mirror* was reporting that over a two-day period, some '100,000 parcels were sent in two days to soldiers at the front.' With 'the whole of the postal work for the British Expeditionary Force on the Continent done under military control', the system relied on eight hundred Post Office Clerks sorting the post and parcels at Mount Pleasant, with 'another 1,000 men engaged in receiving and distributing on the other side of the Channel,' who would nevertheless be expected 'when occasion needs, to drop mail bags, seize their rifles and help in defence work.'[226] The pressure of delivering the Princess's gift

was extreme, with at least one officer charged with organising its delivery complaining, on 13 December 1914, 'You have given us simply an appalling task in connection with the distribution of the Princess Mary's Fund gifts… I really don't know how we are going to tackle it.'[227] Tackle it they did; for the majority of men, in France and Flanders at least, would receive their gift at Christmas.

Nevertheless, the volume of traffic was staggering, with 300,000 letters sent to the front daily in 1914, and some 18,000 parcels; and over half a million parcels of Christmas Gifts were despatched 'to the front' in the two and a half weeks before 17 December, with sailors, also 'receiving great shiploads of Christmas gifts.'[228] In the aftermath of Christmas, this figure was revised dramatically upwards:

Two and a half million letters and a quarter of million parcels! This enormous Christmas mail was despatched by the General Post Office, London, to the men of the British Expeditionary Force in time for the Christmas festivities at the front. It was the expression of Great Britain's feeling for her sons enduring the hardships of active service in the most fiercely fought campaign on record.[229]

This included at least 2,500 parcels sent to prisoners of war in Germany. To meet this challenge, and to fill a shortfall made by men joining the colours, 'thousands of temporary workers' were employed to meet the demand.[230] A dim view of this was taken by Major 'Ma' Jefferies of the Grenadier Guards in his diary entry for 18 December 1914:

Everything seems hung up just now for all the Christmas parcels, which are becoming a positive nuisance…Our enemy thinks of war, and nothing else, whilst we must mix it up with plum puddings![231]

Certainly, the staggering concentration of gifts and cards sent from home, and the proliferation of well-meaning schemes can only have added to this postal burden, a veritable Yuletide log-jam.

But amongst this profligacy, Princess Mary's gift remained something special, a gift from the Royal Household itself. It would be treasured; it is no wonder that so many survive today.

The Princess's Gift Box, 1914

BIG GALE BLOWING, with very large sea and squalls. I had a most pleasant middle (I don't think!). Came down at 4 am to find my hammock sopping with water, a whole sea having come down the hatch.

Midshipman A. Scrimgeour, HMS *Crescent*, 10 November 1914[232]

Front Line. It is thawing, with some rain; and the parapets are beginning to slide into the trench. Everything and everybody plastered with mud: mud on your hands and face, and down your neck and in your food, and bits of mud in your tea.

Pte D.H. Bell, London Rifle Brigade, 27 November 1914[233]

The military backdrop to the development of Princess Mary's Gift Fund was one of many challenges. As with all wars involving the British Empire, the Royal Navy, the 'Senior Service', was the 'bulwark of the nation'; protecting its island shores and those of the Imperial possessions overseas.

The Royal Navy, the strongest in the world, was mobilised on 1 August 1914, and almost immediately it guaranteed the safety and security of the French coast facing the English Channel and North Sea. Under Admiral Sir John Jellicoe, the Grand Fleet was embodied and was to carry out its duties from the high seas to the inshore waters from almost the start; the first RN ship to founder was that of HMS *Amphion*, off Yarmouth, sunk by mines; the first German U-Boat to be sunk by the British being *U-15*, which fell victim to HMS *Birmingham* on 9 August. What would follow were hard months at sea, and many challenges, not least the loss of HMS *Aboukir*, *Cressy* and *Hogue* in

THE SINKING OF HMS *ABOUKIR* September 1914

September, defeat at the Coronel in November, and the triumph of the destruction of Admiral von Spee's squadron at the Falkland Islands on 8 December 1914.

The army under Sir John French had already endured the harsh retreat from Mons in August and had helped turn the tide that was flowing against the Allies, fighting alongside the French Army at the Marne and on the Aisne. What followed was a desperate struggle to prevent the Germans from outflanking British Expeditionary Force in the 'Race to the Sea', and ultimately to the establishment of trench warfare that would hold almost to the end of the conflict. And one place in particular would become the epicentre of British endeavour: the Ypres Salient. Here, to the east of the city of Ypres, once a mediaeval jewel set in the clay plain of Flanders, the British and French fought the Germans over the possession of the low ridges that dominated that plain. To those who had helped defend it in that first great battle, Ypres itself was approaching a ruin:

As we drew near to the old walled and moated town we thought it had not been worth defending, for it was already in ruins, and it looked as if every house and building had been destroyed by shell or flame.[234]

The Salient that was formed as a result became a drain on resources, and all men who served there in 1914 suffered from the icy conditions of a Flanders winter, exacerbated by the cloying embrace of the icy mud that gave rise to 'Trench foot', a 'serious evil' caused by men standing for 'days and nights up to their middle in water' with communication trenches 'made impassable because of the depth of water.'[235]

The Expeditionary Force that fought here was not British alone; for alongside doughty soldiers from the home countries of the United Kingdom, came the Indian Army, men of diverse backgrounds and religions who had been thrust into conditions the like of which they had never seen before. The Princess's Christmas Gift Fund appeal of 1914 transcended race and, ultimately, gender. Despite the statement that it was 'decided that every man, whatever his rank and without distinction of race' was to 'receive a precisely similar gift' (subject to when he was to receive it), the result was a scheme that was sensitive to religious observances and the growing diversity of Britain's Imperial forces.[236] Mary's appeal would

THE CLOTH HALL BURNS,
Ypres November 1914

try and cater for all – and it was down to the Executive Committee to deliver the ideals of the Fund; a task that was frankly quite enormous, given what was needed to be done in order to provide gifts for all, by Christmas Day. Its centrepiece was the brass box – a box of intricate design reflecting the Edwardian aesthetic, which rejected Victorian heavy gothic for a more modern style in everything from buildings to interiors – that was issued eventually to all eligible recipients of the Fund.

In many ways, this embossed brass box identifies with the war as it was being fought in 1914; in 2014, *The Daily Mail* certainly thought so. A hundred years from the commencement of the Great War, the newspaper created a carefully produced replica of the box to be given away to its readers, perhaps recalling the contribution of its co-founder, Lord Rothermere, who put a thousand pounds into the pot at the inception of the fund. With boxes being delivered directly to individuals, the choice of this gift to mark the Centenary was also personal, the boxes: 'still cherished in many homes, treasured reminders of a long-gone member of the family who answered his country's call. A century on, they remain as poignant and evocative as ever.'[237]

Central to the box – and its replica – is a representation of the Princess herself, depicted in profile, and surrounded by a laurel wreath. This echoes the gilded image of Queen Victoria at the centre of her Chocolate Box, issued in 1900. This is more than coincidence, a nod towards the influence that the Queen's chocolate box had, without doubt, in the formulation of the idea – a fact that was not lost on contemporary commentators:

> The box in which Princess Mary sent a Christmas present of tobacco to every British sailor and soldier at the Front… is embossed with the Princess's portrait and the flags of the Allies, and looks remarkably like the one in which Queen Victoria sent chocolate to the soldiers in South Africa during the Boer War.[238]

That the Princess sat for a special photographic portrait for the purpose was reported in the press in late October, and particularly in Society Magazine, *The Tatler*:

THE *DAILY MAIL* REPLICA GIFT TIN, 2014

Central to both Princess Mary's and Queen Victoria's gift boxes is a raised cartouche with each of their profiles in bas relief

Princess Mary has adopted the suggestion that the photograph of herself should be embossed on the covers of the boxes which will contain smoking requisites which her Royal Highness has provided as a Christmas gift for the troops at the Front. Princess Mary recently sat in the studio of Mr E. Brooks, of Buckingham Palace Road, for a special photograph, and it is this photograph which is to be reproduced on the boxes.[239]

Either side of this striking portrait is Mary's distinctive monogram in the form of a flourished M – very much

associated with the Princess's own identifiable yet simple signature.

Topping the box lid design is a shield with the Latin inscription IMPERIUM BRITANNICUM – British Empire – in keeping with the forces on active service. Clockwise, depicted in the four rounded corners of the box are

MARY'S DISTINCTIVE SIGNATURE and the basis for her monogram; this is from the frontispiece of her gift book

The distinctive components, in line with the 'Edwardian aesthetic' of Professor Adshead's design

cartouches carrying the names Belgium, Japan, Montenegro and Servia (as Serbia was called in 1914) – three of them allies by fact of invasion or threat from the Central Powers, with only Japan representing an ally by treaty. Britain's principal allies of France and Russia are shown in the left and right uprights of the box lid respectively, depicted on roundels and each overlaying three flags – no doubt indicative of the Triple Entente of Britain, France and Russia. It is interesting that, though the Royal Navy is specifically placed first in all official correspondence and announcements, it is actually an unsheathed bayonet, entwined with a laurel branch, and with its scabbard overlain by a wreath, that is depicted at the top of the design. However, the prows of two Dreadnoughts ploughing through the wave-tops are depicted at its base, situated either side of a central plaque bearing the words CHRISTMAS 1914, curiously out of centre.

The design was heralded in the press, a box worthy of those serving at sea, or at the front:

The brass box in which Princess Mary's Christmas gift is to be sent to our bluejackets and our troops is strong and well made, and yet not too heavy. Even apart from its associations, it would be worth keeping: with those associations added, we can easily imagine how it will be treasured in many a little home years after its recipient has enjoyed the contents. On the lid appears in bold relief the profile of the Princess, which seems to unite the charm of childhood and the grace of womanhood…The design is simple and dignified, and a credit to British workmanship.[240]

What is absent from the records, however, is how the designers, reported as 'Messrs Adshead and Ramsey' were selected to carry out the commission.[241] In fact, it was Stanley Davenport Adshead himself who was the designer of the box – and the curious asymmetry of the term CHRISTMAS 1914 upon its plaque was actually a design feature of his making – with a purpose:

The box in which the tobacco will be enclosed will be a permanent souvenir of a Christmas spent in the field or on the seas. The box is of brass, and has been specially designed by Professor Adshead. On medallions are engraved 'Impericum Britannicum' and the names of the Allies, and in the middle is a portrait of Princess Mary, from an engraving especially made. Beneath the portrait is the inscription: 'Christmas, 1914,' and a space is left for the owner to scratch his name or initials.[242]

It is likely that this purpose was opaque to the average Tommy or Jack – as it is more common to find boxes that have been crudely inscribed in the field, or carefully engraved when

Adshead had proposed that recipients could inscribe their name in the lower central cartouche, above the words 'CHRISTMAS 1914'. Driver John Blake of the RFA has added his regimental number there; most men inscribed their names wherever they saw fit.

out of it – but not usually in the designer's intended location.

In a period known for its industrial and domestic design, there were surely no shortage of designers, so the matter of how and why Adshead himself was appointed to the task is open to interrogation. The Professor was 'an architect and a highly sort after perspective artist,' whose drawings were exhibited regularly at the Royal Academy Summer Exhibition in London.[243] In his obituary, Professor Adshead's architectural style was described, in general terms, as 'an adaptation of classical modes to modern needs, with special attention to significant detail', with a typically Edwardian aesthetic that fits well with his design for the box.[244] But the most obvious link between Adshead and the Princess Mary Christmas Gift Fund is William Hesketh Lever.

Lever had made his fortune in establishing the Sunlight Soap brand and had determined that he would create a model village on the Wirral Peninsula to house his workers – a village that would naturally become known as Port Sunlight. Lever had a passion for architecture, and in many ways, the Edwardian aesthetic used by Adshead in the Princess Mary

WILLIAM HESKETH LEVER
Lever had endowed Adshead's professorial chair at Liverpool University, and is likely to have recommended the professor to the Executive Committee, of which he was a member

Gift Box can arguably be seen in some of the design flourishes in the village itself.[245] William Lever was a supporter of wartime charities, and specifically the Prince of Wales' National Relief Fund, to which he was a 'generous donor.'[246] Lever had also made a substantial donation to the Fund from its outset, gifting five-hundred pounds as one of its earliest donors. With this level of interest, and given his drive, it is perhaps not surprising that Lever would be appointed to several wartime committees, the first amongst them was the Executive Committee of 'Princess Mary's Soldiers and Sailors Christmas Fund [*sic*]'.[247] And to complete the link, it was Lever himself who appointed Professor Adshead to an endowed chair in Civic Design at Liverpool University, the first of its type, in 1909.[248] Though Adshead moved to a chair at London University in September 1914, there seems little doubt it was Lever who proposed – or even invited – the Professor to submit a design to the Committee. It seems unlikely that this was an open call, and more so a direct commission on Lever's own recommendation. At least once, Lever himself took the chair of the Executive Committee and was clearly a significant member, his views likely to be respected.

With the design set, the matter of who was to produce the box in sufficient numbers to be delivered in time for Christmas, was paramount. In early December, the press announced widely that 'the brass boxes, of which 500,000 have been ordered, are now being made in four important centres of industry in Great Britain.'[249] Those centres aligned with the main manufacturers of printed tin-ware in the United Kingdom, manufacturers who had contributed so wonderfully to the success of Queen Victoria's chocolate box, which was clearly such an inspiration for the design of Princess Mary's own box.

Tin box manufacturing in Britain was very much a Victorian innovation, and the invention of offset lithography by British manufacturers meant that plain looking tins could be decorated by a riot of colour. It was this type of ware that British tin manufacturers specialised in, and the main names were Barclay & Fry of Southwark, Hudson & Scott of Carlisle and Barringer, Wallis & Manners of Mansfield.[250] It was Barclay & Fry that had presented the winning design for Queen Victoria's Chocolate Box in 1900, and it was fitting that this firm would also provide for Princess Mary's successor gift – as would the other major tin-ware manufacturers. Barringer, Wallis and Manners were especially proud of their involvement in both endeavours:

It may not be generally known that a large proportion of the gift boxes to be filled with tobacco, etc. for presentation at Christmas to our sailors and soldiers on active service, from the Fund so thoughtfully inaugurated by Princess Mary, has been made at Mansfield by Barringer, Wallis and Manners, Ltd., who in 1903 [*sic*] supplied one-third of the chocolate tins sent by Queen Victoria to the troops in South Africa. The present boxes are made of brass, and bear an embossed medallion of the Princess, and will doubtless be treasured by the recipients and afterwards by their descendants.[251]

On 17 November 1914, the Executive Committee was informed that the Secretary, Rowland Berkeley, had entered into contracts with these three prominent companies for the production of the box, with each firm contracted to produce 166,000 at a net cost of 6¼d per box.[252] This amounted, at this stage, to 498,000 boxes at a cost of £12,968 15s to the Fund. With the later expansion of the distribution, and by the end of the production of the box, it seems likely that ultimately there were as many as six companies engaged, with other major companies, including E.C. Barlow & Sons, G.H. Williamson & Sons and F. Atkins & Co.[253] However, what is

certain is that by November 1915, Barringer, Wallis & Manners alone had produced 'over 750,000 solid brass boxes for Princess Mary's gift to the troops.'[254]

In late December, the *Illustrated War News* illustrated the box to be given on Christmas Day, accompanied with a caption that gave of its form:

A ROYAL GIFT FOR OUR HEROES: PRINCESS MARY'S CHRISTMAS BOX

The box, which will hold a gift of tobacco, is of lacquered metal, five inches long by over three wide, and an inch and an eighth deep. Princess Mary is sending each of our sailors and soldiers one of these boxes as a Christmas present.[255]

The production of brass boxes by all these firms was a departure from their usual patriotic wares, such as producing a decorative 'Warfare Box', a tea caddy depicting scenes from the war produced by the ever-industrious Barringer, Wallis and Manners, and other wares by Hudson & Scott that depicted the destruction of Ypres.[256] Naturally, all went on to produce munitions of one form or another in the course

THE BOX DESIGN AS PUBLISHED IN THE *ILLUSTRATED WAR
NEWS*, 19 DECEMBER 1914

of the conflict.[257] At least one of
them (the ubiquitous Barringer,
Wallis and Manners), went on to
produce a gloriously Art Nouveau
inspired tin in 1915, destined
to house a present of Cadbury's
chocolate using a patriotic gift of
raw cocoa to the value of £40,000
made by the West Indies:[258]

Three of the Crown Colonies,
Trinidad, Grenada, and
St Lucia; are sending to the

soldiers large quantities of
chocolate, made from material
grown in those countries, and
that Messrs. Barringer, Wallis
and Manners have already
made 900,000 large fancy tin
boxes for containing the gifts.[259]

This particular tin, commonly
encountered, is yet more evidence
of the general distribution of gifts
to the troops, though this time in
1915. No doubt these firms were

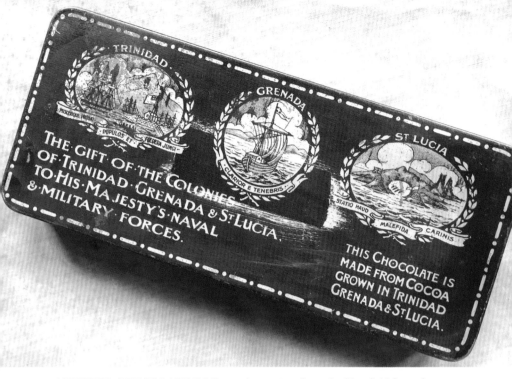

ANOTHER CHOCOLATE BOX – and an output from the Mansfield firm of Barringer, Wallis and Manners. This box contained chocolate made by Cadburys from cocoa beans gifted to the war effort by the Caribbean islands listed on its lid

also involved in the production of the decorative tins used by the Grocer's Federation and the City of York for their own Christmas gifts, already described.

Nevertheless, despite the obvious industry shown by the main manufacturers, there was one critical point at stake: while Queen Victoria's gift had been produced from tin-plate, Princess Mary's box was to be of 'solid brass'. The *Final Report* of the Princess Mary's Gift Fund in 1920 looked back on the challenges of using brass, rather than decorative tinplate, commenting that 'previously the manufacture of brass boxes had only been carried out in this country to a limited extent'.[260] Nevertheless, the companies soon rose to the challenge of adapting their manufacturing process to the production of Princess Mary's box – as distinguished visitors were to observe:

Her Grace the Duchess of Portland and Lady Victoria Cavendish-Bentinck paid a private visit to the Works of Barringer, Wallis and Manners Limited, on Friday last, to see the Princess Mary's Brass Boxes for the Troops, being manufactured. They expressed themselves as being very pleased with what they saw, and were much interested in the numerous processes through which the boxes pass. The embossing of the design on the lid bearing a medallion of the Princess Mary, attracted their particular attention.[261]

Surviving in the collections of the Imperial War Museum in London is a steel die for the box lid (actually two, the positive and negative dies needed to make a stamping), presented to the then National War Museum by the Secretary of the Princess Mary Fund on 9 April 1920.[262] It is one of at least twelve die pairs (comprising positive and negative dies) that were available for distribution to museums after the war, a number that therefore must represent the minimum that must have existed to stamp out in brass the lids of each box. Each lid top was stamped separately from the remainder of the box and was attached to the

lower portion of the lid, the brass rim of the lid top folded around that of the lid bottom. The cost of manufacturing the dies was calculated at twenty-five pounds.[263]

The surviving dies show the scars of multiple stampings, and of the work of the die-makers themselves in tooling the die. Today, collectors seeking to make sense of slight variations in these lids have performed a detailed 'spot-the-difference' that distinguishes variations in head size, the number of laurels and stalks on the wreath, the narrowness of the Princess's cipher, the size of font used for 'CHRISTMAS 1914', the use of a san serif font for 'IMPERIUM BRITANNICUM' and whether there is a full stop after 1914 – amongst other details of the strike and form of the design, and have determined that there are at least seven separate versions.[264] These show varying levels of skill in the rendering of Professor Adshead's design – though finding a possible correlation between 'type' and date of production would surely not be an easy task.

One enduring view is that there are some boxes of inferior quality – and the question of the supply of brass seems to indicate that there

STEEL DIE (POSITIVE) OF THE GIFT BOX LID
Note the standard size of the Princess's head, and the font size of 'Christmas 1914'. There is also a full stop after 1914. These any other details vary across some the range of boxes, indicating different dies (and possibly manufacturers)

STEEL DIE (NEGATIVE) OF THE GIFT BOX LID
The two dies together were used to stamp out the brass lids

LID OF A POLISHED VERSION SHOWING SOME OF THE DESIGN DIFFERENCES BETWEEN THIS AND THE DIE ILLUSTRATED OPPOSITE – such as the smaller size of the Princess's head, and the font size of 'Christmas 1914'. This is the external face of the box illustrated below

The box lid comprises two parts. This is the interior of the stamped lid

This is the second part of the lid. The external, design-stamped lid is designed to fit over it

TYPICAL BOXES SHOWING DESIGN VARIANTS
particularly the detail of the Princess's profile, wreath and font.

Top: wreath 'stalks'   *Bottom:* 19 leaves on right side, no stalks

Top: No full stop after 1914.
Bottom: Smaller profile and font, narrower cipher, wreath rose

was some form of alternative alloy or 'brass substitute' having been used in its place. It is more likely that any inferiority relates to the use of scrap brass, and given that 'brass' is a broad term applied to a range of copper-zinc alloys – usually between 56–95 per cent copper – there is the possibility of variation in quality.[265] Typically, boxes are found with splits in their four rounded corners – most likely associated with weakness of the brass at this point. In addition, there is physical evidence of some boxes having been 'plated' with bright brass or gilt – as many boxes are encountered with this plating worn off, but there is no evidence that the metal beneath this plating is anything other than brass.[266] Other boxes are encountered that are 'silver' plated (or chromed in some way) – leading to a mythology of specially produced boxes for senior officers. However, as there is no evidence that any such plated boxes were issued, this is a post-war whim of the owners, not a conscious effort on behalf of the Fund in order to produce distinctly different boxes for officers (though they are often listed as such by dealers). There

Some boxes are recognisably plated; this one is losing its plating with wear. Many others have been polished by their owners

Opposite: Silver (or chromium) plating of boxes was carried out at the whim of the owner, and was never a feature of an original issue

was no distinction made for rank, gender, race or religion.

The box manufacturers may well have been complacent in 1914. For while there was to be 'no crippling shortage of tin-plate', in 1914 at least, finding a supply of brass would be an entirely different matter.[267] Brass was a significant alloy used in a variety of munitions – and its primary components, copper and zinc – were also essential. With a shortage of shells on the horizon there was little to be spared for endeavours peripheral to winning the war. While manufacturers were also to prove they were skilled enough to produce brass boxes for the Gift Fund, they would soon find the challenges of sourcing the brass strip needed to be an altogether more difficult proposition. For example, with Christmas 1914 fast approaching, and with 370,000 of the required 500,000 gifts assembled, both Hudson & Scott and Barclay & Fry were finding it difficult to meet their orders due to the brass shortage. Fortunately, the ever-resourceful Barringer, Wallis and Manners 'agreed to meet the deficiency' and to make some 63,000 more boxes.[268]

Given the insecurity of brass supply to the contracted box manufacturers at such a late stage, the Secretary, Rowland Berkeley, set out to obtain a reserve of brass to be controlled by the Gift Fund directly. At the December 15th meeting of the Executive Committee, Berkeley reported that after consultation with the Chairman and Sir Edward Coates, he had arranged for the direct purchase of some 218 tons at 7 3/8d a pound of brass through O.T. Banks Ltd, with a view to holding that reserve in Birmingham – and obtaining a further 100 tons for delivery in February 1915.[269]

This experiment would ultimately prove to be a failure.[270] More brass would be needed – and if that brass could not be sourced from home foundries then it would have to be sought elsewhere – but that would become a story of the extension of the Gift Fund, and of 1915–16.

Fulfilling the increased aspirations of giving gifts to all men in uniform was going to be a significant challenge for, as reported by the Executive Committee, it would prevent the full distribution of the gifts to those serving overseas until August 1915; those who were in uniform at home would not see a completed distribution before June 1916 – again a direct result of brass supply.[271]

The meeting of 19 February 1915 resulted in a set of minutes that were stark in detail, reporting on the 'Failure of Brass Supply'. Rowland Berkeley's minutes did not mince its words, as he 'reported that all the firms with which they had entered into contracts for the supply of brass' had 'broken their contracts' – before listing the offending companies (see table on page 112).[272]

These bald figures are indicative of the issues that the Committee was facing. With an actual supply rate of just a third of what was contracted, things were only going to get worse. The message from all the firms concerned was clear, it was 'partly due to the want of labour, partly due to the requirements of the War Office and Admiralty.'[274] In reality, the plan to extend the scheme meant that those deserving of a box would also have to wait, and this meant that the idea of a gift emanating from Christmas 1914 would be stretched across the whole period of the war.

With the formation of the Ministry of Munitions and the mass recruitment of women in its wake some way off – it is perhaps unsurprising that there was not enough labour available to produce the brass required. Indeed, as the *Final Report* of the Gift Fund was at pains to point out, competition with the general war effort was not desirable, and on that basis 'no work would be carried out that should interfere in any way with the output of war material'; therefore it was difficult to press the point.[275] Nevertheless, the main offenders, Stubbs Metal Co and F.L. Atwood – both contracted to provide brass for the embossed lid – actually claimed it was cost that was the main factor, as though they had been contracted to supply brass at a rate of 7⅜d per pound, it was now more like 9d or 9½d.[276] Legal action against the defaulters was considered, but dropped.[277]

It was not surprising then that following further consultations, the Executive Committee came to the conclusion that it was 'impossible to obtain any supply of brass in England' and set about obtaining the alloy from America – 150 tons in the first instance. It was hoped that 'the Admiralty might be able to arrange for the shipping of the brass'.[278] Further orders were placed with an American firm to the tune of 200 tons, and Captain Lambert, on behalf of the Admiralty, and the Gift Fund, confirmed they could

Firm	Contracted (Commencing 11 December 1914)	Expected (E) and supplied (S) to Thursday 19 February 1915 (10 weeks from 11 December)
Evered & Co	30 tons at 2 ½ tons a week (12 weeks)	E: 25 tons S: 11 tons 6 cwt 27½ lbs
Carl Case & Co	50 tons at 5 tons a week (10 weeks)	E: 50 tons S: 26 tons 14 cwt 3 qtrs 1½ lbs
Hughes Stubbs Metal Co	48 tons at 4 tons a week	E: 40 tons S: 3 tons 19 cwt 1 qtr 5 lbs
F.L. Atwood	8 tons in December 1914 and then 5 tons weekly (4 weeks)	E: 28 tons S: 9 tons 16 cwt 2 qtrs 13 lbs
Earle Browne & Co	25 tons at 1 ½ tons a week (16.5 weeks)	E: 15 tons S: 6 tons 1 cwt 3 qtrs 6 lbs
Charles Ellis & Co	5 tons at 1 ton a week (5 weeks)	E: 5 tons S: 1 ton 5 cwt 3 qtrs 6 lbs
Totals	**(Expected, full 12-week supply):** 166 tons	**(10-week supply to 19 February)** E: 163 tons S: 59 tons 4 cwt 2 qtrs 3 lbs
Shortfall to 19 February 1915		**104 tons 4 cwt 2 qtr 3 lbs**

Firms contracted to supply brass: status of supply as of 19 February 1915[273]

arrange for shipping, picking up the brass from New York.[279] It would be a fatal mistake.

Lambert was true to his word, but a tragic train of events would see brass amounting to some 140 tons transferred from ship to ship – eventually reaching the hold of the RMS *Lusitania*.[280] Though it was stated that the brass had been consigned to SS *Portsmouth*, and had left port on 9 April, this was not true, as the *Portsmouth* was carrying sulphuric acid and it was likely that any fumes emanating from this cargo would 'spoil the brass'. Not surprisingly, the contractors declined to let this happen – and the brass was once again moved on, this time to the SS *Den of Airlie*, before passing to the *Lusitania*. The ill-fated liner was torpedoed on 7 May 1915, with the loss of almost 1,200 souls and, as a collateral, the brass. This much needed supply of the coveted alloy would, in Rowland Berkeley's words now lie 'at the bottom of the sea off the coast of Ireland' – the plans to provide additional brass from America in tatters.[281]

The loss of the *Lusitania* – torpedoed as part of the German policy of unrestricted submarine warfare – would have far-reaching implications for the conduct of the war, straining relations with the United States due to the

RMS *LUSITANIA*, which was torpedoed with great loss of life on 7 May 1915
It was also carrying brass strip for use in making more gift boxes

numbers of US citizens lost. Not surprisingly, justifications for the sinking of this vessel centred upon its cargo deep in the hold of the ship, and particularly whether this could be considered to be military contraband; according to one expert at least, 'on this trip almost the entire cargo was to be contraband', containing materials from food stuffs to munitions that could aid in the Allied war effort.[282] The day after the sinking, *The New York Times* published a loading manifest for the ship that included 260,000 lbs (116 tons) of sheet brass, with a total cost of $49,565, seemingly the second most expensive cargo onboard.[283] Undoubtedly, this was brass that had been destined for the manufacture of the gift boxes. Berkeley was able to source other suppliers (including some that had withdrawn their cargo in the light of German threats to the liner).[284] But once again, the Secretary would have to make good the losses by entering into contracts with British firms – but with the result that the Executive Committee had no choice but to wait until this could be supplied.[285]

Nevertheless, reflecting upon its actions, the Executive Committee was reassured that its efforts had not been in vain, as the view was taken that, if left to the brass box manufacturers themselves, it would have become prohibitively expensive to fulfil their promises.

The whole story of brass supply is complex, weaving backwards and forwards from early optimism of the box manufacturers, their failure to gain brass, the competition with munitions manufacturers; the naïve early attempts of the Committee to gather its own stocks; and the foundering of the idea of supply from the USA in the icy waters of the Atlantic. It was a battle against cost, and the struggle to provide enough alloy to support an innocent desire to provide a Christmas gift became a dead, metallic, weight around the neck of the Executive Committee. In a report in the aftermath of the *Lusitania* tragedy, Rowland Berkeley identified the remaining need for brass: 185 tons, which would be met by American contractors (54 tons), British manufacturers (86 tons), scrap (45 tons), plus a supply of 28½ tons of 'cast strip'.[286]

In the end, supplying sufficient materials was all down to cost, raw materials, and the provision of labour. Certainly, the cost of brass had increased steadily due to war conditions, rising from an initial £68 6s 8d a ton, to a staggering £110 16s 8d for the last contracts placed. Brass was found, and boxes were manufactured; some 314 tons 14 cwts and 26 lbs of brass strip were obtained directly by the Committee to try and bypass the manufacturers; and though this was a risky step, ultimately the sale of surplus brass at the end of the life of the scheme helped offset some of the challenges.[287] They had done their job, and 2,504,677 boxes were completed.[288]

There would be one additional, and very special version made that would be given to a very special recipient: a 'silver gilt reproduction of the brass box in a leather case', its blue leather lid blocked out in gold with the names of the committee.[289]

This sumptuous present, made specially by the London firm of Mappin & Webb, silversmiths to the King, was set to sparkle in its silk-lined case. In this way, Princess Mary would receive her own gift, a fitting recognition of her efforts in providing for all those who served in that first year of the war.

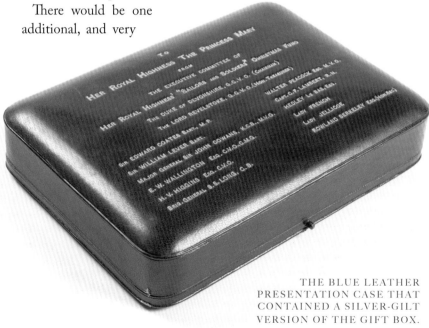

THE BLUE LEATHER PRESENTATION CASE THAT CONTAINED A SILVER-GILT VERSION OF THE GIFT BOX.
Lined with silk, it contained a remarkable version of the box, which is still at Harewood House. This presentation case carries the names of the Executive Committee

The 'Standard Gift', Christmas 1914

As ALREADY DESCRIBED all – or at least, almost all – gifts would have the Adshead-designed brass box as their centrepiece.[290] With so many surviving today, the box design seems forever fixed, the Princess herself frozen in time, her youthful gaze projected in hope to her left; whilst below, Dreadnoughts plough on forever, west and east, and above, there lies a bayonet never to be sheathed. It remains a very familiar representation of the early days of the war. But beyond its solid existence, a mythology of what actually represents the contents of the gift has grown up, derived in part from the vivid imaginations of authors attracted to this very touching story, and to that of the Christmas Truce, leading to a fogging of detail.[291] Nevertheless, the intention of the Committee was to deliver a gift of a set number of components, an intention that had been announced widely in the press, and stated in the most definite terms:

Each of the Christmas parcels will contain five articles, including tobacco or cigarettes and a tinder lighter, and every man on active service, from Sir John French and Sir John Jellicoe down to the most humble member of the Forces, will receive a similar gift.[292]

Over time, no doubt fuelled by the evolving decisions of the Executive

Within the image:

HER ROYAL HIGHNESS
THE PRINCESS MARY'S
CHRISTMAS FUND
1914

ARETTES

·1914·

THE CONTENTS OF THE 'STANDARD',
'FULL' OR 'SMOKER'S GIFT', 1914

Committee to cater for a range of different recipients, the absolute clarity of this statement has become blurred; this blurring is perhaps driven by the circumstances that created a number of variations. These have been embroidered in romantic allusion to the hope of this first Christmas at war; but what is clear is that from the outset, from the very first meeting of the General Committee on 14 October 1914, the nature of the gift was set. The gift was to take the form, 'should the funds permit' of 'an embossed brass tobacco box, pipe, tinder lighter, tobacco, cigarettes and a Christmas card.'[293]

Though this configuration has since become known as the 'Smoker's Gift', in essence it was the *standard* or *full* gift, intended for the majority of eligible recipients on Christmas Day. Variations to this norm, reflecting the changing opinions of the Executive Committee as they considered likely recipients, were simply derived from the meetings that followed that first, pivotal, gathering at the Ritz, and perhaps commenced with the first mention of the needs of the Indian Army recipients in the first meeting of the Executive Committee, the day after the initial announcement.[294]

Discussion of these variants would exercise the minds of the Executive Committee in the coming weeks, but first there were bigger matters to resolve, particularly the questions of who and how these objects would be manufactured, collected and put together in order for them to be delivered in time for Christmas. Certainly, though this was a short timeframe, the flurry of orders made by the Committee was also to provide substantial employment for British firms on the Home Front in 1914:

The present for those at the front consists of embossed brass box, tinder lighter, a pipe, cigarettes, and tobacco, with various alternatives for non-smokers, together with a Christmas card. The brass boxes, of which 500,000 have been ordered, are now being made in four important centres of industry in Great Britain. The manufacture of the tinder lighters is providing work in three localities also in Great Britain. Tobacco is being supplied by three firms, cigarettes by two, and pipes seven. The covers for the packets of cigarettes and tobacco are being printed by a London firm. The orders for the Christmas cards and the cardboard boxes for packing the present have also been placed in London.[295]

It didn't end there. As the details unfolded, so the amounts ordered started to look insubstantial. With Christmas looming, the Committee deemed it essential that a further 220,000 gifts should be assembled, beyond the original 500,000, in order to meet the needs of the navy, and to support all eventualities. As with the brass box, there would be challenges in meeting all of these orders; but it seemed there were always deserving cases to be met.[296]

Today, typing in 'Princess Mary's Christmas Gift' into an internet search engine will bring up very many webpages and lines of text dedicated to the gift, such is its popularity with the public. The box appears in at least one children's book and the linkage with the extraordinary events of the Christmas Truce, a connection inevitably made, has raised it to almost mythological status.[297] But, often, there has been extrapolation, and misinterpretation of the gift. Therefore it is important to break down the contents of the 'Standard' or 'Smokers' Gift as was given to the majority, in order to more fully understand the extent of the commitment made by the Executive Committee. The components of this gift are discussed in some detail below.

BRASS BOX AND OUTER CARDBOARD BOX

The nature of the signature brass box has already been described; but for many who encounter the box for the first time, the obvious question arises, 'how did all the separate pieces of the gift fit into it?' The answer is simple; they didn't. For smokers, the brass box was designed simply to contain just the two packets of tobacco products, which fitted snugly inside – together, it must be presumed, with the Princess's Christmas card in its envelope laying on top of the packets. Certainly, the inner brass box lid is recessed to receive it.

There are no doubt photographs of soldiers receiving their gift, perhaps taken by an amateur photographer using a Vest Pocket Kodak, or VPK – a camera no bigger than the average smart phone today. But perhaps one of the best-known representations of a soldier enjoying his gift on what must be presumed to be Christmas Day in 1914, is that of a corporal in the Army Veterinary Corps. Seated on his greatcoat, shod in wellington boots fitted, incongruously, with spurs, he is wearing home-knitted gloves that could well have been supplied by the Queen Mary Needlework Guild.[298] Around him, the grass bears the frosting of winter. He has his new pipe clasped in his teeth, and he holds the brightly-gilded brass box open to examine the packets of tobacco and cigarettes within. Placed to one side is the Princess's Christmas card in its envelope, and next to it, the

A SOLDIER OF THE ARMY VETERINARY CORPS EXAMINES HIS GIFT IN FRANCE, CHRISTMAS 1914 Missing is the tinder lighter, and no 'replacement gift' is present

cardboard box and separate lid that once contained the entirety of the gift. There is no tinder lighter to be seen. In many ways, the cardboard box is the most significant player in this scene, having delivered its contents to all recipients – but it was no doubt quickly discarded.

This cardboard box was simple in construction, designed to contain the gift and protect it on its journey. It has reinforced corners, and a strip of gummed tape (of which 1,202 reels were purchased) wrapped around its centre, designed to hold the lid to the box. The outer box was $2^{5}/_{8}$ inches (6.7 cm) deep, $5^{3}/_{16}$ inches (13.2 cm) long, and 3½ inches (9 cm) wide, and the depth of the lid was $^{3}/_{8}$ inch (1 cm) deep.[299] This simple protective box was capable of holding the brass box, with the tinder lighter and pipe placed on top – in fact, it was capable of holding two gift boxes stacked one on top of the other, but there is no evidence that the gifts were sent to the front to be assembled as separate items.[300] Nevertheless, it appears to have had no other packing to prevent these looser items moving around, though a surviving example of the tinder lighter shows that its rope was neatly bound with a simple piece of thin red string.[301] The boxes were made by the London firm of Johns, Son & Watts Ltd of 40-50A City Road, London EC, simply and appropriately listed in 1914 as 'Cardboard Box Makers'.[302] The cost to the Princess Mary Gift Fund for the 500,000 cardboard boxes required at this stage was 17 shillings per thousand (and therefore a total cost of £425).[303] Very few boxes actually survive today, though it is likely that those that have survived were used to send their gifts home, intact.

Each box was packed by hand at the Supply Reserve Depot at Deptford, a large wharf that was once a place where foreign cattle were brought ashore in the nineteenth century, and which, in 1914, had been transformed into a depot for all variety of military stores. With the gift comprising a number of articles derived from several suppliers, it was a matter of some concern to the Executive Committee that a location with

ORIGINAL 'FULL-DEPTH' CARDBOARD BOX USED WITH THE FIRST ISSUE OF THE GIFT This is has a non standard label attached; it is presumed that this was to be used for the recipient to send his box home

By the first day in December – through prodigious efforts – the 'bulk of the goods for the first 500,000 presents' had been delivered to Deptford, and packing for the front had commenced. The gift was becoming a reality, and an official Army Council Instruction issued on 10 December announced that each man of the Expeditionary Force would receive one.[305] Each gift was to be packed into its own separate cardboard box, each box packed within one of 10,000 wooden packing cases.[306] Some contemporary photographs show the wooden cases bearing the label 'HRH THE PRINCESS MARY'S CHRISTMAS GIFT FUND GIFTS 56', suggesting fifty-six gifts per case.[307] It was well that the cases were of sturdy construction, no doubt nailed closed and bearing a large label that read, in block letters, 'HRH The Princess Mary's CHRISTMAS GIFT FUND'. Certainly, the January newspapers carried pictures of such cases being man-handled for the camera in a none-too gentle way.[308]

The packing was supervised by Lady Kathleen Lindsay, who was the Manageress of the Supply Reserve Depot at Deptford (as well as a Superintendent of the

STANDARD BOX LID OF THE CARDBOARD CONTAINER, WHICH WAS TAPED IN PLACE. The box is the later, half-deep version used for individual issue to returning prisoners of war, and for boxes that were issued to the family of the deceased. The cardboard boxes were manufactured by the London firm of Johns, Son & Watts Ltd

sufficient space and capability to handle and pack the good securely should be found. General Long, a military member of the Executive Committee, suggested application should be 'made to the War Office for their store in Deptford', and that he himself could assist in the arrangements for packing 'if this was done'.[304]

ISSUE OF THE GIFTS IN FRANCE; the taped, cardboard outer boxes can be seen stacked on top of the packing cases used as an issuing table. These are former biscuit cases, and are not original cases used to send out the gift.

Woolwich Arsenal), responsible for some twelve hundred staff by the war's end – service for which she received the OBE.[309] Lady Kathleen supervised 'a large staff of packers' all of whom were engaged in 'assembling, packing and despatching the gift', significant given the large number of items – over eleven million – which arrived from a number of manufacturers. Packing was an involved business, requiring '358 reams of wrapping paper, 36,000 labels… and 1,202 coils of gummed tape'.[310] Loss of the boxes themselves amounted to just an estimated 0.0093 percent according to the *Final Report* of the Executive Committee.[311] It is interesting that with so many tempting items that could go astray, the Gift Fund paid £20 for three months insurance – though the number reportedly lost in transit from the depot was actually very small – just 215 out of 650,000.[312] Nonetheless, in the closing days of the Executive Committee's work, when there was need to take stock of remaining gifts, it became apparent that 'a very considerable amount of pilfering had taken place at Deptford' and that 'it must have mostly occurred in the course of packing there in 1914.'[313]

In time, at the conclusion of the gargantuan task presented by the extension of the gift to all those in uniform on Christmas Day, Lady Kathleen received the 'cordial thanks of the Committee' for her work, which amounted to 'supervision of the assembling and packing of the gifts to the number of 2,652,000 distributed by the Fund from the Reserve Supply Depot at Deptford'.[314]

At least two of the gifts were packed at Deptford by the Royal Family, with one assembled by the Queen, and another packed by the Princess herself. It was a matter of chance who would receive them, and they were marked only with packing slips to distinguish them – somewhat in the manner of a prototype 'golden ticket'. The Princess recorded this visit to Deptford in her diary – and it must have been quite an occasion for all those who were engaged there:

16 December 1914. In the afternoon I motored with Mama, Lady Bertha, Melle. D, and Mr Wallington to the Army Supply Reserve Depôt and the Horse Transport Depôt at the Foreign Cattle Market, Deptford, where we inspected the packing of the gifts in connection with the 'Princess Mary's Sailors and Soldiers Xmas Fund'. It was a wonderful sight and most interesting. We met Sir John Cowans, General Long, The Duke of Devonshire, Sir Edward Coates, Mr Berkeley, Mr Peacock etc...[315]

The Princess's gift was given, by chance, to a soldier of the Royal Munster Fusiliers – and the press across the Empire delighted in the soldier's laconic reply to his royal donor:

LUCKY FITZGERALD
When Princess Mary's gifts to the troops at the front were being despatched from Deptford, her Royal Highness deposited in one box a slip with the words, 'This box was packed by H.R.H. the Princess Mary. The recipient should acknowledge its receipt to H.R.H Princess Mary, Buckingham Palace.' Recently the slip was received at Buckingham Palace, and written on it were the words, 'Thank you. Received by me, 9780 Pte. Fitzgerald, B Company, Royal Munster

Fusiliers.' A note from the Quartermaster-Sergeant states that the box was handed to Pte. Fitzgerald on Christmas night when rations were sent up to the trenches.[316]

Pte Peter Fitzgerald was serving with the Second Battalion of the Royal Munster Fusiliers in December 1914; his battalion was to move into trenches to take part in the Battle of Givenchy with an attack at Festubert on the 22nd. The scene that greeted him was typical of that first winter:

No line of trenches existed, the whole country had been shelled and shelled again. It was impossible to dig more that eighteen inches as the subsoil water was always found at depth. The companies advanced in extended order, slowly dragging their feet, weighted with immense clods, stumbling into water-filled holes, silent, but determined to stick it out.[317]

Under such conditions the attack was a failure; a costly one, at the loss of two hundred other ranks and eleven officers – and the battalion was withdrawn to the equally sodden reserve trenches the day after, where they spent their Christmas – and received their gift.[318] The reporting of the receipt of the special gift packed by the Princess has an extra poignancy. Pte Fitzgerald's regimental number was 9790; the reported 9780 was actually Pte William Meaney's number. Meaney had been killed in action on 27 August 1914, the battalion's first action in France at Etreux, during the retreat. Here it had been instructed to hold the line until relieved, and this it did with great loss of life.[319] Was this misreporting a careless mistake, or a deliberate remembrance of the life of one soldier who did not live to receive his gift from the Princess?

Pte Fitzgerald was not the only Irish soldier to receive a gift hand-packed by a member of the Royal Family, but this time, the recipient was more forthcoming:

Among the Princess Mary's gift boxes of pipes, cigarettes, and tobacco sent to soldiers at the front was one packed specially by the Queen. In it was a card stating this [fact]. The recipient of this package at once wrote thanking the Queen, but thinking his letter might have gone astray he sent a second letter to her Majesty's private secretary. This letter, stamped. 'Passed by the censor,' was as follows:

C Company, 2nd Battalion, The Leinster Regiment, Expeditionary Force, 6th February, 1915. Sir,—I have the honour to acknowledge the Princess Mary's Christmas gift packed by Her Majesty the Queen's own hands. I was a very lucky man to have received it. It reached me in the trenches on Christmas evening, and I wrote and thanked Her Majesty myself the next day, but I think the letter must have been lost, in the post. JOHN DUFFY, Pte. No. 356.[320]

Unlike Pte Meaney, both men, Fitzgerald and Duffy – 'Old Contemptibles' and eligible to wear the 1914 Star – would survive the war, their gifts no doubt retained and cherished.

TOBACCO, CIGARETTES AND A CIGARETTE CARD

The brass box was specifically designed to hold tobacco products, and there was just room for a

CIGARETTE AND TOBACCO PACKETS DESIGNED TO FIT SNUGLY WITHIN THE BOX. The original issue brass box contained these, and the Christmas card in its envelope. The Princess's photograph was provided as a 'cigarette picture' sealed within the cigarette packet

Manufacturer	Tobacco	Cost
British American Amalgamated Tobacco Co	15,000 lbs tobacco at 2/6 per lb	£1875
R.J. Hill & Co, Ltd	10,000 lbs tobacco at 1/9 per lb	£875
Cope Brothers Ltd	6,250 lbs tobacco at 1/9 per lb	£547
Manufacturer	Cigarettes	Cost
R.J. Hill & Co, Ltd	5,000,000 cigarettes at 8/s a thousand	£2000
Major Drapkin & Co	5,000,000 cigarettes at 10/2 a thousand	£2542

Tobacco & cigarette suppliers for the original batch of gifts [324]

packet each of tobacco, and of cigarettes. It is presumed that its designer thought that the box would continue to function in this way long after the Princess's gifts had been consumed.[321] These products were given to the majority of recipients; but as described in the next chapter, there would be exceptions – and for good reason.

While the nature of the gift had been announced at the inception of the fund, the final decision was actually made after some deliberation, on 3 November: 'It was decided that the brass tobacco box should contain two packets, one of tobacco and one of cigarettes…'.[322]

Nevertheless, given the Princess's original conception this must not have been in doubt, and it made sense that, in providing a pipe and a lighter, a 1 oz packet of tobacco would also be given; alongside that was a packet of twenty cigarettes. This would mean that a supply of at least 500,000 ounces (almost 14 tons) of tobacco and 10,000,000 cigarettes would be needed in the first instance.

The main source of tobacco, purchased by the Committee and contracted by Rowland Berkeley on its behalf, came from several manufacturers in the first instance, with the ten million cigarettes being

Manufacturer	Tobacco	Cost
British American Amalgamated Tobacco Co	2,900 lbs tobacco at 2/3 per lb 100 lbs tobacco at 2/9 per lb	£326 5s £ 13 15s
Cope Brothers Ltd	2,000 lbs tobacco at 1/9 per lb	£175 0s
J. Bear & Company Ltd	7,500 lbs tobacco at 2/3 per lb	£806 6s
Manufacturer	**Cigarettes**	**Cost**
R.J. Hill & Co, Ltd	2,000,000 cigarettes at 8/- a thousand	£800 0s
J. Bear & Company Ltd	1,000,000 cigarettes at 11/- a thousand	£550 0s

Tobacco & cigarette suppliers for the additional 220,000 gifts [327]

divided between two suppliers: R.J. Hill & Co of Shoreditch, and Major Drapkin & Co of Bishopsgate.[323]

This was yet another huge commitment, and in the end, Major Drapkin was unable to fully meet its obligations and made a modest payment of £18 6s 11d, 'as liquidated damages for failure to deliver cigarettes according to their contract,' as well as presenting 50,000 cigarettes to the Fund.[325] These original figures were expanded when it was decided to make up an additional 220,000 gifts in December 1914, to meet all eventualities, and particularly given the fact that the Committee had decided the month before to extend the issue of the full gift to the 'whole of the Fleet'.[326] While this would stretch resources and capabilities, supply of tobacco and cigarettes was not an issue, it seems – though, increasingly, cost would be. More suppliers would have to be contracted to meet the demand.

Though the supply of tobacco and cigarettes could be resolved easily, maintaining a specific identity associated with the Gift Fund was more problematic. With so many other schemes designed to supply 'smokes for Tommy and Jack' – such as that devised by the *Weekly Dispatch* newspaper already discussed – it was important that those provided by the HRH The Princess Mary Fund should be distinctive. Probably for this reason, both tobacco and cigarettes were packed in unique, elegant and uniform golden-yellow stiff paper wrappings, with, on one side, and printed in dark blue, the name of the fund and the contents of the pack, and on the reverse, the Princess's monogram in an oval, surmounted by her coronet.[328] And the branding went further than this, as each individual cigarette was marked with the same device, in dark blue. There was a lot of intricate attention to detail.

From the inception of the fund, the Committee had accepted gifts of cigarettes and tobacco 'in kind'.[329] As these were usually wrapped in commercial wrappers, they were not ideal; and though no appeal had been made for them, the Committee nevertheless decided to 'accept all that came'.[330] These gifts would later be distributed separately, given specifically to hospitals 'in the name of Her Royal Highness The Princess Mary', as

FRONT FACE OF THE TOBACCO PACKET, showing the foil at its sides

REAR OF THE TOBACCO PACKET, SHOWING THE DISTINCTIVE MONOGRAM
The same monogram appears on the rear of the cigarette packet, and on the cigarettes themselves

The distinctive diamond pattern of the tobacco foil

Monogrammed cigarette

they could not easily be redeployed as part of the gift itself.[331] A large number of cigarettes given 'in kind' were used in this way, for the wounded in France and at home, and, at the request of Sir Hedley Le Bas, to be distributed 'amongst recruits in Ireland' – presumably as an incentive.[332]

The contents of both standard and distinctively wrapped packs of tobacco products were kept fresh through the use of a foil inner wrapper, this foil impressed with an unusual pattern of alternating stippled and smooth diamonds. The paper wrapper of the tobacco was accessible from the two sides of the pack while that of the cigarettes, at the top of the wrapper. While tobacco packs are often found

unopened, it is rare indeed that cigarette packets are found intact – even if the cigarettes are still present.[333] As we will see, there is a distinct reason for this.

Cigarette cards became a phenomenon soon after the inception of the packaged cigarette in the late nineteenth century. In part designed to protect the contents of the flimsy packaging, they were also there to develop brand loyalty, creating a desire to 'complete the set' that is common to most collectors. The earliest known cigarette card was produced in 1879 in the United States, and within ten years the Bristol firm of W.D. & O.H. Wills had produced their own versions, from humble cards with some printed words, to the

fully illustrated and sophisticated sets of cards illustrating everything imaginable, familiar as objects of desire for collectors. With men being the majority users of cigarettes in the early part of the twentieth century, it is not surprising that themes commonly depicted on cards were sporting pursuits, military subjects, and society beauties in order to encourage purchase of specific brands.[334] This continued during the First World War, though the contents became subject to censorship, and were finally discontinued for wartime economy reasons in 1917.[335]

With cigarette cards so prevalent, it is hardly surprising that the Gift Fund would incorporate its own version in the packet of cigarettes. In this case, the card was a side profile photographic portrait of the young Princess, sitting on a padded

by plain card inserts – these inserts are often found separate from the pack, used to protect the Princess's picture.[336] But what puts this out of doubt is the reference to the card in the Minutes of the Executive Committee for 22 December 1914. This specifies the need to purchase sufficient contents to make up an additional 220,000 gifts – and identifies the cards as 'Cigarette Pictures', produced by the firm of F. Eldred & Co at a cost of 2/9 per thousand.[337] The photograph would therefore principally be issued with the Smoker's Gift, and only to those who qualified as being 'afloat or at the front' on Christmas Day 1914 – what was termed 'Class A' in the *Final Report of the*

stool. The photograph was taken by the society photographer Ernest Brooks – the same photographer who produced the image that was reproduced in bass relief as the centrepiece of the brass box. The card, reproduced in black and white with a black border, measures 2⁶/₁₀ inches (65 mm) by 1⁹/₁₀ inches (49 mm), and bears the Princess's signature, Mary, in white. That this was intended as a cigarette card is demonstrated by surviving examples that have the card in place within the packet, protected

The photograph is often found associated with the Christmas card, sometimes, as in this case, with the original stiffeners from the cigarette packet

HRH The Princess Mary's Gift Fund. There is no wonder, then, that the vast majority of surviving cigarette packets have been opened.

The photograph of the young Princess made a lasting impression on the often equally young and mostly male audience who received it. In his novel *A Fox Under My Cloak*, Henry Williamson – a participant in the Christmas Truce as a private in the London Rifle Brigade – describes a meeting of his main character with German soldiers in no man's land. Opening the box, Williamson's character indicates Princess Mary's photograph to his former enemies, now fleeting friends. 'Prinzessin! Schön!' comments the German; 'She is beautiful, Princess Mary, I think' muses his new friend.[338]

The photograph would also find its way as a separate piece into at least some of the Non-Smoker's Gifts described below. That this is rare, but appreciated, is understood from Morgan Crofton's *Ypres*

Diary: 'I was one of the lucky ones, for inside the writing case I found an extremely pretty little photo of Princess Mary.'[339] That the photo was prized is also illustrated by the fact some examples are encountered in small frames of the same dimensions – presumably made to preserve the image of the beautiful princess, the benefactor of the Gift Fund.[340] In total, some 836,470 'Cigarette Photographs' featuring the Princess would be produced – and it would only figure in the gifts given to the original intended recipients. 'all those afloat, all those at the front' – and not with the gifts given following the expanded distribution.[341]

THE CHRISTMAS CARD

The Christmas Card to be sent with the gift – and treasured by its recipients – was to be printed by the well-known firm of De La Rue. It was decided on 27 October 1914 that Stuart De La Rue should be asked to 'furnish designs for the Christmas Card to be sent with the present'.[342]

With

Best Wishes

• for a •

Happy Christmas

• and a •

Victorious New Year.

From

The Princess Mary

and Friends at

• Home •

✦ ✦ ✦ ✦

THE INTERIOR OF THE 1914 CHRISTMAS CARD

Today, De La Rue remains the 'world's largest commercial banknote printer'.[343] Founded by Thomas De La Rue in 1830, the company made its name in the printing of playing cards, before diversifying into a wide range of printed materials from wedding cards to railway tickets. Its reputation was enhanced by a number of innovations, from the development of the first envelope making machine – capable of producing some 2,700 an hour – in 1846, through to the printing of postage stamps in 1855. By 1880, De La Rue had 'cornered the domestic postal market.'[344] Concerns over this virtual monopoly led to questions in Parliament in 1896, and eventually, through poor management decisions, this lucrative market was lost. In 1914, the company claimed expertise in a wide range of activities: 'The Engraving and Printing of Bank Notes, Bonds, and other Securities; the Printing of Postage and other Stamps, the Manufacture of Playing Cards, Drawing Boards, Cardboards, Envelopes, &c., and of Account Books, Albums, Index Diaries, and Fancy Leather Goods, &c...'[345] But it was achieving a commission

THE 1914 CHRISTMAS CARD AND ENVELOPE

to print ten shilling bank notes for the Bank of England at the outbreak of the war that meant the company was more financially secure, though an attempt to diversify the firm away from its standard output – embraced by Stuart De La Rue himself – was to lead once more to financial difficulties.

Once approached, De La Rue responded to the needs of the Princess Mary Gift Fund by agreeing to supply Christmas cards (and envelopes) to be included with all the gifts given out on

THE RECESSED LID was no doubt designed to accept the Christmas card when the lid was closed.

or around Christmas Day. The contracted amount was 25/s per thousand, De La Rue agreeing that 'should the cost work out at a less figure [*sic*] the Committee would secure the benefit' – meaning that this saving would be passed back to the Fund. In fact, De La Rue went further still, committing to supply the first 250,000 free of cost to the Fund, followed by 250,000 at the cost price quoted. The Committee therefore ordered an additional 100,000, making 600,000 in all from this initial tranche of cards.[346] A further 220,000 cards was ordered from

De la Rue in December, this time at an improved rate of 21s 10d per thousand – though without envelopes.[347]

Princess Mary's Christmas card for 1914 consists of a folding card, possibly cut to metric dimensions of 6 cm (= 2⅜ inches) by 9 cm (= 3½ inches), with a separate paper insert, sewn simply in with cotton. The outer card is distinguished with a red coronet over a stylised version of the Princess's distinct 'M' monogram; beneath is the date, also in red: •1914•.[348] The sewn-in insert depicts a sprig of holly, with red berries. It bears a message in stylised Old English Gothic script: 'With Best Wishes for a Happy Christmas and a Victorious New Year from The Princess Mary and Friends at Home', emphasising not only Mary's initiation of the Fund, but also all those who had contributed to its success.[349] This card was presented as part of the gift contained within a suitably sized, but otherwise plain, envelope. That it was expected to sit on top of the tobacco products within the brass box is demonstrated by the distinctive recess, designed to receive the card on the inner lid.

This attractive and personal card should not be confused with the separate card sent out by the King George V and Queen Mary already described; indeed, this card has *nothing directly to do* with the Princess's gift, other than perhaps the fact that soldiers and sailors often brought the King's card and the Princess's box home together.

THE TINDER LIGHTER

The aspiration of the Gift Fund had always been to supply a tinder lighter – designed to be sparkless and therefore especially valuable in time of war, preventing possibly fatal enemy attention in trenches or onboard ship. Such devices deployed a rope that, when lit using a spark generated by the action of a wheel or from the physical act of striking the 'flint' against steel, would smoulder, capable of lighting both cigarette or pipe. That tinder lighters were commercially available at the time is apparent from newspaper advertisements and from their inclusion in other comforts funds, such as the tobacco box fund organised by *The People* newspaper.[350] But the over-riding issue for the Gift Fund was how it would source the 500,000 lighters needed for all those at sea and at the front on Christmas Day 1914; it was to be a tall order.

The *Final Report* of the Princess's Gift Fund, published in 1920, talks in carefully measured tones about the source of the lighter. It explains that the Executive Committee had examined examples of lighters that were for sale commercially – and had settled upon one type. As 'the quantity of tinder lighters required being very large' the report explained, 'it was necessary for the manufacture of them to begin at once'. And then came the crunch point; 'arrangements were made with the contracting firm that this should be done without waiting for the formal execution of the

With such a warrant, it is perhaps not surprising it was Asprey who would be selected to carry out the commission.

For such a fancy supplier, the lighter was simple in construction, comprising around ten inches of orange rope with a nickel-plated steel sleeve (bearing the distinctive mark 'Asprey LONDON') and removable cap. The cap carried a channel for the 'ceric stones', which would be used to strike a spark on the steel, and thereby light the end of the rope. (The 'stones' are now, almost invariably, missing in surviving examples.) Replacing the cap would extinguish the glowing embers; and this cap bore a large coronet and a small representation of the Princess's 'M' cipher over the block-letter words 'XMAS FUND 1914'.[353]

But it was the 'ceric stones' that would prove to be the downfall of this endeavour. Not stones at all, they are composed of a chemical alloy of thirty per cent iron, and seventy per cent cerium – a rare earth.[354] Known as 'ferrocerium' the alloy was patented by Austrian

contract'.[351] This un-named firm was none other than leading New Bond Street firm of Asprey & Co, listed in the 1914 *Who's Who in Business* as 'Goldsmiths, Silversmiths, Watch and Clock Makers, Travelling Bag and Dressing Case Manufacturers, Fine Leather Workers, and Stationers'. It was 'One of the oldest London firms in this trade' and carried a Royal Warrant, 'Special Appointment as Travelling Bag, Dressing and Writing Case and Despatch Box Manufacturers to His late Majesty King Edward.'[352]

industrial chemist Carl Auer von Weisbach in 1903, and was manufactured principally by his company, *Treibacher Chemische Werke GesmbH*, founded in 1907, still functioning today.[355] It was the cerium content that made the sparks when struck; with Austria (and its inventor's factory) being the main source of the 'Ceric Stones' it was not surprising that any British firm dependent upon the supply from an enemy country might be in for a trying time. It was perhaps no wonder, then, that Asprey would 'decline to sign the contract on the grounds that they were unable to obtain the necessary quantity of stones.'[356]

THE ASPREY TINDER LIGHTER, WITH ITS CAP REMOVED. A spark was induced by striking the 'ceric stones' (here missing) against the steel, thereby causing the rope to smoulder

The careful wording of the *Final Report* relating to the supply of the lighter is not to be found in the minutes of the Executive Committee, which did not hold back in its views. As Christmas loomed, at the meeting of 1st December, Mr Berkeley reported that 'Messrs. Asprey had completely failed in their Contract for the supply of tinder lighters, and had stated that there was no binding contract between themselves and the Committee.'[357] Ruefully, the secretary noted that the nature of the 'transaction' between him and Aspreys had simply been by 'letter, and partly by interview' and as such 'it was correct to say that technically there was no contract'.[358] Legal action against Aspreys was not really an option, and would not resolve the difficulties the Executive Committee now faced.

In desperation, the Committee realised that the original plan to supply a distinctively designed and branded tinder lighter was not likely to happen, and that only a fraction of the quantity of lighters that had been promised by Asprey could be supplied. There was nothing for it, and on 1 December 1914, the Executive Committee resignedly resolved to despatch the gift without the lighter, with the forlorn hope that if Asprey came up with the goods in due course, they could be sent on.[359] This would, quite literally, become a pipe dream.

Nevertheless, as late as 15 December, the Committee was reporting that the company had agreed to deliver 100,000 lighters within three days, and an additional 23,000 within a week.[360] These would be the only ones Asprey produced, and they were distributed exclusively to the army.[361] As a consequence, today, they are scarce and highly sort after by collectors. Rowland Berkeley was left having to consider other options to fulfil the ideal of the complete gift – and time was against him.

REPLACEMENT GIFTS
FOR THE ARMY

With Asprey's failure to supply sufficient tinder lighters, the Executive Committee no doubt felt duty bound to make good the promises made in the early days of the announcement, following the initial meeting of the General Committee on 14 October 1914. The dispute with Asprey had consumed a great deal of time, and two months on from this meeting, there was still no sign of a resolution. In the meeting of 15 December 1914, the hard-working Secretary reported that he had 'endeavoured to obtain' a further 50,000 generic tinder lighters 'at a price not exceeding 1/-', and that he had been successful in gathering at least '10,000 from Messrs Wilson & Gill at 8/6 a dozen' and a further '1,000 from Messrs Barclay & Co at 11/6 per dozen', with the promise of more to follow.[362]

Without attributed examples, it is difficult to determine what these generic lighters looked like with any certainty, though a typical example that could be bought as part of '*The People* Tobacco Fund', was illustrated in that newspaper, no doubt representative of the type then available, comprising a rope, metal housing and abrasive wheel.[364]

This commonly encountered type may well be the one

TINDER LIGHTERS		
Manufacturer	**Number**	**Cost per lighter**
Asprey & Co [Gift Fund branded]	137,000	5½ d
Perkins & Co [non-branded]	1,000	11½ d
British American Co. [non-branded]	3,600 2,880	1/- 7½ d
L & A Arkle [non-branded]	15,084	9d
Wilson & Gill [non-branded]	9,980	8½ d
Total Number	**169,544**	**Ave. 6 ¼ d**

Tinder lighters finally sourced by the Gift Fund[363]

TINDER LIGHTERS The Asprey type *(right)*, compared with the commercial type *(left)* which is fitted with a wheel to cause friction. This was often given in other gifts, and is probably typical of the replacements sourced by Rowland Berkeley

purchased by Rowland Berkeley for the Gift Fund.

Even if Berkeley was successful in fulfilling his order of 50,000 generic lighters, there would be significant shortfall, as these and the Asprey originals combined were 123,000 plus 50,000 (173,000) delivering nowhere near the magic number of 500,000. If the men at sea and at the front were to receive their due, a more pragmatic solution needed to present itself. As such, in the same meeting it was agreed that 'tinder lighters to the number of 150,000 or more were to be sent to the men in the trenches' and that 'a further 150,000 gifts of various kinds should be sent to the remainder of the troops in France'.[365] Once more it would be down to Rowland Berkeley to source these items, and time was pressing. The Secretary certainly got busy. Within a week he had sourced some 169,544 miscellaneous items, which, together with the tinder lighters already obtained, meant that there were altogether 370,635 items to make up the gift.[366]

The items that Berkeley had sourced were commercially available and bought off the shelf – and these would be destined for the army in the field; the navy would have their own requirements. Given the Executive Committee had first charged the Secretary with purchasing the additional items on 15 December, with the orders placed and reported just a week later, there was no time to create special 'Princess Mary Gift Fund' branded items, other than the monogrammed bullet pencils already planned. Of paramount importance was price – an average of 5d per item – and availability. It is fortunate that a list of them was made at the time, especially as these items have been subject to considerable speculation, with objects attributed to the gift that have little evidence to support them. They were a hotch-potch set of mostly commercially available items that seem to fall into three categories: smoking requisites, grooming items, and stationery.

Without direct association with a given Gift Box – often framed – it is difficult to determine exact provenance for these items, other than the distinctively branded bullet pencils. It is perhaps possible to speculate on the nature of the other type of pencil (to be given with the postcards), as it is reasonable to think that these would be similar to those given away as part of the

REPLACEMENT ITEMS		
Number purchased	**Item**	**Comments**
51,567	Tobacco pouches	Smoking requisite
2,160	Cigarette cases	Smoking requisite
10,000	Shaving brushes	Grooming
30,660	Combs	Grooming
1,074	Scissors	Grooming
20,232	Knives	Grooming/stationery
20,000	Bullet pencils	Stationery. Presumed to be in addition to those obtained for the Navy.
17,712	Pencils	Stationery. Assumed not to be the bullet pencil type
29,360	Sets of postcards	Stationery. Intended to be given with the pencils [as specified in the minutes]

Assorted gifts purchased (for the army) in lieu of tinder lighters [367]

stationery set described in the next chapter. There is, however, plenty of room to speculate on the matter – but without attributed provenance it is a probably a fallacy to do so. And perhaps one item above all others that has been subject to a great deal of speculation is the form of the 'gift knife', which was given in large numbers.

This speculation has tried to visualise what the knife looked like, and one source in particular identifies 'two versions of the knives that were believed to be packed in some of the gift boxes given to troops in World War One.'[368] These depict robust, bone-handled clasp knives of a military pattern, rather than the more likely, cheaply

KNIVES *(clockwise from top left)* Standard army issue 'clasp knife' pictured here for comparison. 'Duralumin War Knife, 1914', a commercial knife with aluminium grips. There is no evidence that this no-doubt expensive knife was the one bought as a replacement item, though this has been speculated by some collectors. Bone-handled clasp knife with copper loop; it has been suggested that this type is a 'replacement gift', but this seems unlikely, given its probable cost. At the centre: a fruit/penknife with provenance that is the most likely replacement gift knife produced and commercial pen, or fruit knife.[369] More reliable is a specimen that belonged to a soldier of the 2nd Royal Irish Rifles, who has marked his box with his initials and battalion, and who, with the same hand, has inscribed his simple, two-bladed, bone-handled, $2^5/_{16}$ inch-long penknife with regimental insignia and battle honours.[370] This, surely, is the more likely candidate for the 'typical' gift knife, with similar examples found with other gift boxes, and is taken as typical here.

Provenance of the gift knife, here 'scrimshawed' by its owner, a soldier in the 2nd Royal Irish Rifles. This man, 'WA', has inscribed his initials on the base of his gift tin. The battalion was in France in December 1914

However, more difficult to determine would be the combs, scissors and shaving brushes; and the tobacco pouches and cigarette cases – but no doubt these were cheap and commercially available. Other items with provenance have also been identified – with Soldier's Testaments being encountered associated with the gift, in frames, or sometimes with inscriptions. With so many gifts being given out at Christmas, from different agencies, it is likely that these have different sources. It is also difficult to know whether these items, or at least some of them, were delivered to the troops at Christmas, or whether they were sent on later. It seems likely that, like the silver

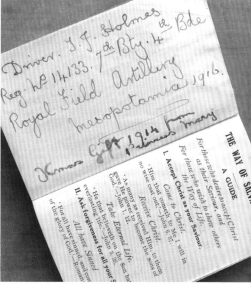

Many other items have been speculated upon as replacement gifts. This pocket testament is inscribed by its owner, 'Xmas Gift 1914 from Princess Mary', but it is equally likely that this was a coincidental gift from another donor

bullets for the navy, these were delivered at a later date.

SILVER BULLETS FOR THE NAVY

The number of alternative gifts and tinder lighters that were available would not make up the shortfall to meet the needs of the army and navy combined. The 'Grand Fleet' alone under the command of Sir John Jellicoe would require 160,000 replacement gifts to make up the shortfall. When the Executive Committee was established, the navy's representative was Captain Cecil Foley Lambert RN, a Commodore who would become a Rear Admiral by the war's end.[371] Lambert's view, originally, was there would be 'approximately 145,000 Naval men, including the Marines', and this was the primary basis for calculations.[372] It was the meeting of the 24 November 1914 that extended the range of the naval gift, and this meant that 'the whole of the Fleet, including mine-sweepers and dockyard officials' would now be entitled to the full gift, replete with all its smoking requisites.[373]

However, the Royal Navy's long history of recruiting boys under eighteen to the Service provided a complication with regard to the suitability of a gift packed with smoking materials. Most boys carried out their duties at home, on training ships, and with ranks rising to 'Boy First Class', before moving to the sea-going rank of Able Seaman. Perhaps the most famous of these young men was John Travers Cornwell, who received the Victoria Cross posthumously for his bravery during the Battle of Jutland in June 1916.[374] When they reached their eighteenth birthday, these young men automatically became Able Seamen, and, like Cornwell, many served at sea.

The Executive Committee deemed that boys serving in the navy would, perhaps naturally, not be allowed to receive the full Smoker's Gift – but simply the box, Christmas card and bullet pencil. However, a suggestion that Midshipmen should receive an unspecified 'separate present' – presumably for the same considerations – was not adopted.[375]

In January 1915, the full extent of the distribution to almost all branches of the navy was outlined in some detail, far in advance of the original 145,000 sailors originally specified by Captain Lambert.

Catering for them, in supplying all of the gift's intricacies, was clearly a challenge.

The concept of the origin of the bullet pencil is discussed later, but its use as a replacement gift clearly relates to the intervention of Lady Florence Gwendoline Jellicoe, a dedicated member of the Executive Committee. On 15 December, no doubt conscious of the need to protect the interests of the sailors under her husband's command, and fearing that they would not receive the tinder lighter, Lady Jellicoe had suggested that sailors should receive pencils in their place.[377] The idea was further advanced in the meeting

GIFTS TO THE ROYAL NAVY

'Squadron, etc'	'Total No of presents'
Grand Fleet at Scapa	55,819
Destroyers, Trawlers, etc at Cromarty	2,046
3rd, 5th, 6rd Battle & 3rd Cruiser	22,227
Ships at Home Ports, etc	19,530
Armed Merchant Cruisers, Fleet Messengers, etc	8,141
11th & 12th Cruiser	5,328
1st & 3rd Flotilla	5,914
6th, 7th, 8th & 9th Flotilla	7,600
Air Service	2,176
Submarines	4,051
Royal Marine Division	11,938
Trawlers, yachts, etc	8,866
"Pembroke", "Vivid", Shotley, etc*	37,712
C.C. Cruisers, etc	1,241
Admiralty, miscellaneous ships	1,911

'Squadron, etc'	'Total No of presents'
Atlantic Cruiser Forces	16,686
Ships on Foreign Stations	24,088
Royal Naval Division	10,513
Total number of presents	**245,787**
Less Boys, Shotley, "Impregnable" & "Powerful"*	3,034
Additional Issues for Ships (807), Coastguard and R.N. Division (3,677)	4,484
Total [Full gift]	**247,237**
'Required for Boys' [box, card & bullet pencil]	3,034
'Widows' [box & card]	5,000
Grand total [Full gift plus gift for boys & widows]	**255,271**

* Shore establishments
The extent of the Gifts made to the Royal Navy, after extension of the scheme [376]

that followed, and this defined the gift to be finally delivered to sailors, at least those who had been at sea on Christmas Day. Perhaps befitting its status as the Senior Service, the navy would neither receive the tinder lighter, nor any of the miscellaneous replacement items purchased by Berkeley, but in their place were given bullet pencils, with Sterling silver pencil holders – some 240,000 being purchased at a cost of 5½d.[378] In April 1915, a picture of the silver pencil for the men of the Royal Navy was published in the *Illustrated War News* – though the report displayed evident confusion between the Princess, and her mother:

A ROYAL GIFT AND A ROYAL INSPECTION

Queen Mary [*sic*] has presented the men of the Navy each with a pencil-case made from a cartridge actually used 'somewhere in France' with a silver holder representing the bullet. The cases are engraved with the letter M and a crown.[379]

Arguably, the presence of the silver bullet pencil makes the Navy's full gift unique, as sailors received only the silver version. Often, these are identified through them being framed with the otherwise separate, Admiralty, version of the King and Queen's Christmas Card, the frame having, in addition to the box, pipe, cigarettes, tobacco and Christmas card, the silver topped bullet pencil.[380] However, though it is recognised that some soldiers would eventually receive silver pencils too, there was no pattern to this. Nevertheless, this was surely a nice addition to the gift, but given the fact that Christmas was almost upon them, the chance of manufacturing sufficient pencils in time was receding fast. The expanded figures were also a cause for alarm, as too few had been ordered even through some 20,000 had been added to the revised figure of 220,000 as a contingency.

LADY FLORENCE JELLICOE
Originator of the idea that bullet pencils should be given as replacement gifts for sailors

It was determined by Captain Lambert that it 'was not necessary to send the pencils to the depots', and men serving at shore stations would miss out on this part of the gift. In any case, sailors would have to receive their gift without the pencil, which were reported as being 'ready for distribution' in late January 1915.[381]

THE SILVER BULLET PENCIL
As depicted in the 'Illustrated War News', April 1915

GIFT TIN AND ASSOCIATED 'BULLDOG' TYPE PIPE

And at the final meeting of the Executive Committee, in 1919, an application for a pencil was made from a sailor who had, indeed, served at a depot. The Committee was realistic – there were many specimens still remaining at Deptford, and there was no chance of a new distribution. Nonetheless, the sailor got his pencil.[382]

THE PIPE

The question of what type of pipe was issued with the Princess Mary Gift has also exercised the minds of anyone who has taken the trouble to consider the matter.[383] Certainly, pipes that can be attributed to the Gift Fund and which are associated with men who received them are startlingly random in form, perhaps not surprising given the manner in which they were acquired. In October, the Executive Committee had sourced some 708,000 pipes at prices ranging from 4½d to 9d (which would

CONTRACTED PIPES, NOVEMBER 1914

Pipe Supplier	Number of pipes	Total cost
Harrods Ltd	207,280	£5,107 16s 8d
R.J. Hill & Co. Ltd	120,000	£3,625 0s 0d
Fribourg & Fryer	23,040	£595 0s 0d
Charatan & Son and The Amalgamated Briar Pipe Factories	16,128	£520 10s 0d
Venis & Co	10,312	£222 7s 8d
Marechal Ruchon & Co	38,247	£970 3s 4d
Charles Maas & Co	14,400	£420 17s 6d
The London Pipe Co and E. Degningand	70,596	£1899 6s 3d
Totals	**500,003**	£13,361 1s 5d

Pipe wholesalers, the numbers of pipes they were to supply, and the total cost [388]

amount to some £13,275 to £26,550 dependent on price) and had arranged for samples to be supplied. It was agreed that the Duke of Devonshire, Walter Peacock and Rowland Berkeley would handle the negotiations.[384]

As in all his dealings, the Secretary Rowland Berkeley was given authority by the Executive Committee to supply the goods, and he was remarkably industrious. In the minutes of the Committee of 17 November, Berkeley provided a list of the contracts issued to the suppliers of items that would become a significant part of the gift received by the men.[385] Amongst those to be acquired were half a million pipes, with some eight separate wholesale suppliers listed. Given the huge numbers of pipes required and the fact that there was little over a month to go before they had to be supplied to the men at sea or at the front, the secretary

CONTRACTED PIPES, DECEMBER 1914		
Pipe Supplier	**Number of pipes**	**Total cost**
Harrods Ltd	150,000	£312 10s 0d
R.J. Hill & Co. Ltd	73,442	£4,218 11s 2d
Fribourg & Fryer	3,448	£223 16s 0d
Amalgamated Briar Pipe Co	25,128	£761 8s 0d
Marechal Ruchon & Co	29,315	£719 4s 11d
Charles Maas & Co	2,160	£45 0s 0d
The London Pipe Co	60	£1 17s 0d
Frischer & Co	15,730	£140 15s 9d
F.W. Cole	3,024	£95 11s 0d
L & A Orlick	5,772	£168 7s 0d
Cape & Peter & Co	7,920	£228 0s 0d
Totals	**500,003**	£13,361 1s 5d

Numbers of contracted pipes after extension of the scheme, and the total cost [389]

had set to work to obtain them from wherever he could. Not only that, gifts of pipes 'in kind' were also accepted, increasing the diversity of types likely to be distributed. There was no standard pattern to work from, and with such a short time frame available, and the fact that they were obtained from many suppliers, it is safe to conclude that no pipes were likely to have been engraved with the Princess's distinctive monogram, or even carry a 'Princess Mary Gift Fund' label.[386]

The same suppliers – and more besides, would be called upon to supply yet more pipes in December 1914, to meet the extension of the gift to all sailors, at home or at sea, and to meet any further

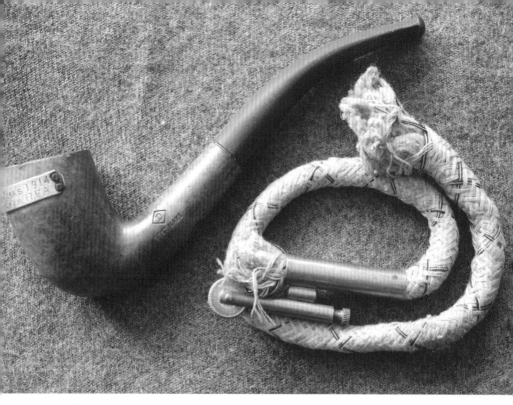

'DUBLIN TYPE' ATTRIBUTED PIPE that was given to (and engraved by) Bombardier W. Tucker of the Royal Field Artillery

eventualities. Perhaps because of this, Berkeley had clearly over-ordered, just in case.[387]

For those with limited experience of tobacco pipes, it might come as a surprise that there are actually many different types – today as there were then. Pipes differ in terms of materials (e.g., briar, clay, porcelain, meerschaum, etc), and in terms of design.[390] At one point, the minutes of the Executive Committee record the consideration of a uniform purchase of 'Calabash pipes', those so often associated with the fictional character of Sherlock Holmes, with a sinuous stem and a flamboyant two-tone colouration and flaring bowl, traditionally manufactured from the calabash gourd predominantly harvested in South Africa.[391] Rowland Berkeley had entered into a correspondence with the South African Trades Commissioner about the supply of such pipes; though undoubtedly these could have been provided, the Committee agreed that at 3/- each, they would be too expensive –

amounting to a staggering £75,000 for the half-million pipes required.

With so many suppliers, and with such a demand to be provided over such a short period of time, the reality was that any pipe that could meet requirements would suffice. And if we look back at this and consider those requirements, it is most likely that they were simply: cost, availability, and size – the latter due to the need for them to fit inside the cardboard box used to house the brass box itself, and, it was hoped, the tinder lighter. This meant that the pipes had to be compact, not exceeding a length of some 5 to 5½ inches.

A survey of surviving examples shows a diversity of briar pipe shapes. Given that they were obtained from several suppliers, it is difficult to map type to a particular one. Mostly smoothly finished, some have plated silver bands. Commonly accepted pipe shapes include straight and bent 'billiard' styles, as well as 'apple', 'bulldog' and 'Dublin' types. The billiard style is a simple, unfussy and relatively short-stemmed pipe with a cylindrical bowl, which can be straight or curved. These are commonly seen in attributed gifts

'BILLIARD' (TOP) AND 'BULLDOG' (BOTTOM) TYPE PIPES
Attributed to soldiers who served in the Ypres Salient

'BULLDOG' (TOP) AND 'APPLE' (BOTTOM) TYPE PIPES

and with their simplicity, were no doubt value for money. 'Apple' pipes have a similar style, but a distinctly rounded bowl. 'Bulldog' pipes are short, and typically have a section with a distinctive 'diamond' shank and grooved bowl, while 'Dublin' pipes have a conical bowl and curving stem.

All versions are seen in surviving, attributed gifts – often in frames, sometimes carved by the soldier or sailor in honour of its receipt – or even labelled with mounted silver plaques. For the most part, however, they became an anonymous item of the soldier's kit, sometimes, no doubt, sent home with the personal effects of a man killed in action, or died of wounds.[392]

Assembled from many suppliers in the closing weeks of 1914, the complexity and intricacy of the Princess's Christmas Gift has been discussed ever since. This, perhaps, is just one of the reasons why the gift retains its enduring fascination for collectors, despite the large numbers produced.

Reactions to the Gift, 1914-15

THE PRESS ASSOCIATION is authorised to state that the distribution of gifts from Princess Mary's Christmas Fund has now been made to the whole of the Navy, the whole of the Expeditionary Force, and to the wounded in this country, also, with a few exceptions, to the next of kin of those who have lost their lives on active service. Gifts have also been reserved for those men who are prisoners of war. The gift will be forwarded as soon as possible to all those, other than those wearing the King's uniform on Christmas Day, who were, or had been, at the front.[393]

CARD SENT HOME FROM ABLE SEAMAN CROUCHER OF HMS *HIBERNIA*, DEPICTING THE GIFT HE RECEIVED

According to Rowland Berkeley's report of 8 April 1915, 'practically all the men with the Expeditionary Force on the 24th December had received the gift'.[394] Its distribution had sent the Army Postal Service into overdrive, but the system had held, and soldiers were appreciative of the gifts they received in the field. For the navy, however, getting any form of mail in time for Christmas was a much tougher proposition. It was inevitable that those sailors on Active Service would have to wait for their gifts. While many were on Home Stations, there were others serving with distant patrols or in far off actions across the globe. For example, while the Royal Navy's first major action was the Battle of Heligoland Bight, fought in the North Sea on 28 August 1914, by the end of the year it was operating in South American waters, first suffering defeat off the coast of Chile in the battle of the Coronel, on 1 November, before, a month later, destroying the German East Asia Squadron at the Falkland Islands – all part of the developing 'global war'.[395]

GIFT BOX carefully inscribed by sailor E.S. Johnson of HMS *King Edward VII*, which served with the Third Battle Squadron in Home Waters

Nevertheless, by April 1915, 'the whole of the gifts, including the cartridge pencil cases' had been 'handed over to the Admiralty, and had been distributed except in one or two isolated cases.'[396]

As Christmas approached, the Royal Navy ensured that age-old traditions were followed. Sailors like Willie Hartnell of HMS *Argyll*, serving on a Home Station, wrote home to express delight at receiving whatever home comforts could be spared 'I have just received your letter and parcel and the Babe's Photo... I am delighted with the Photo and more than that with the presents just fancy you sending me all those things...'.[397] One sailor, on board HMS *Albemarle* and part of the 6th Battle Squadron

ONE SAILOR'S GIFT
KEPT SAFE AND GLAZED
IN A CUSTOM-MADE OAK
FRAME INDICATIVE OF
'HEARTS OF OAK'

PRESENTED BY
PRINCESS MARY
XMAS 1914.
H.M.S.ALBEMARLE

This man was serving on board HMS *Albemarle* when he received his gift

serving as a defence against possible German invasion in the channel ports was so taken with his gift that he crafted a wooden 'Hearts of Oak' frame to house it.[398] For Lieutenant Scrimgeour, on board the former Allan Line ship and now Armed Merchant Cruiser HMS *Alsation* at Scapa Flow there would be 'an excellent Xmas dinner' and 'a musical time afterwards with pianola and gramophone' (though with no record of receiving his gift).[399]

Those on more far-flung stations would have to improvise and await the possibility of mails arriving with other ships – the men of HMS *Kent* 'gathering greenery from a Chilean hillside' in order to decorate their ship.[400] Petty Officer Samuel George Hobbs, also off the coast of Chile, spent his Christmas 'very quietly' on board HMS *Glasgow* whilst at

Vallenar Roads Coaling Station, though his calm was interrupted when, at 4 pm, the ship 'had to go to sea in company with BRISTOL having received orders to join CARNARVON in Magellan Straits.'[401]

For PO Hobbs and his ship mates there was no issue of Princess Mary's Christmas Gift that day – that would have to await the arrival of the ship *Otranto* in the River Plate six months later, which 'arrived from England … bringing mails and three Ratings' and, mentioned without fuss, 'Princess Mary's Christmas presents.'[402] By then, the impact of the gift had perhaps been lost.

The discussion over the suitability of boy sailors receiving the gift meant that some, despite sharing the same conditions and dangers as their more mature shipmates, missed out altogether.

Ordinary Seaman D.A. Lee wrote home to Harrogate with some very direct requests:

Dear Mother,—Just a line to let you know I received your welcome letter. I hope all are well at home. I have not heard from Mr. Mawson. Tell Will and Gladys 1 am allowed to smoke. I am now an ordinary seaman. You can send me some fags if you can spare them. You can send the scarf – 1 can do with it. It's cold where I am now. I did not get Princess Mary's gift. I was only a boy then, and we were not allowed them. Never mind about chocolates, send fags. I did not receive papers and books I think at all this time from Your loving son, Douglas.[403]

Tragically, Douglas Arthur Lee was killed at the Battle of Jutland; his ship HMS *Black Prince*, separated from the main fleet, was sunk in an engagement with five German ships, with the loss of all hands.

Sailors who survived the loss of their ship in action also suffered the loss of their treasured gifts from Princess Mary. The pre-Dreadnought battleship HMS *Formidable* was conducting gunnery exercises off Portland on 31 December 1914, when she was hit by two torpedoes and sunk in the early hours of New Years' Day, with the loss of 547 men. The survivors were landed at Brixham. Such was the significance of the gift that a local resident was moved to write to Rowland Berkeley in order to highlight the sailors' loss:

The survivors of the *Formidable* who were landed at Brixham having expressed their keenest disappointment the loss of their Christmas gift from Princess Mary's Christmas Fund, Miss Ruby Curtis, the Bolton Hotel, Brixham, interested herself on behalf of the men, and has received the following reply from Mr. Rowland Berkeley, the secretary to the fund: in reply to your letter with reference to the survivors of his Majesty's ship *Formidable*, I regret to inform you that it will not be possible to send a second gift to these men. Although the case appears to be a hard one, I do not think it any different from that of the soldiers who have been unhappily killed in France within a few days of

POSTCARD FROM 'FRED' SENT HOME TO KENT
IN DECEMBER 1914. 'This is some of our happy party'

receiving the gift, and whose gifts, in consequence, may be lost. If we were to commence sending a second gift, I fear the claims would be unending.[404]

Nonetheless, Berkeley was able to offer some consolation:

I may say that the survivors of his Majesty's ship *Formidable* will still receive a gift from the Princess Mary's Fund in the form of a pencil, as these have not yet been distributed to the men.[405]

But, arguably, Princess Mary's Gift would make its biggest entry into the iconography of the Great War as part of the idealised view of Christmas 1914 'in the trenches' which has attained a mythological status; the events that led to the Christmas Truce, and the Truce itself that occurred in pockets along the line, has seen to that. It is to be remembered that at this stage of the war the majority of the troops in 'the trenches' were regulars, men who were already serving in the army as the war commenced. The business of war was their business, and in Flanders in December 1914 that business was fighting – but there was always time to pause for breath, to bury the dead, and to reflect on the enemy. Old soldier Pte Frank Richards of the Royal Welsh Fusiliers took it in his stride:

I am quite well. *Wishing You a*
I have been admitted into hospital *Jolly*
{ sick } and am going on well. *X mas*.
{ wounded } and hope to be discharged soon.

I am being sent down to the base. *and*

I have received your { letter. *a*
{ telegram. *Happy*.
{ parcel.

Letter follows at first opportunity. *New*

I have received no letter from you
{ lately.
{ for a long time. *Year*

Signature }
only. } *Jas Sinclair*

Date____ 20 12 14

[Postage must be prepaid on any letter or post card
addressed to the sender of this card.]

(24386) Wt.W3497-293 1,000m. 9/14 M.R.Co.,Ltd.

FIELD SERVICE POST CARD

Miss Sinclair
80. Amphill Road.
Beaford.
England

FIELD SERVICE POST CARD SENT
HOME ON 21 DECEMBER 1914
These cards were intended to indicate
the status of the individual, but gave
little away. It was forbidden to write
anything on them other than address,
name and date; this soldier has risked
censure and added his own message

'On Christmas morning we stuck up a board with "A Merry Christmas" on it. The enemy had stuck up a similar one.'[406] And while the war would pause, briefly, along the line, though some battalions concentrated upon maintaining their trenches, others faced stiff opposition. Though in truth much offensive action had died in the mud at the close of the Battle of Ypres at the end of November, there were still fierce fights that resulted in casualties. Major 'Ma' Jefferies, serving with the Grenadier Guards near Bethune experienced this first-hand:

24th December. There was a general scramble in the mud and water and Nos 2 and 3 retired from their front trenches into the second line, which the

Opposite: THE KING AND QUEEN'S CHRISTMAS CARD
Though not part of the Princess's Gift Fund, they were also prized, and often framed.
The rear of the picture is also glazed so that the intimate message may be read

enemy then attacked but was driven back with heavy loss. But we lost heavily…Other ranks, 15 killed, 29 wounded and 9 missing… We ought never to have held such a line, but taking over in the dark we could not see the lie of the land.[407]

Regulars or territorials, the winter war continued to pit men against each other, the environment conspiring to create a greater level of misery than could reasonably be expected. In all original accounts of the day, this misery is a repetitive theme. Captain J.L. Jack, serving with the 1st Battalion Cameronians at Houplines, recorded, what, for the men, was an all too familiar experience:

December 24th. The lines are in a terrible state. The incessant rain has caused large portions of the trench walls to subside. We are hard at work revetting

the broken edges and filling sandbags to stop the breaches after dark.[408]

Certainly, these conditions favoured no one side. That the Truce would be experienced by some, though not all, was truly remarkable; but perhaps more remarkable was the fact that, in December 1914, the 270,000 officers and men estimated to have been serving in France and Flanders with the British Expeditionary Force (BEF) and its Indian contingent, would be supplied with a gift that had been born in the fertile mind of a young princess, just three months previously:[409]

On Christmas Day every officer and man in the field received two acceptable gifts. From the King and Queen came a card…From her Royal Highness Princess Mary's Soldiers and Sailor's Christmas Fund came a present…In quarters, in the trenches, and in the hospitals these tokens of the kindly thought of their Majesties [sic] gave the most intense pleasure. In fact, the eagerness shown by some of the wounded to receive their presents was almost pathetic, and many soldiers have written personal letters of thanks to their Majesties.[410]

Future novelist Private Henry Williamson was serving with a territorial battalion, the London Rifle Brigade in France. Like his friend and comrade, Private D.H. Bell, Williamson not only received the gift from the Princess, but also experienced the Christmas Truce first-hand. He wrote home to his parents on Boxing Day to express his excitement and surprise at the events that unfolded, in a letter published in *The Daily Express*:

I am writing from the trenches. It is eleven o'clock in the morning. Beside me is a coke fire, opposite me a dug-out with straw in it. The ground is sloppy in the actual trench, but frozen elsewhere. In my mouth is a pipe, presented by Princess Mary. In the pipe is tobacco. 'Of course!' you say, but wait! In the pipe is German tobacco. 'Ha!' 'Ha!' You say, 'from a prisoner or found in a captured trench.' Oh dear no! From a German soldier. Yes, a live

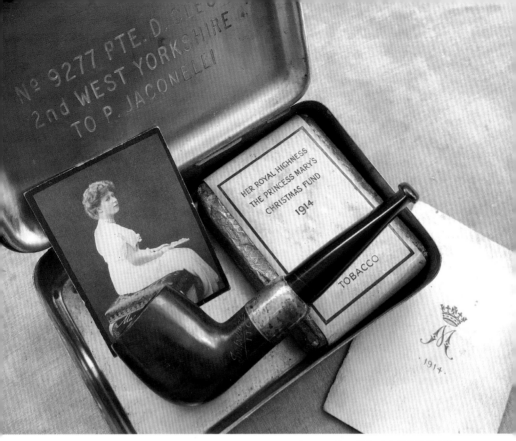

GIFT SENT HOME BY A SOLDIER AND ENGRAVED BY ITS RECIPIENT
Pte Darius Clegg landed in France on 5 November 1914; he survived the war

German soldier from his own trench. Yesterday the British and Germans met and shook hands on the ground between the trenches and exchanged souvenirs. Marvellous, isn't it?[411]

But it was not just the private soldiers in the trenches who received the gift with such interest. Though Field Marshal Sir John French, Commander-in-Chief of the BEF was evidently too

busy to record its arrival in his diary, Major-General Sir Henry Rawlinson, Commanding the IV Corps in Flanders, took time to write to the King's secretary to record his delight at the receipt of this practical gift, on 26 December:

I received last night a charming little packet containing pipe tobacco and cigarettes which I am told that is sent me by Princess Mary. It is just what

I want, for my old pipe is rapidly coming to an end, and tobacco is not too plentiful. The least I can do to shew my gratitude is to return to HRH one of my Xmas Cards. Will you give it to her for me and say how much we all value her kind gift of tobacco and cigarettes.[412]

Princess Mary's gifts were highly valued; whether any of them were traded with German soldiers during the Truce is unknown. However, they were certainly valued enough to be sent from France to soldiers' loved ones at home. Sergeant Blundell of the 1st Bedfordshire Regiment was a witness to the Truce, and wrote to recount some details – and to announce he had sent his gifts home:

I am writing this to you as I have just heard that letters posted on Dec. 26th were lost. There was a breakdown with a motor lorry, which got on fire, and all letters were burnt. I was sending Princess Mary's gift and the King's and Queen's Christmas card to you. I don't know whether they were lost or not. We were in the trenches all Christmas week, and the weather was awful. On Christmas Day we had a lot of firing over us, and shells, too. All at once it ceased, and I looked up and saw the Germans on top of their trenches shouting to us, and asking us to meet them. All our brigade went, and were talking to them about two hours. They asked us not to fire that day, and said they would not; and no firing was done until next day, and then we were fighting for all we were worth. Times are very hard here. In the trenches we are up to our waists in water with shells bursting over us, and no sleep.[413]

Behind the lines, the men of the support services were also appreciative of the gift, and perhaps had more opportunity to enjoy them. Driver W. Powell of the Army Service Corps was able to reassure his wife in South Wimbledon that his Christmas had been a reasonable experience:

Our Christmas was better than we could have expected. Our officers made us as happy as they could, and we had a very nice dinner, tea, and concert.

GIFT BOX RETAINED BY GUNNER SHELLIS OF THE ROYAL FIELD
ARTILLERY The box was often used as a means of retaining memories

But the best surprises of the lot were the card from the King and Queen and the present from Princess Mary. This is a lovely gift, and I am sending it home that you may keep it safe, for I would not part with it for anything in this world.[414]

Sapper D.A. Jones of the Royal Engineers was also moved to write home to express his satisfaction with events of the season:

I hope you all enjoyed yourselves at Christmas. We had a decent time under the circumstances. The weather was absolutely great on Christmas and Boxing Days. We had two very sharp frosts, followed by a light downfall of snow, but this eventually turned to drizzling rain. Christmas morning we had a game of football to get us in form for our dinner, which we put

NAVAL GIFT SENT HOME BY A SAILOR TO BE KEPT
AS A SOUVENIR OF SERVICE

away in style. The Christmas pudding, etc., was a treat. . . I am sending you my gift from Princess Mary, as I think it will be worth keeping, also the Christmas card from the King and Queen. The tie pin I had given to me by a French artilleryman. . . . Things are a bit different this Christmas, but still we enjoyed ourselves, and I never thought for one moment that we should have had such a decent time.[415]

Soldiers not only wrote to their families about the gift; they also felt the need to write to the originator of the scheme and express their thanks for the kindness. Many of these reside with Princess Mary's correspondence in the archives at Harewood House.[416]

But the intersection of the war in Flanders with Princess Mary's gift became stark when soldiers started to report that the gift box had helped save their lives, and remarkable stories started to fill newspapers in January with a steady stream of letters to the local press. Pte William Chambers' account of serving with 2nd Battalion Worcestershire Regiment was typical:

> We are having two days' rest after having been in the trenches for a week. I haven't had a wash or a shave for a week and am caked all over with clay. We all look like a lot of tramps. I have had a bullet go through my ruck-sack. It went through a box which the 'Evening Despatch' sent me, through some tobacco that Princess Mary sent us, and through another tin box, and broke my watch and strap and

smashed a set of rosary beads. I am going to try and have it sent home for a souvenir.[417]

Chambers had a lucky escape. He had joined the army as a seventeen-year-old in 1911, and was an experienced – and married – soldier in 1914. His luck would not hold, however, as he received a severe facial wound at Richebourg on 11 May 1915. Eventually, he was released from the army to work in munitions two years later.[418]

The flow of battle and the intensity of the actions of 1914 – with the reward of the Princess's Christmas gift – was recorded for one soldier of the Queen's Regiment:

> Private Stephen Hughes, of the Queen's Royal West Surrey Regiment, has been invalided home from the front... Private Hughes, who was educated at the Bath Blue Coat School, joined the colours in the autumn of last year, and went out to the front on November 18th. He landed at Havre, and went into the trenches at Fleurbaix, where he experienced the usual trench warfare until

December 18th. On this day a violent attack took place on the German front, and a week after this the truce came, Christmas Day being spent burying the dead. Private Hughes subsequently found himself at Laventie, where he was attached to the Royal Engineers and took part in the conflict at Neuve Chapelle and his regiment formed part of the reinforcements sent to Hill 60, but never reached there, having been called back. In a subsequent engagement, when the Allies were successful, Private Hughes was wounded in the left elbow. But for his knapsack he would probably have lost his life, the bullet being embedded in it, smashing his Princess Mary gift box beyond recognition. He was hoping to keep this as a souvenir of his escape, but while in hospital it disappeared. He remained in hospital at the front for some time, and eventually transferred to a convalescent home in North London, where his recovery was completed. He is now spending a few days in Trowbridge before rejoining his regiment.[419]

Private Hughes survived the war. Another press report was singular in reporting how not only the box – but also the precious image of the young princess – was struck by the random death-dealing violence of the Front:

Gunner F. Cooper, writing to a friend in Harrogate, describes how a comrade's life was saved by one of Princess Mary's gift boxes. A rifle bullet, says the gunner, passed right through the box and just lodged in his comrade's skin, where it could be pulled out easily. The box was in the upper left pocket, which covers the heart. 'Another funny thing about it,' the letter proceeds, 'that the portrait of the Princess, which shows her seated on a chair, was so struck that it cut her clean off the chair without damaging the portrait. Don't you think that rather remarkable? I am pleased you remember me in your prayers. It is pleasant to think someone remembers you when you are in such danger. You never know when some stray bullet may give you your deathblow – waiting for death, as it were, but being lucky enough to cheat it.'[420]

Damage to the delicate brass box of Princess Mary's Gift by shellfire was typical, and was often reported in letters from soldiers 'at the Front':

Colour-Sergeant E. Seal, Royal West Kent Regiment, who has arrived at his home at Dover a brief leave of absence from the battlefield, has brought with him a very interesting souvenir of the war. It was one of Princess Mary's gift boxes of tobacco, &c., which was the means of saving the life of the soldier to whom it was presented, Private H. Metcalfe, Royal West Kent Regiment, of Ewell Minnis, Dover. Metcalfe was carrying his much-prized gift box when shrapnel shell burst over the trench and a bullet struck the tin, ploughed its way through the tobacco and cigarettes, and smashed the pipe. It then passed through another portion of the box and killed a man who was in the fighting line alongside Metcalfe. But for the presence of the gift box Metcalfe would have been killed. He has sent the box home to his people.[421]

In some cases, gifts – or photographs of the gifts – that had miraculously saved the lives of their owners were sent on to Princess herself:

Private J. Norman, D Company, 1st Northamptonshire Regiment, probably owes his life to the gift he received from Princess Mary. He was one small party of the Northamptonshire Regiment engaged in digging

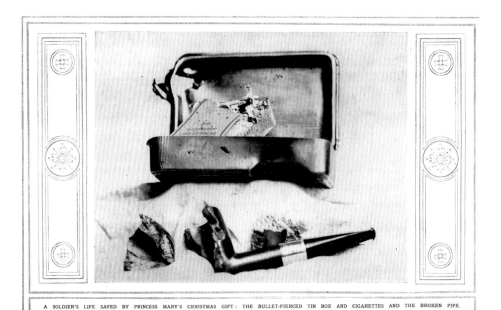

GIFT BOXES THAT HAD 'SEEN ACTION' OR THAT HAD SAVED THE
LIVES OF THEIR RECIPIENTS WERE OFTEN REPORTED IN THE PRESS
This example saved the life of Colour Sergeant Seal of the Royal West Kent
Regiment, and was depicted in *The Illustrated War News*

trenches, when they were surprised by the Germans and compelled to retire. Private Norman's haversack was riddled with bullets. The photo of Princess Mary was damaged, the pipe which the casket contained was smashed, the tobacco was cut into two portions, and a piece was shot out of the handle of Private Norman's shaving brush. The ruined casket and its contents have been sent to Private Norman's parents at Irchester, and a copy of the photograph...has been sent to Princess Mary.[422]

A similar picture was sent by Matron Miss Beardmore to the Princess – this time recognising its role in saving the life of Pte A. Maynard of the Queen's Regiment – on 22 January 1915.[423]

Perhaps the most celebrated

story of one such escape – and of the return of the box to the Princess herself – destined to be repeated in several newspapers, was that of Private Mike Brabston of the Irish Guards:

Private 'Mike' Brabston, of the 2nd Company 1st Battalion of the Irish Guards, thinks that he is the luckiest soldier in the British Expeditionary Force. He was in the fighting at Givenchy last February, and considers that his life was saved by Princess Mary's Christmas Gift Box which he carried in his left breast pocket, the box preventing a German bullet from penetrating his heart. Writing home at the time Private Brabston stated that the bullet struck the box in his pocket on February 2, but a few days after he was struck above the left eye. Having been nursed at Edenbridge Hospital, Kent, he has now recovered and is at Barracks, Brentwood.

The matron at Edenbridge forwarded the box and the bullet which it stopped to Princess Mary, and a letter was received in reply from Windsor Castle stating that Her Royal Highness was delighted to hear that one of her boxes had saved Brabston's life. The box, added the letter, 'was shown to their Majesties, who hope that Private Brabston will soon recover from the wounds.' Brabston will soon return to the front.[424]

But not all men who carried the gift were lucky enough to escape death. One of them, Private Jacob Rivers, was to be awarded the Victoria Cross for his gallantry at Neuve Chapelle in 1915. On this occasion, the Princess's box was not able to save him:

There is a pathetic interest attached to one of the tobacco boxes, a gift from Princess Mary which has been sent to Derby. It belonged to Private Jacob Rivers, of the 1st Sherwood Foresters, who won the V.C. at Neuve Chapelle, but was killed in that battle. He was a native of Derby, and was 34 years of age. He had completed 12 years' service with the Royal Scots Fusiliers when the war broke out, having served seven years in India and five in the Army Reserve, and was one of the first to volunteer for service in August. He re-enlisted this time in the Sherwood Foresters, and, being an experienced soldier, was sent with one of the earliest drafts to France. He had three brothers-in-law in the same regiment. His mother has been notified of his death, and his box containing Princess Mary's Christmas gift, has been forwarded to her. This has been pierced by a bullet, and the presence of a hole right through it shows that Rivers was shot, through the heart. Rivers lived with his widowed mother, whose other son is in the Grenadier Guards.[425]

A battle-scarred object exists in the King George V's own collection of military artefacts. Mary's father visited the Western Front on a number of occasions; as a collector he gathered objects relating to the war as he travelled, and inevitably, as word spread of his interest, so objects found their way to him, sent from the front. These became part of the King's own war museum, curated by the Royal Librarian Sir John Fortescue, which was housed in the Brunswick Tower at Windsor Castle. Each was displayed with a handwritten label.[426] The collection grew to contain some significant pieces, many of which were transferred to the Imperial War Museum on the instructions of his son, David, the future Edward VIII, when he succeeded him to the throne in 1936. Not surprisingly, the collection contains three specimens of Princess Mary's gift, including a bright gilt one with cigarettes (opened, as the vast majority are) and tobacco.[427] Another, just the box 'encrusted with the earth of the trench it was found in,' was sent to the Royal Family on 9 February 1915, by Captain Hubert Roberts of the Army Service Corps who was serving at the 2nd Corps Railhead, and who had served in France since August 1914. More intriguing, though, is the battle-damaged specimen, which is severely battered and crushed by the violence of shellfire. Though no further details are available, it is surely likely that this is one of the examples that was sent home from the front after saving the life of its owner.

But for one soldier, at least, the box was too precious even to send back to its originator:

A Bradwell wounded soldier whose life was saved by

Princess Mary's gift box did not act on the advice of his officers that he should send the bullet-pierced box to Her Royal Highness. The measure of gratitude to the Princess is indicated by the statement that he would not part with the souvenir for a fortune. The soldier is Lance-Corporal A.G. Hallam. York and Lancasters, brother of Private T.E. Hallam (who was recently killed in action) and son of Mr. Stephen Hallam of Bradwell. Writing from a hospital in a letter dated

BADLY DAMAGED GIFT BOX, FORMING PART OF KING GEORGE V'S OWN PERSONAL COLLECTION OF WAR RELICS
It is possible, perhaps, that this was one of the boxes sent to the Princess as evidence of its life saving potential

11 August he says: "You will perhaps be a little surprised to hear I have got wounded, but thankfully the wound is not serious, and I am living in hopes to be discharged before long. It happened yesterday about 3-30 in the afternoon and I am more than satisfied with what I have got. I just managed to be wounded in the thigh, and if it had not been for Princess Mary's Christmas gift box I should not have been here to tell the tale. A bullet passed right through the box, and of course it was stopped from going too far."[428]

Nevertheless, in the field at least, it seems that Princess Mary's Gift was saleable – just as Queen Victoria's chocolate box had been in 1900. Certainly, Major Burgoyne of the 2nd Royal Irish Rifles was enterprising in this regard; he purchased two additional boxes for 2/6 – presumably from fellow soldiers, and sent all three back, one for his father, one for his brother, and the third, most valued of all as it was sent to him directly, he sent to his wife.[429] In another instance, the man who sold his gift box to a fellow soldier had occasion to rue his decision. Pte Harry Towers of the Lincolnshire Regiment wrote home to his father in order to describe how he escaped being wounded – by good fortune of having purchased a box from a fellow soldier:

I have had a very lucky escape from being wounded. I was walking behind another fellow when a bullet came straight through his leg, and I felt it strike me. I looked and found it had gone through my overcoat and pocket, and the Princess Mary box was dented, and I found the bullet in my pocket. It had struck it sideways somehow, and it had turned it. The most curious part about it all was that the very man whose leg it had come through was the man I had bought the box from.[430]

Whether Private Towers was purchasing a box because he hadn't been issued with one – or whether he was taking a leaf out of Major Burgoyne's book – is difficult to determine. It would appear though, perhaps, that it was bad luck to sell one – at least at the front.

Gifts for The Indian Army, 1914–15

IN 2014, JUST north of the once beleaguered Belgian city of Ypres, a short section of trench in a piece of formerly devastated landscape was found by a small team of archaeologists.[431] Alongside the detritus of war were found the sad remains of men; men who had fought and fallen in these battlefields; men whose names were recorded on memorials to the missing, but whose graves were no more. A wartime cemetery had been lost in the actions that

INDIAN
SOLDIERS IN
FRANCE, 1914

followed, and with them these men, lost for a century.[432]

Identifying fallen soldiers recovered from the battlefields of Flanders is notoriously difficult. Both men wore uniforms of the British Army, but peculiarities of their equipment, and the fact that one at least carried distinctive 'One Anna' coins in his pocket, indicate that they were probably Indian.[433] Both soldiers were most likely killed during the Second Battle of Ypres in April 1915; and both carried the revered gift from the Princess in their breast pockets.[434]

The importance of the gift to its Indian army recipients is difficult to determine at this distance; but

even today it holds some meaning, so much so that it was a matter of some interest to *The Hindu*, an Indian national newspaper. In 2016, under the headline 'This "tin" is filled with memories' an article described the desire of one young man to 'take care' of the '102-year-old brass tin gifted to his great-grandfather by Princess Mary in 1914.'[435] That the brass box was of some continuing

significance to the family was clear from the published image of Mohammed Babavali 'protecting' his brass 'tin'. This care continued the tradition of his father, Abdul Raheem, who had also 'protected it all through his life' having salvaged it from a cyclone that had 'swept away everything in his native village' in 1977; and, in turn, his grandfather,

Abdul Azeez, who 'had also protected it all through his life'. Such a lot of attention was given to the 'tin', which, 'with a shape of a small tiffin box' was not an 'ordinary item, for it has a long and interesting legacy connected with the British...'.[436] And in present-day Pakistan, a similar, distinctive brass box has pride of place in the village military museum in Dulmai, Punjab. The village sent 460 soldiers to fight in the war, the box having been brought back from Europe by one of the those who served. It still has great meaning:

The gift box is a small but important symbol of the relationship of the Indian troops to the British during the Great War. It was a token

TWO ONE ANNA COINS FOUND WITH A SOLDIER, HELPING TO INDICATE THAT HE WAS INDIAN
One Anna was broadly equivalent to one penny

of appreciation for soldiers who travelled thousands of miles to support the Allies. The fact that the tin has been looked after for over 100 years and now preserved in a Punjabi village museum shows that people still remember the sacrifices of their ancestors.[437]

These boxes, preserved in India and Pakistan today, and those carried by soldiers recovered from Flanders, link to the lives of those men who came such a long way to fight, and who were rightly feted.

Apart from a single deployment to Malta in the late nineteenth century, this was the first time that the Indian Army had been committed to a campaign 'west of the Suez Canal'.[438] The men of this army were to meet with significant challenges:

They came from a country where the climate, the language, the people, the customs, were entirely different from any of which they had knowledge. They were presently faced with the sharp severity of a Northern winter. They, who had never suffered heavy shell fire, who had no experience of high explosive, who had never seen warfare in the air, who were totally ignorant of modern trench fighting, were exposed to all the latest and most scientific developments of the art of destruction.[439]

The Corps now committed to the dreadful winter conditions of the Western Front comprised the Lahore and Meerut divisions, each consisting of three brigades, plus divisional troops and artillery.[440] Each infantry brigade was made up of three Indian battalions and one British battalion that had been serving in the subcontinent; for instance, the predominantly Sikh Jullundur Brigade (Lahore Division) was formed of the 15th Ludhiana Sikhs, 47th Sikhs and 59th Scinde Rifles (Frontier Force) – together with the 1st Battalion Manchester Regiment; while the majority Gurkha Dehra Dun Brigade (Meerut Division) comprised the 1st Battalion 9th Gurkha Rifles, 2nd Battalion 2nd King Edward's Own Gurkha Rifles, the 6th Jat Light Infantry – and the 1st Battalion Seaforth Highlanders.[441] Those men had arrived in the sun of Marseilles with much fanfare in September;

A SOLDIER OF THE 2ND BLACK WATCH AT FACQUISSART, WITH INDIAN SOLDIERS BEHIND HIM The 2nd Black Watch was a battalion of the Bareilly Brigade (Meerut Division) and an integral part of the Indian Army alongside the 41st Dogras, 58th Vaughan's Rifles, and 2nd/8th Gurkha Rifles

but by December they were serving under the grey, damp skies of Flanders:

The communication trenches, where they existed, were very imperfect, and there were many instances of wounded men being drowned in them when attempting to find their way back from the firing line. It would be impossible to imagine conditions more terrible for Eastern troops. No language can describe their sufferings, carried swiftly from fierce tropical sun to the wet and winter of Flanders.[442]

Captain Arthur Ion Fraser was in the trenches in the Rue du Bois on 21 December 1914 near Givenchy, and was a British officer serving with the 4th Cavalry (Hodson's Horse). A letter to his brother, Commander James Gordon Fraser on board HMS *Shannon* gives some flavour of the conditions experienced by the men of this Indian cavalry regiment:

Shortly before Xmas we were in the trenches again…One man in my squadron was killed & five others wounded, while a good many including myself got our feet more or less frost bitten, having them so much under water in this weather. Some men near us were stuck in mud up to their chests all night….It is difficult keeping rifles clean enough to use in such mud. We saw the Germans fire a lot of 'Jack Johnsons' & shrapnel…It takes a long time getting one's feet right again.[443]

Under the Command of Sir John French, all ranks of the Indian Army not only received their share of *Daily News* Christmas pudding and the King and Queen's Christmas card, but were eligible to and deserving of Princess Mary's Gift.[444] This was explicitly stated and, indeed,

CHARACTER STUDIES FROM LIFE OF A SIKH SOLDIER (LEFT)
AND A GURKHA SOLDIER (RIGHT), 1914

expected. From its inception, the Executive Committee of HRH The Princess Mary's Gift Fund was determined to supply gifts to the men of the Indian Expeditionary Force, men who had landed at Marseilles in September 1914, and who were committed to battle in France and Flanders:

There are among the men who are fighting for us brave soldiers from the East to whom Christmas has not the same

OPPOSITE: INDIAN SOLDIERS TRAINING WITH MAXIM GUNS

meaning as it has to us; but they are sharing our sorrows – she wants them to share our joys. India has stood for the King; the King's daughter has not forgotten India.[445]

The exact form of the gift that they would receive was, however, subject to discussion, especially given the Indian Corps was composed of men of widely differing ethnic and religious backgrounds, with its 'class' system organised 'on considerations of race, religion and locality.'[446] Typical of the first of these were regiments composed of Rajput, Pathan, Jat and Gurkha ethnic groups, largely from the northern areas of the subcontinent; characteristic of regiments organised on religious grounds were those composed principally of 'Sikhs, Hindus and Mahomedans'; while those formed of Mahrattas, Dogras and Punjabis reflected the location of their recruitment.[447] It was a complex business.

One matter that had clearly influenced the Executive Committee of the Princess Mary Gift Fund was the fact that for Sikhs, 'the smoking of tobacco was strictly forbidden'. In its efforts to explain the nature of the Indian Army for British troops, the contemporary War Office guide *Our Indian Empire* was explicit, stating bluntly that for Sikh soldiers, 'The very sight of tobacco is considered an insult.'[448] Given that Sikhs 'bulk[ed] more largely than any other class in the Indian Army', it was imperative that no offence should be given.

With this in mind, and in order to ensure that the needs of the Indian Corps as a whole were met, the Executive Committee commenced a journey that would see them consulting those who knew India and the Indian soldier best. The matter was a point of discussion on their very first meeting of the Committee, 'It being understood that the Indian Corps should have sweet-meats instead of tobacco and cigarettes, Mr Le Bas undertook to make enquiries of Sir John Hewett 'what form of sweet-meats' the Indians would prefer.[449]

It was probably not surprising that Hewett's opinion should be sought. Afterall, Sir John Prescott Hewett had been a senior member of the Indian Civil Service, an institution he had joined in 1875. He had only just retired, in 1913, having steered the coronation 'durbar' of King George V and Queen Mary in Dehli, when he was instrumental in 'creating a tent city housing 200,000 people, spread over twenty-five square miles'.[450] Given the complexities of the Indian army 'class' system, drawing upon his experience would be necessary.[451] Hewett had another string to his bow, however; for in 1914 he had taken the chair of the Indian Soldiers' Fund Committee, yet another fund that would provide 'comforts' for the troops. Hewett was thus well qualified to assist.

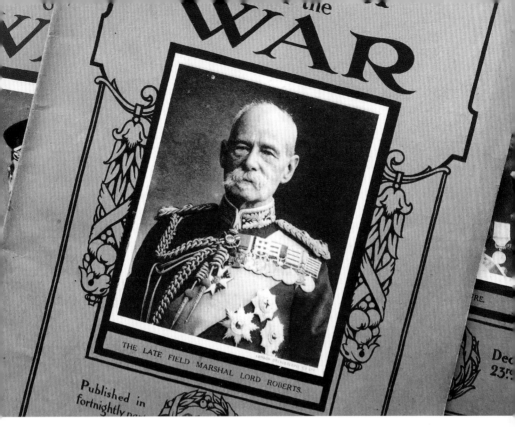

'BOBS', FIELD MARSHAL LORD ROBERTS VC
A highly respected soldier who did much to support the Indian Army. He was patron
of the Indian Soldiers Comforts Fund, but died of pneumonia in St Omer in 1914

The Indian Soldiers' Comforts Fund – formed just fourteen days before Princess Mary's own fund – was to be of the greatest importance in supporting the Indian Army in France and Flanders. This Fund was particularly special in that it was supported by Lord Roberts, an old soldier who inspired great affection across Britain and the Empire. His participation was reported widely, the story picked up in the United States:

Earl Roberts is raising a fund which will be delivered exclusively to the use of the Indian forces, in the present war. Already he has received $250,000…The Fund will be used to provide warm clothing especially suited to the Indian troops. Rations of the English Army are wholly unlike the customary diet of the Indians and special dishes will be provided for them out of the fund.[452]

'Bobs' would not live to see the fruits of his inspiration, as he died of pneumonia at St Omer, on 14 November 1914, while visiting the Indian Army in France. The Fund's committee was composed of men and women who had a significant connection with India, and who were 'anxious to do everything possible to assist our Indian troops in their severe trials in Europe.'[453] While much of the work of the Fund was to support hospitals and the wounded, it was also there to 'supplement the clothing and comforts supplied by Government,' and was responsible for supplying some 78,000 pairs of socks and 12,000 balaclava helmets to the men in France and Flanders.[454] Local initiatives across Britain also focused on aiding the Comforts Fund in order to support Indian soldiers. In the northern town of Birkenhead, for example, a Mr Rogers of Devonshire Road advertised that he would 'gratefully receive gifts of warm clothing, or money to buy the same, for the 36th Garhwal Rifles, a Gurkha Regiment at the front. Vests, pants, sweaters, and large coloured handkerchiefs are the most useful articles.'[455] In line with the diversity and customs of the men it served, the Indian Comforts Fund also provided over twenty-two million cigarettes and 125,000 lbs of sweets for the soldiers' consumption; and it was

PRINCESS MARY GIFT PIPE FOUND WITH THE INDIAN
SOLDIER RECOVERED FROM THE BATTLEFIELDS IN 1914
The soldier must not have been a Sikh; there is every possibility, due to the
location of the man's body and other details, that he was a Gurkha.

principally for advice whether the Indian troops should receive sweets or smoking materials that the Princess's own Fund was to consult its chairman.

Sir John's deliberations were read aloud to the Committee a week after Le Bas had contacted him. Unfortunately, the letter received has not survived, but it is clear that the complexities of the needs of the Indian Army were deemed significant enough to be 'adjourned for further discussion'.[456] Once more, Rowland Berkeley was called upon to assist. He approached the prominent Indian philanthropist and heir to the Tata fortune, Sir Ratan Tata.[457] Sir Ratan was evident in London Society, and though wealthy, had already funded a number of worthy charitable concerns relating to the well-being of citizens in India, and of London. No doubt well connected, Tata was asked to recommend a supplier of suitable 'sweet-meats', and Berkeley acted on this advice to commission some samples from one Nizam Dreen. That these were not considered satisfactory is evident from the fact that a further suggestion was made by the Executive Committee, that 'the Indian troops should receive the brass box, a looking glass and a silk handkerchief with the Princess Mary's monogram', instead of the 'pipe, tinder lighter and tobacco or sweetmeats'.[458] These suggestions were not adopted.

Once again, the matter was adjourned for 'further enquiry', and this time a consortium of five retired senior officers of the Indian Army was consulted, again as recommended by Sir John Hewett. Prominent among them was General Sir Alfred Gaslee, former commander of the Northern Army in India; Colonel C.S. Wheler, formerly of the Indian Staff Corps; Colonel Richard Ridgeway, a senior staff officer who had been awarded the Victoria Cross in India in 1879; Lt-Col. O.C. Bradford and Brevet Col. N.A.K. Burn.[459] To move the matter to its conclusion, the Duke of Devonshire, Sir Hedley Le Bas and Rowland Berkeley met with these officers at the Ritz, and their advice was to be the germination of the idea behind the various gifts be given to the Indian soldiers in France.[460] This was a matter of some interest to the press, and seemingly particularly so in the United States:

Indian Army 'class' groups	Gifts advised 10 November 1914
Gurkhas	'Same as the British Army'
Sikhs	'Brass box and Saccharine Tablets'
Brahmins, Rajputs, Dogras, & Jats & Mahrattas	'Brass box, barley sugar, cigarettes & tinder lighter'
Pathans, Punjabi Mohammedans & Hindustani Mohammedans	'Brass box, cigarettes & tinder lighter'
Authorised followers	'Also to receive the present'

Gifts advised to the Committee by former Indian Army Officers

Princess Mary and her advisors are making special preparations to send the Indians Christmas gifts which will especially appeal to them. It is likely the gifts will take the form of boxes of candies and other sweet meats particularly relished by the men from the Far East.[461]

These extended deliberations of the special group of retired officers so well acquainted with India and Indian troops were to lead to some definite decisions being made. In that all important meeting of 24 November 1914, Rowland Berkeley reported the resolutions of the Executive Committee:

In regard to the Indian Troops, the Gurkhas would receive the same present as the British troops, the Sikhs, the brass box filled with sugar candy and a box of spices, the remainder the brass box with a packet of cigarettes, sugar candy and a box of spices, and the camp followers a box of spices.[462]

BRASS BOX AND SPICE TIN

The Adshead-designed brass box was, as always, at the centrepiece of the gift. It did not differ for Indian soldiers, or those serving in British battalions as part of Indian Brigades. However, it is notable that non-combatant 'camp followers' were not granted the gift of a brass box; instead, they would receive the tin box of spices together with the Christmas Card.[463] The Indian

GIFT BOX GIVEN TO PTE WILLIAMSON OF THE 2ND SEAFORTH
HIGHLANDERS Like the 2nd Black Watch, the 2nd Seaforths were an integral
battalion of the Indian Army (Indian Expeditionary Force – IEF), serving in the Dehra
Dun Brigade alongside the 9th Gurkha Rifles, the 2/2nd King Edward's Own Gurkha
Rifles, and the 6th Jat Light Infantry. It is presumed that Pte Williamson received the
standard gift, as would his Gurkha comrades

Army relied to a certain extent on non-combatant labour, engaged in activities from cooking through to water-carrying and cleaning. Though sometimes identified as *Bhistis* – traditional water carriers – there were many other groups, and as the war progressed, this labour would be required in many theatres.[464] It is difficult to determine how many non-combatant followers received the spice tin, but it is clear that the total number of tin spice boxes that were manufactured totalled at least 39,480.[465] Nevertheless, it was later found that this number was in excess of what was actually needed, and with so many left in storage, the spices were later distributed to wounded Indian soldiers in England.[466]

The spice tin is perhaps the least common item encountered of all the gifts produced by Princess Mary's Fund. The only one seen is typical of the standard output of the tin manufacturers that had made such a name for themselves in late Victorian times. It was not designed to fit inside the brass box, and was broadly cubic, consisting of tinware, not brass and bearing a paper label with the name of the Gift Fund, similar to that used on the nurses' chocolate packets.[467] The spice tin remains a very illusive object.

It is difficult to specify whether this tin was packed in a cardboard container with the brass box, though it seems unlikely, given its size and shape; and it is also difficult to specify the contents of the tin, other than they were 'mixed spices', and that each tin contained at least four ounces.[468] Presumably they were representative of such Indian staples as turmeric, cumin, coriander and cardamom, flavoursome spices with known medicinal benefits.[469] Berkeley secured contracts to supply '39,400 boxes of spices at 8½ d', and '394,000 [*sic* – actually 39,400] tins for spices at 14/- a gross and labels.'[470] This was 'exclusive of the cost of filling', presumably also carried out in Deptford, as well as delivery. In all, 5,640 lbs of spices were purchased to fill these boxes.[471]

SUGAR CANDY

The exact suppliers of the 'sugar candy' for the non-Gurkha Indian soldiers is now obscured with time, but the candy supplied differed in cost, and therefore quality; the total ordered was 5,137 lbs.[472] It is not known who was the supplier of these candies, but there were plenty to choose from, including Needlers of Hull who, like many confectioners of the time, packaged their sweets in patriotic tins depicting Field Marshal French and Admiral Jellicoe. Nevertheless, pinning down the exact manufacturer is challenging.

It is to be assumed that these sweets represented some form of hard candy, created by boiling sugar syrups at a high temperature, though which flavour those supplied to the Gift Fund is lost in time. Certainly, modern home-grown Indian candies are

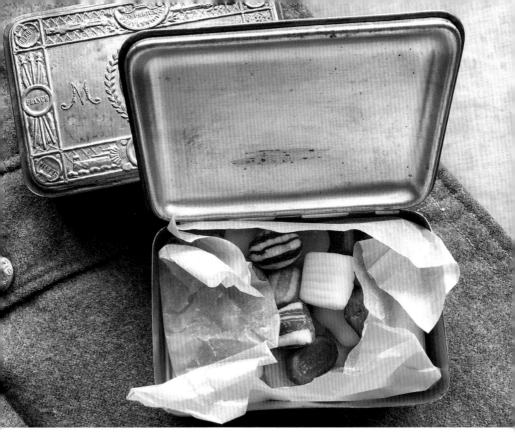

RECONSTRUCTION OF THE 'SUGAR CANDY' THAT WAS GIVEN TO
SIKH SOLDIERS ALONGSIDE THE SEPARATE TIN OF MIXED SPICES
At this distance, it is not possible to determine the nature of these candies, but
undoubtedly they were boiled sweets. This reconstruction uses traditional hard sugar
candy, and shows that the box could indeed house four ounces of sugar candy

representative of the Indian palate, but as these were derived from British sources, it is possible to speculate that they were given typical citric or even aniseed flavouring. Nevertheless, as the Committee had previously taken advice on which 'sweet-meats' would be acceptable, it is also possible that they could have had other flavours.

It is unlikely that there was specialist packing for these sweets, but it is known that 'the embossed brass box contained, either as four ounces of broken sugar candy' for the non-smoking Sikhs, or 'two ounces of candy and a packet of twenty cigarettes' for other non-Gurkha, Indian fighting men.[473] Certainly, when measured with available hard candy today, four ounces is the

Sugar candy ordered	Cost (per cwt)
31 cwt, 21 lbs	40/- cwt
6 cwt, 1 quarter, 12 lbs	46/6 cwt
4 cwt, 1 quarter	43/9 cwt

Sugar candy ordered for Indian troops

quantity it can hold comfortably. It is not unreasonable to assume that there was a greaseproof paper liner or similar in order to keep the candy untainted, and now and again boxes are found with remnants of a paper lining, suggesting just such an origin.[474]

REFLECTIONS ON THE INDIAN GIFT

The two probable Indian soldiers recovered from the battlefields of Ypres in 1914 were not only in possession of Princess Mary gift boxes, but also pipes. Both pipes were of a similar pattern, with a curving stem and simple bowl; it seems more than probable that these men are Gurkhas, given the fact that no other Indian ethnic groups were given the same gift as that of the British soldier.[475]

Though it is clear, on religious grounds, why Sikh soldiers were given an alternative to tobacco products with their gift, at this distance from the events of 1914 it is a little more difficult to see why (in the language of the day), the other 'fighting classes' should be given such a mixture of goods. It may simply have been a question of variety, but there is no doubting the sincere wishes of the Executive Committee to meet the needs of the diversity of Indian soldiers who were fighting for the Empire in France and Flanders. And this sincerity was no doubt appreciated – even though the Christian festival it recognised may not have meant much to the average soldier of the Indian Army. As Gordon Corrigan has commented:

[Christmas] meant nothing to the sepoys, of course, but they were delighted with the small gifts…sweetmeats, cigarettes,

PRINCESS MARY'S GIFT BOX, GIVEN TO AN INDIAN SOLDIER IN 1914
No doubt once treasured, it was recovered with the soldier's remains a hundred years later

postcards and the like; each present contained in a small, flat, square tin. Even today homes in India and Nepal will produce the tin with great pride to show to visitors.[476]

This view certainly echoes that of the official correspondent with the British Army in 1914, 'Eyewitness', who communicated the following to the press on 28 December:

The Indian troops exhibited their boxes with an undisguised pride and glee, which showed how these prizes would be treasured and handed down as heirlooms.[477]

What is certain, however, is that two soldiers of India carried their boxes with pride into battle, and losing their lives, were buried to lie for evermore in the Ypres Salient, with the gift from the young English Princess, daughter of the King-Emperor, in their breast pockets.

And for men like Mohammed Babavali, protecting his 'brass tin', as his father and grandfather did before him, is a very important thing indeed.

Gifts for Nurses and Non-smokers, 1914

AT SUCH A distance from events of 1914, it seems surprising that the Executive Committee of the Princess Mary's Gift Fund should devote more time to the consideration of the needs of non-smokers, rather than those of military nurses in uniform, in France, and close to the front. But surviving records suggest that this was indeed the case, with the nurses seemingly almost an afterthought. Whether this was by design, or by accident, is difficult to determine – though it is particularly surprising given Princess Mary's subsequent work as a nurse in 1918.

When Princess Mary met with her mother, her brother and Sir Walter Peacock on 8 October 1914, it was to discuss the matter of 'sending pipes and tobacco to the sailors and soldiers at the Front'.[478] The choice of gift was unsurprising. The majority of men were smokers, and smoking was very much the norm, encountered in every walk of life, in streets, houses, bars and cafés. From clay pipes to fine cigars, smoking was expected, and soldiers could equally expect to receive tobacco as part of their ration. Indeed, as the war progressed, the packaging of cigarettes became increasingly aligned with the military masculinity.[479] Not only that, there was even a view that the smoking was a beneficial activity, a means of providing a mild calming effect for the average serviceman on frontline duty. And there was considerable pressure in the correspondence and opinion columns of newspapers to the effect that non-smoking railway carriages should be dropped in favour of smoking ones to meet demand.[480]

A WOUNDED SOLDIER PAUSES TO RECEIVE A LIGHT FOR HIS CIGARETTE FROM A YOUNG CHILD This seems odd to us today; but back in 1914, some ninety-six per cent of soldiers smoked, and it was taken as the norm. By contrast, then very few women partook of the habit

This was the backdrop to the Princess's gift, a backdrop supported in October 1914 by respected medical journal *The Lancet*, which at least in part suspended some of its antithesis to the habit due to the war conditions.[481]

Yet the fact remained that despite considerable peer pressure, some men may not have wanted to receive smoking materials as part of a Christmas gift, through health concerns, religious beliefs or personal preference. But with the population of non-smokers being such a minority, it is important to ask why the Executive Committee spent so much time in considering its needs?

It would seem most likely that there was a vocal pressure group reacting to the announcements of the gift's contents, perhaps a group associated with religious abstinence that was at the root of Victorian–Edwardian anti-smoking campaigns, rightly ascribing a great deal of ailments to the practice of smoking.[482] The British Anti-Tobacco Society had been formed as early as 1853, a combination of scientists, moralists and evangelicals, and by 1890 it had evolved into the British Anti-Tobacco and Anti-Narcotic League – a group with 'a strong nonconformist element' that was concerned with combating 'moral decline' in the nation.[483] That this lobby had influence is demonstrated by the fact that at the second meeting of the Executive Committee, early on in the life of the Gift Fund, it was noted that 'Mr Berkeley had received numerous letters on the question of non-smokers'. That these ultimately proved to be influential is indicated

WORRY?

I DON'T THINK.

Smoking was not only expected, the habit was also condoned due to its 'calming effect' – and non-smokers were very much in the minority in 1914

by the discussion that ensued, in which 'the Committee decided unanimously that, if it were possible to differentiate, non-smokers should receive boxes of sweets, or chocolates, instead of pipes, tinder lighters, and tobacco'.[484] It was no doubt a high ideal to support a minority, particularly if they had influential lobbyists as members. Nevertheless, this idea was soon dashed, as at the very next meeting the enormity of the task of determining just how many non-smokers were serving in the armed forces was deemed almost impossible, leading to the resolution that 'it would be impracticable to make any special arrangements for non-smokers'.[485]

With such effort given to support the needs of a minority group, it is important to consider that there were other potential recipients who were deserving, arguably *more* deserving, of a dedicated gift at

Nurses of the Queen Alexandra's Imperial Military Nursing Service (QAIMNS) and the QAIMNS Reserve pictured with their patients, c. 1915

Christmas 1914. Particularly significant is the fact that the British Expeditionary Force – and the Indian Army that fought alongside it – did not solely consist of male soldiers. There were also nurses, members of the Army Medical Service who served alongside the doctors and orderlies of the Royal Army Medical Corps. These were regular army nurses belonging to Queen Alexandra's Imperial Military Nursing Service (QAIMNS), and the volunteer, part-time, nurses of the Territorial Force Nursing Service (TFNS). They were part of the army establishment and were despatched to France accordingly (together with members of the QAIMNS Reserve) to serve in the base hospitals and ambulance trains.[486] Surely their needs deserved to be met too?

'o prophet's needed here to tell
The joyful news that all is well !
Sweet Peace,
a fragrant whiff,
and Nursie
For "lighting up"—
her work of mercy !

'MINISTERING ANGEL'
Patronising contemporary view of the role of nurses as the simple purveyors of cigarettes. The stark reality was that QAIMNS nurses were very much in the war zone, and the lives of their patients depended upon them. It is surprising that nurses were not initially considered eligible for the Gift Fund

The question for the Executive Committee of the Princess Mary Fund was, therefore, whether nurses should be considered as eligible for a gift – particularly as its original definition was for 'sailors afloat, and soldiers at the Front,' and particularly as they were 'limited to sailors serving under Lord Jellicoe, and soldiers serving under Sir John French.'[487] Whether military nurses were to be considered as 'soldiers at the front' was one matter, but as personnel of the British Expeditionary Force, nurses were very much under the command of Sir John French, and their experiences alone in caring for the wounded, surely placed them as worthy of recognition.

Nurses arrived in France in August 1914 to serve at base hospitals, and from September 1914 on the ambulance trains that brought the often heavily wounded men to them. One of them, Adelaide Walker, was an experienced military nurse who had served in South Africa before joining the QAIMNS in 1903. She was deployed to France in August and was very soon 'in action' amongst the wounded of the autumn battles in France and Flanders, in charge of one of the Stationary Hospitals on the French coast. Her experience must be typical of the many others who served to tend to the wounded, close to the battlezone:

> Number 14 Stationary hospital was found to be in a large hotel on the sea-front at Wimereux... Every place was packed with sick and wounded lying on the floor; you stepped between them, and over them, to get along... Operations went on unceasingly. As fast as one patient could be taken off the operating table, another was placed on – and so on all through the night: the surgeons had been at it the whole day.[488]

Wounded men poured into the hospitals in a pitiful state, and the nurses were there to receive them:

> The sugar sheds on the Gare Maritime were to be converted into a hospital, No.13 Stationary hospital. What an indescribable scene! In the first huge shed there were hundreds of wounded walking cases (as long as a man could crawl he had to be a walking case). All were caked with mud, in torn clothes, hardly any caps, and with blood-stained bandages on arms, hands, and legs; many were lying asleep on the straw that had been left in the hastily cleaned sheds, looking weary to death; others sitting on empty boxes or barrels, eating the contents of a tin of 'Maconochie' with the help of a clasp knife. Dressings were being carried out on improvised tables; blood-stained clothes, caked in mud, which had been cut off, were stacked in heaps with rifles and ammunition.[489]

Work on the ambulance trains was similarly taxing, particularly as they carried medical staff into close contact with the front line – especially so as trains pulled into the beleaguered city of Ypres, and were immediately subjected to the threat of shellfire:

Great work was accomplished by the Sisters on Ambulance Trains in 1914. They worked under enormous difficulties, and with, for themselves, the barest necessities, and no comforts. The loads carried were heavy, and the journeys long. They worked too under dangerous conditions and there is no doubt that there were many examples of brave conduct which passed unrecorded.[490]

Despite such dedication to duty, surprisingly, the first mention of Princess Mary's gifts for nurses was at the Executive Committee for 27 October 1914, some two weeks after the launch of the Gift Fund. Evidently nurses had *not* been considered from its outset. In this meeting, it was reported that

INTERIOR OF A HOSPITAL TRAIN TAKING WOUNDED MEN BACK TO THE BASE HOSPITAL The conditions on board for men and nurses were harrowing

'a proposal had been made that the Committee should purchase silver pincushions to be sent to the nurses at the front'.[491] Who proposed this idea is not recorded, but on this occasion, the Committee unanimously 'agreed not to proceed with the suggestion'. There could be no doubt, surely, that these nurses were deserving of the gift; but the idea, briefly mooted, was now shelved. It would take a change in fortunes to re-emerge.

The meeting of the Executive Committee of the 24 November was a momentous one. Donations had now reached a total of £108,197 – close on twice the original £55,000–60,000 estimate of cost for the Gift for 500,000 recipients that had been set over a month before in the ballroom of the Ritz – and this total was set to rise.[492] A direct result of the burgeoning number of donations was that the Gift Fund was set to expand its reach. The minutes of that momentous meeting make interesting reading, for not only do they confirm the extension of the Gift to all those serving in the King's uniform on Christmas Day 1914, but they also counteract and rescind previously made resolutions no doubt designed to at least

enforce some considerations of frugality, when finances were more uncertain, in the meeting of the 27 October. The resolution that no special provision was to be made for non-smokers was overturned. They would now be eligible to receive a present consisting of the 'brass box filled with sweets, and some other gift to be determined', to be sent to them in the proportion of two non-smokers to every fifty-six smokers' – in other words, just over three-and-a-half percent of the total recipients.[493] And, arguably more significantly, now nurses 'at the front' were also to be in receipt of a gift, the ultimate form of which was yet to be determined.[494]

For both non-smokers and nurses, alternative gifts to the standard tobacco products were eventually identified, and were itemised in the final meeting of the Executive Committee before Christmas, on 22 December 1914. The fruits of these deliberations would be received, gratefully, by both non-smokers and nurses overseas at Christmas, such as at the Casino base hospital in Boulogne:

Each man had a square [*sic*] cardboard box, in which was pipe and an artistically-finished brass box, bearing the portrait and monogram of the Princess. The box contained a packet of tobacco and one of cigarettes. If the recipient was a nurse, chocolate was substituted for tobacco. If he was a male non-smoker he received a neat khaki writing case, completely equipped for field correspondence.[495]

PRESENTS FOR
NON-SMOKERS

At 12 o'clock [on 26th December] we received Princess Mary's present. There were two sorts, one for smokers, and the other for non-smokers. Each contained an embossed brass box which held in one case two packets of tobacco and cigarettes and in the other, a large packet of acid drops. To which was added a pipe and a case containing writing materials. I chose the non-smokers' present and

got the brass box and acid drops and the writing case.[496]

The principle having been accepted that non-smokers should receive a different gift from that of the smokers, the question arose as to what that gift should be. With the standard gift comprising the box plus five items (Christmas card, tobacco, cigarettes, tinder lighter and pipe) it followed that the smoking materials should be replaced with other gifts.

In the last meeting before Christmas, the Executive Committee listed out the remaining contracts it had filled in order to deliver on its commitments. This itemised 18,000 'khaki cases' for non-smokers, which were ordered from De La Rue & Co at a cost of 11½ d each.[497] With the number required being just

THE KHAKI WRITING CASE produced by De La Rue, to be given to non-smokers in lieu of the smoking requisites

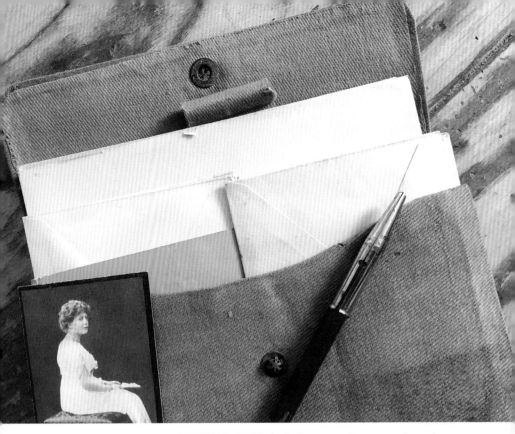

over three and a half percent of the total number of 500,000, this is a small percentage – showing, once again, just how small yet influential this minority group was.[498] The *Final Report* published by the Gift Fund provided specific details of this item:

The writing cases, in envelope form, were made of khaki cloth with Her Royal Highness' monogram, the date, and 'Christmas Fund' stamped in red lettering on the outside. They were fitted with stationery and an indelible pencil.[499]

The writing case, expanding with a central divider, is closed with a press stud, measures seven inches by four and a half inches (17.5 x 11.5 cm). Inside the flap, there is a loop for a pencil, which typically was a red-lacquered indelible pencil with a bright nickel cap to protect the tip, stamped 'EAGLE PENCIL CO LONDON.'[500] The case contained a standard pad of unlined writing paper (together with a ruled sheet to aid the writer), as well as two packs of envelopes that were kept together with blue gummed paper bands, to complete the set.[501] Supplied with the writing set was the 'cigarette photo' of Princess Mary, though it appears this might have been variable; Morgan Crofton certainly thought that this was the case, noting 'I was one of the lucky ones for inside the writing case I found and extremely pretty little photo of Princess Mary. There were only very few packets which had the photo'.[502]

With the writing set replacing the pipe and tinder lighter, the tobacco-related contents of the box were replaced by a four-ounce packet of 'acid tablets', again contained within the box itself. These are rare survivors today, though some 18,200 packets were ordered, in excess of the 18,000 required – once again presumably to cater for wastage.[503] The term 'tablets' has been interpreted by some as comprising solid slabs of sour-sweet boiled sugar; but Morgan Crofton was clear that he received 'acid drops'; then, as today a familiar term used for

PACKS OF ENVELOPES FROM THE WRITING CASE

RECONSTRUCTION OF THE NON-SMOKERS GIFT, INCLUDING WRITING CASE, BRASS BOX AND 'ACID TABLETS'. These were likely to be citrus-based boiled sweets in round tablet form, rather than a solid block

circular, citrus-based boiled sweets that were once a stable of any traditional sweet shop.[504] Though it is not known which company supplied them, surviving examples show that the packet comprised individual sweets contained in a cardboard wrapper bearing a very simple label, less elaborately lettered than the chocolate packet given to the nurses, outlined and bearing the name of the Fund and date at the top of the packet, and 'Acid Tablets' at its base.[505]

That such acid drops were appreciated by the men is noted by one nursing sister serving on an ambulance train, who recorded that 'one little Gurkha with his arm just amputated, and a wounded leg, could only be pacified by acid drops being put in his mouth and being allowed to hug the tin.'[506]

CHOCOLATE FOR NURSES

Though not discussed as such by the Executive Committee, it can be taken for granted that smoking

A RARE SURVIVOR: A GIFT BOX WITH ITS ASSOCIATED PACK OF
'ACID TABLETS' The poor preservation is deceptive; though it appears to be
'Tablet' (singular), it actually reads Tablets' (plural)

materials had been deemed inappropriate for nurses. With smoking then overwhelmingly a male habit – and the use of tobacco seen as morally ambiguous – it is not surprising that the number of women who engaged in smoking pre-war was insignificant. It would take the increased emancipation of the female workforce during the war and after to change these attitudes as regards whether the habit was 'suitable' for women.[507] Something else would have to be found, and with the mooted silver pincushions ruled out, it would seem that once again, sweets would provide the answer.

Though providing a gift for military nurses overseas had only been considered in late October, there is relatively little on record as to how the Committee came to the idea that they should receive chocolate as part of their gift – though sweets seemed always to be a default option when discussing alternatives. The *Final Report* of the Committee emphasises the military nature of the nurses' duty, as uniformed members of the British Expeditionary Force, and reports simply the items received – and their restricted distribution to those in France alone:

NURSES AT THE FRONT (FRANCE) The embossed brass box, a packet of chocolate, a Christmas card[508]

The nurses' gift contains fewer items than the standard gift; and fewer items than was contained in the non-smoker's version of that gift. It is interesting to reflect on why the quite complex gift given to the non-smokers was not extended to nurses, who would no doubt have found equal value in its acid tablets and stationery pouch. Perhaps the daintily wrapped chocolate was considered to be more feminine than the khaki-covered stationery pouch; but it is possible to consider the brass box itself as a masculine object. It is difficult to determine the reasoning in the absence of correspondence.

The number of nurses who would receive the gift was also open to interpretation. In August 1914, the total number of trained military nurses was 3,246, with the majority being members of the TFNS,

intended to staff military hospitals at home.[509] But the Gift now to be awarded was only for those nurses in France (with no subsequent extension to those at home); considering their eligibility, the Executive Committee suggested that in 1914 there were just 400 nurses who might be eligible.[510] Nevertheless, it was important to be sure, and so on 3 December 1914 the Matron-in-Chief of the British Expeditionary Force received a request 'for a nominal roll of all nurses serving in France for Queen Mary, as Princess Mary wishes to send them all a present from her fund.'[511] The actual number nurses who received the gift was specified in the *Final Report* of the Executive Committee as 1,500.[512]

The chocolate supplied for the nurses' gift was provided by two firms: De Bry & Co, who was to supply 1,000 packets at 7d, and 585 packets from Pascalls, at 4d/8.[513] De Bry (de Paris) was a French chocolatier that offered quality chocolate at two addresses in central London, of which its 64 New Oxford Street address was the most well known. The firm of James Pascall supplied 'sweets, chocolate and novelties' from its shop in Blackfriars, and its main location

AN EVEN
RARER
SURVIVOR:
A PACK OF
CHOCOLATE AS
GIVEN, WITH
THE GIFT BOX,
TO NURSES
Only some 1,500
were supplied.
This packet
contains two layers
of 'CHOCOVUM'
brand chocolate
made by London
manufacturer
De Bry

in Mitchum, Surrey; as its price-point indicates, Pascall's product was less 'up market' than that of De Bry.[514] With a total number of 1,585 (compared to the 1,500 nurses identified), the additional order was probably made so as to make good any wastage. The chocolate itself was a four-ounce packet wrapped in a form of greaseproof paper, tied with a pink ribbon that was secured under a label bearing the usual wording 'Her Royal Highness The Princess Mary's Christmas Fund, 1914', its block letters rendered in a pleasing Edwardian font.[515] It is expected that there would be minimal differences between the packets of chocolate supplied by the two firms, and these packets were designed to fit snugly within the standard brass box.[516] Examples are correspondingly rare.

Receipt of the gift was well organised, and the Matron-in-Chief recorded their arrival (for distribution), in Boulogne on

CHRISTMAS IN A STATIONARY HOSPITAL, QAIMNS NURSES
AND MEN IN ATTENDANCE

23 December, allowing the majority to be distributed to the hospitals for Christmas Day.[517] On the ambulance trains, its receipt on Boxing Day punctuated the routine scenes of pain:

Saw my lambs off the train before breakfast. One man in the Warwicks had twelve years' service, a wife and two children, but 'when Kitchener wanted more men' he re-joined. This week he got an explosive bullet through his arm, smashing it to rags above the elbow…We had Princess Mary's nice brass box this morning…[518]

The occasion was marked by the Matron-in-Chief of the British Expeditionary Force, who telegrammed the Princess on Christmas Day 'The QAIMNS and Reserve thank your Royal Highness for their Christmas gifts and wish you every happiness.'[519]

With the gifts distributed to all who were eligible, it was to be expected that no further distribution would be needed. But in March 1915, the redoubtable Lady Jellicoe, consistent in her support of her husband in matters naval, felt it necessary to write to the Secretary of the Executive Committee to express the view that

PRINCESS MARY AS A VAD NURSE,
PICTURED WITH HER MOTHER, 1918

Front, there can be no doubt that the nurses at sea deserved to be recognised, but it is to be presumed that the Committee was fearful of a spectre of an ever-evolving and expanding envelope of gift giving, and had decided enough was enough. Nevertheless, Lady Jellicoe was not one to give way lightly, and after pressing the point at a later meeting, these deserving nurses, who also 'wore the King's uniform at Christmas Day' were added to those who would receive the gift.[521]

Princess Mary's gift should also be given to the nurses who served at sea – on Hospital Ships. It seemed that requests for recognition of nurses continued to fall on deaf ears, as it was deemed that 'the gift was only promised to nurses at the Front' and that 'naval nurses could not be included'.[520] Once again, nurses were almost the last to be considered. However, as with their compatriots on the Western

Nurses, serving their country and the sailors and soldiers who defended it, finally received the recognition they deserved. That this must have surely pleased the Princess must be acknowledged, as she herself, her sense of duty as strong as ever, would ultimately join the ranks of the Volunteer Aid Detachments (VAD) to 'gratify her dearest wish – that she should enter a hospital and do regular work as an ordinary nurse.'[522]

Casualties, 1914

THE BRITISH EXPEDITIONARY Force landed in France on 16 August 1914. From the first engagements at the Battle of Mons on the 23rd of that month, the war ran hot for the BEF, with a succession of battles and engagements that would lead, eventually, to the establishment of the line of trenches that would become a recuring motif for the rest of the war.[523] And with these engagements came casualties, the official term for any soldier who has been rendered ineffective, or incapable of carrying on the fight, whether he be killed, wounded or taken prisoner. In the three months to the close of 1914, the British and Indian troops in France and Flanders had suffered heavily, with for every man killed in action, three would be wounded. Total military casualties in this period amounted to 95,654 men: 18,174 died (including 14,135 killed in action); 50,969 wounded and 26,511

missing or taken prisoner.[524] And this was just the army.

Captain Aubrey Herbert of the Irish Guards was wounded on the retreat from Mons – and would be taken prisoner:

WOUNDED MARINE OF THE NAVAL BRIGADE ON HIS WAY BACK FROM ANTWERP, 1914

I lay down on the ground and an RAMC man dressed me. The Red Cross men gave a loud whistle when they saw my wound, and said the bullet had gone through me. The fire was frightfully hot…The doctor gave me some morphia and I gave them my revolver. They put me on a stretcher, leaving another empty stretcher behind me. This was hit several times. Shots came from all directions…After about an hour and a half, I suppose, a German with a red beard, with the sun shining on his helmet and bayonet came up looking like an angel of death… He said: '*Wir sind kamaraden.*'[525]

Herbert was lucky, though a prisoner, he and his captors would be overtaken and released by French troops. Less fortunate was Lieutenant Malcolm Hay of the Gordon Highlanders, who was also badly wounded and captured:

SOLDIERS WOUNDED AT MONS ACCEPT APPLES FROM A WELL-WISHER

The bullets began to spray too close to my left ear, and laying my glasses on the parapet I was about to sit down for a few minutes' rest… when the machine-gun found its target… The blow might have come from a sledge-hammer, except that it seemed to carry with it an impression of speed. I saw for one instant in my mind's eye the battlefield at which I had been gazing through my glasses the whole day. Then the vision was hidden by a scarlet circle, and a voice said, "Mr H. has got it."[526]

Nevertheless, Hay would eventually be released as part of an exchange with German prisoners. Both men were eligible to receive the Princess's gift.

The focus of the Executive Committee in its early days was inevitably the delivery of gifts to those men serving at sea and at the front; but given the significant number casualties, and recognising the sacrifices they had been made, these men and their families could hardly be excluded from the distribution. Accordingly, the question of the supply of gifts to the wounded and returned soldiers, prisoners of war – and even men 'on furlough' – became a matter for some discussion by the Executive Committee. Once again the steady growth of the fund beyond its projected £55,000-60,000 gave some confidence that if donations continued to be received, then 'the wounded, prisoners and men interned [in the Netherlands] should receive if possible the full gift'.[527] Though still tentative, this resolution meant that men who were overseas on Christmas Day and who had given so much in action, would also be rewarded with a gift. This was confirmed a week later, when it was determined that 'the wounded in France and England' would be eligible for the gift. And given that, when convalescing these men were so visible and distinctive – set aside from the average soldier by their bright 'Hospital Blue' uniform – they were also the focus for much attention at a time traditionally associated with good will and good cheer.

Those who had been taken prisoner would have a long wait to receive their gifts from 1914; and for the families of the deceased, the ability to claim these small tokens undoubtedly provided some comfort. Once again, the work of the Executive Committee grew in complexity.

GIFTS FOR THE WOUNDED

In order to determine just how many wounded men this would entail, Rowland Berkeley canvassed opinion from hospitals as to the 'likely number of wounded who would be in hospital at Christmas', using a list that had been supplied to him via the temporary Surgeon-General Colonel M.W. Russell RAMC. In the end, this list was only used as an estimate, the War Office itself dealing with the distribution of gifts.[528] This kindness must have seemed a million miles apart from the conditions in the trenches, or on the high seas, that the men had just left:

[A] lot of patients had Xmas dinner in their Clearing Hospitals today, and the King's Xmas card, and they will get Princess Mary's present. Here they... had oranges and bananas, and hot chicken broth directly they got in.[529]

Following the extension of the scheme, the actual total number of wounded eligible for the gift was calculated at 89,165 sailors and soldiers.[530]

But Princess Mary's gift was not the only one to be received by the wounded in France, who no doubt also took their fair share of the parcels, letters and greetings that were flowing across the Channel at Christmas:

Each wounded man had, besides, all sorts of little presents – tobacco, cigarettes, sweets, warm socks, and so forth from the kindly disposed at home, the nurses being the medium through which the gifts were distributed. On waking, each man found them at his bedside. In one ward they had been stuffed by the sisters into a pair of new socks hung up by each man's bed. A little British flag was pinned on the foot of every bed, with two exceptions. The two undecorated beds were occupied respectively by a Prussian Guardsman and a young Wurtemberger. They had their share of the other gifts, though and seemed contented as their neighbours. A dinner of turkey and plum pudding was being

The King and Queen's Christmas card was also given to wounded sailors and soldiers; both received a card with the King as a Field Marshal, but with a special message

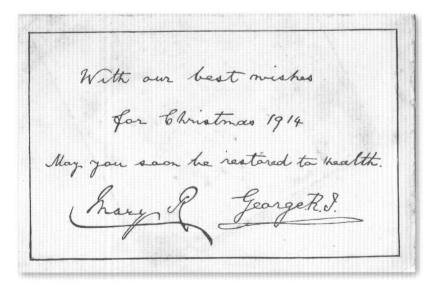

The King and Queen's message to the wounded at Christmas: 'may you soon be restored to health'

served when passed through the wards, and there was bottled beer for those able to take it.[531]

The wounded also were singled out for attention by the Royal Family, who sent a special version of their Christmas card, again separately from Princess Mary's Gift, and in an envelope bearing the Royal Arms. This depicted the Queen and her Field Marshal illustrated on its face, and bore the poignant message: 'With our best wishes for Christmas 1914. May you soon be restored to health. Mary R., George R.I.'[532]

In hospitals at home, the wounded who had made the journey 'back to Blighty' were also to receive gifts in addition to the full gift provided by the Gift Fund. Captain Roly Grimshaw, an officer serving with Indian cavalry regiment The Poona Horse was wounded in the chest on 20 December, near Festubert, a serious 'Blighty wound' that saw him transferred to the base hospital and then marked for home. Grimshaw was *en route* to Southampton the HMHS *Carisbrooke Castle* on Christmas Day when he was 'given Princess Mary's present'. On arrival in England 'Several

girls came along with Xmas cards but the moving me about had so upset me that I fear I took little interest.'[533] He would return to France in March 1915.

As Christmas approached, a brief report appeared across the country in local newspapers. It noted the generosity of one of the nation's most admired chocolate manufacturers, Cadbury's, in providing a gift to wounded servicemen currently in hospital. 'Messrs Cadbury, Bourneville, are sending box of chocolate each of the wounded soldiers and sailors in British hospitals as a Christmas gift.'[534] Cadbury's gift comprised a small ($3^2/5$ inches square by $1\frac{1}{2}$ inches deep – 8.5 cm square by 4 cm deep), colourful square tin with an embossed lid and portrait of the King (but sometimes a circular blue tin with a picture of Britannia upon it), and contained individual chocolates and a card bearing the message: 'Xmas, 1914. With Hearty Christmas Greetings to the Wounded Soldiers and Sailors, and with best wishes for their speedy recovery from Cadbury Bros. Ltd, Bourneville.'[535] The firm and its then majority female workforce – known as 'Cadbury's Angels' – would supply other comforts

CADBURY'S GIFT TO WOUNDED SAILORS AND SOLDIERS individual tins containing chocolates. A round tin featuring an image of Britannia is also known

and gifts throughout the war.[536] Cadbury's gift was well received, in Manchester at least, alongside the other gifts from other sources:

The soldiers in the Whitworth Street Military Hospital will have pleasant reminders of the Christmas season. Many people have taken timely thought of them, including the highest in the land. The King and Queen will send each man a Christmas-card bearing their likenesses and autographs, and the Queen has added a gift of tobacco…A proper Christmas dinner will be served, following the modern instead of the old convention, which substitutes turkey for roast beef but clings tenaciously to the plum pudding, decorated with the twig of holly, and mince pies.

A MERRY CHRISTMAS

With our best wishes
for Christmas 1914.
May you soon be restored to health.
Mary R
George R.I.

XMAS 1914

With best wishes
from Alexandra

MEN IN HOSPITAL
AT CHRISTMAS 1914,
ESPECIALLY THOSE IN
LONDON, RECEIVED A
LARGE NUMBER OF GIFTS
FROM MANY SOURCES

There is almost reason to fear a surfeit of the pudding, one would think, because the *Daily News* will provide each patient with a plateful weighing half a pound; and yet the plentifulness of supplies will be a more positive proof of goodwill.

Messrs Dingley have made the hospital a gift of fruit, and Messrs Cadbury have sent boxes of chocolate.[537]

There were further royal gifts for the wounded, too; though ones likely to have been of limited distribution, and given personally by Queen Alexandra. The Queen Mother had a long history of charitable giving to the armed forces, with her sponsorship of the Field Force Fund, and her New Year gift of chocolate in 1902. It was perhaps natural that she should have an interest in nursing given that the Queen Alexandra's Imperial Military Nursing Service (QAIMNS) was named in her honour in 1902, and in 1914 she sent out an elaborate cloak as a Christmas gift to her regular nurses in France.[538]

But the Queen's plans also stretched to a gift for those who lay wounded in hospital, and it appears that her plans pre-dated those of her grand-daughter. On 4 November, Alexandra's private secretary, Sir Henry Streathfield, wrote to Sir Edward Wallington, private secretary to Queen Mary:

It was settled some time ago that Queen Alexandra should give a little box of cigarettes with her picture on it to the wounded in Hospitals at Xmas – but it has not been made known and was to come as a surprise. Perhaps therefore it would be better if the character of Princess Mary's Fund did not say too much about it as we [do not] want it in the Press at present.[539]

There was no harm done, however, and Queen Alexandra's gift remained a surprise. It consisted of a simple gilded tin with a pasted portrait of the Queen in typical guise, with crown, high-collar and elaborate choker jewellery, and contained twenty-five cigarettes, each one individually signed 'Alexandra'. The tin was small enough to fit in a pocket measuring $4^2/5$ by 3 by ¾ inch (11.2 x 7.5 x 1.7 cm), with the simple message 'Xmas 1914' in the top left-hand corner, and a message 'With best wishes from Alexandra' printed from her own, distinctive, handwriting. And while there has been some speculation about the recipients of this particular gift, evidence suggests that it was intended for wounded servicemen, and particularly those in hospital at home.[540] It seems that this was never a particularly newsworthy event, however; though reports did filter into the local press:

> Queen Alexandra has forwarded Miss Maud Gaitskill, one of the organisers of the Boxing Day entertainments at the Crystal Palace, sixty boxes of cigarettes and fifty boxes of sweets, with a photograph of herself imprinted on the lid. The parcel was addressed, 'For the patients of the Sick Bay, Royal Naval Division, Crystal Palace.' Queen Alexandra also sent every patient at the three military hospitals in the Weybridge district a box of cigarettes with her portrait thereon.[541]

Queen Alexandra's gift was also widely distributed across the London hospitals containing war

QUEEN ALEXANDRA GAVE HER OWN GIFT IN 1914: a tin of cigarettes with her image on the front, each cigarette marked with her distinctive signature. These were given to the wounded in hospital

QUEEN ALEXANDRA'S EFFORTS WERE REPORTED IN THE FRENCH
PERIODICAL *EXCELSIOR* The Queen continued to give out lithographed
boxes with her image on them in subsequent years

wounded; these hospitals at the heart of the Capital were the focus of much attention, so the gifts were plentiful. Hall Caine, literary polymath and journalist, reported on the scene for the *Daily Telegraph*:

The very idea of Christmas… had begun to jar, and [the wounded] had been preparing for a melancholy festival. But, thank God, compensations had come to them. First a Christmas card for every wounded soldier from the King and Queen. Then a box of cigarettes from Queen Alexandra. Then another box of something nice from our charming young Princess Mary. Then, from some unknown Santa Claus, half a sovereign apiece…Then something from the *Daily News*, and something else from the *Daily Express*. And last, but by no means least, "King Albert's Book'..."[542]

Queen Alexandra's gift was also enjoyed as part of the festivities in hospitals across the country:

> The fare at the Cheltenham Racecourse Red Cross Hospital was on Christmas lines, with plenty of plum pudding, cakes, and crackers. The patients received the King's Christmas card and cigarettes from Queen Alexandra, and after dinner there was dancing for such could take part in that social exercise, The 'Christmas tree.'[543]

While the prodigious efforts of the Princess Mary's Gift Fund would not be repeated, there was still room for individual efforts. Queen Alexandra would continue, in a limited way, to give away tins of cigarettes to the wounded at Christmas in the later years of the war, this time bearing her printed portrait and message.[544] Not only that, but Cadbury's would continue to gift boxes of chocolate – though in an unprepossessing cardboard box.[545] No doubt as with all these gifts, they were treasured, remaining as collections of soldier's souvenirs, artefacts of the war in drawers, attics in homes across Britain, even today, each one an important story.

GIFTS FOR PRISONERS OF WAR

There were other casualties of war, and they included those men who had been captured or interned, taken from the battlefield and made to endure the hardships of a prisoner's existence. Those men who had entered captivity on, or prior to, Christmas Day 1914 were also eligible for the Princess's Gift. They had served at Sea or at the Front and had claims to have had suffered more than some; but working out how they might receive the gift was a challenge.

At the 8 December 1914 meeting of the Executive Committee, an unusual suggestion was heard from Mr Edward Page Gaston, an American citizen – therefore representing a neutral country – and social campaigner. Page Gaston proposed that 'a sum of money should be handed over for the purpose of making purchases in Germany' so that prisoners would receive 'some form of gift', and that he undertook to 'make the distribution.' Surprisingly, the

Committee agreed to transfer the sum of £1,250 to the War Office 'for them to hand over to Mr Gaston' for this purpose – though it is not clear whether this actually happened; it would be surprising if it had.[546] Perhaps more significantly, the Committee resolved that 'a box should be preserved for each of the prisoners on his release.'[547] In reality this was a major task, as numbers were huge – particularly as by the end of December, some 16,963 other ranks of the British and Indian Expeditionary forces had been taken prisoner – and the final calculation was more like 18,030.[548]

All those who had been taken prisoner in action in 1914 could reasonably expect to receive the full gift; indeed, the records of the Princess Mary Gift Fund go to great lengths to create a series of list of men eligible to receive the full gift, arranged by regiment, a list of those battalions that represent the 'Old Contemptibles' at the time. Expectations had to be managed, however:

Presents will be given to the wounded, to the widows or mothers of those who have fallen, and to prisoners of war on their return. The committee have been compelled

BRITISH PRISONERS OF WAR AT WORK NEAR DOBERITZ, GERMANY IN 1914, UNDER THE WATCHFUL EYE OF THEIR ARMED GUARD

strictly to limit the distribution of presents to those who are serving who have served previous to and including Christmas Day.[549]

Some prisoners were repatriated, usually due to concerns over health and well-being. In at least one case, the Princess herself took time to visit officers who had been returned, too sick or too wounded to pose a threat to their captors:

Princess Mary visited Queen Alexandra Military Hospital yesterday, and presented gifts from her Royal Highness's Christmas Fund to the wounded officers and men who, as prisoners, have been released by German Government in exchange.[550]

While there were some repatriations, the majority of prisoners had to await the war's end and their return before they could receive their gifts. In practice, catering for the majority of prisoners meant the retention of a full gift for each man, with each of its components. The Committee's resolution would lead to a considerable amount of additional work, tasks that would fall to the various Regimental Associations in the aftermath of the war. Nevertheless, gifts were held back, and Sir Ernest Goodhart, assistant honorary secretary to the Fund, reported to the Committee in 1916 that there were 'a large number of complete gifts at Deptford' put aside for Prisoners of War.[551]

The manner of the distribution of gifts to these men was described in succinct terms by the *Final Report*, which summed up the activities:

The Executive Committee reserved a sufficient number of gifts for distribution to men who had been interned or were prisoners of war at that time after the war had ceased. Accordingly, when the Armistice was declared the names and addresses of the men entitled were obtained through Record Offices and Prisoner Care Committees, and the gift was distributed by the Fund through the Post.[552]

Regimental Care Committees were enlisted to assist with the location of ex-prisoners of war, or the next of kin of soldiers

PRIVATE ANGRAVE'S GIFT BOX in its close-fitting cardboard outer

who had died, in order to better distribute the gifts that were still very much in evidence. After the Armistice, Rowland Berkeley contacted these committees in order to access such men:

A gift from Her Royal Highness The Princess of Wales [*sic*] has been reserved for Prisoners of war on their release. The men entitled to receive the gift are Sailors and Soldiers who had been taken prisoners at any time up to and including the 25th December 1914. In the event of any man, so qualified, having died, a gift will be sent to his next-of-kin. The Executive Committee will be gratified if Care Committees who have records of duly qualified men will send lists giving their names, regiments and home addresses, or where men have died, the names and addresses of their next of kin to Sir Ernest Goodhart, Bart., 43 Wimpole Street, London W1. It is desirable that the lists should be forwarded as soon as possible as the packing of the gift must necessarily take some little time.[553]

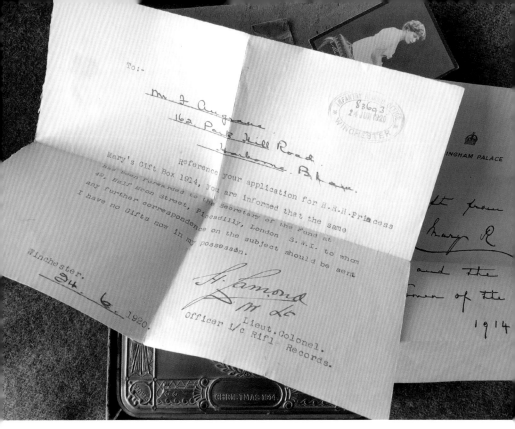

The following text appears within the letter in the image:

To:—

Mr. F. Angrave
162 Park Hill Road
Harborne. B'ham.

Reference your application for H.R.H. Princess
Mary's Gift Box 1914, you are informed that the same
has been forwarded to the Secretary of the Fund at
42, Half Moon Street, Piccadilly, London S.W.I. to whom
any further correspondence on the subject should be sent.
I have no Gifts now in my possession.

Winchester.
24. 6. 1920.

H. Lamond
M & C
Officer i/c Rifle Records.
Lieut. Colonel.

BUCKINGHAM PALACE

(handwritten on card:) ... from
Mary R
and the
... of the
1914

GIFT CLAIMED BY PRIVATE ANGRAVE OF THE KRRC ON HIS
RETURN FROM BEING A PRISONER OF WAR. The gift he received is an
assortment of gift items. Angrave had been posted 'missing, believed killed' in 1914

The resulting lists were huge, the responsibility large.[554] The men concerned still had to make an application to receive their gift. As an example, Private Frank Angrave of the 2nd Battalion King's Royal Rifle Corps was reported Killed in Action on 14 September 1914. Angrave had actually survived, posted as missing, and had spent the war as a PoW before returning home; he applied to the Infantry Record Office in 1920, only to be referred to Secretary of the Gift Fund – the 'Officer in charge of Rifle Records' having 'no Gifts in his possession.'[555] It is interesting that Pte Angrave received a mismatch of the brass box in its closely fitting cardboard outer box, the cigarettes and tobacco, a bullet pencil and the 1915 New Year's card (together, surprisingly, with the letter from Queen Mary's Needlework Guild). It appears that gifts were assembled from whatever was available at the time. This surely must have been typical. Pte Angrave's gift, though claimed, was kept intact, untouched, and possibly unappreciated so far after it had been first issued to the 'Old Contemptibles' in France.

Certainly, the time that had passed since the original gifts were assembled had meant that much of the reserve of cigarettes and tobacco was now no longer in a fit state for consumption, having been deemed 'dangerous to health if smoked' by the War Office Inspection Department, due to the materials having been 'denicotinised'. In addition, a review of the remaining gift items to assemble Prisoner of War gifts had revealed, unfortunately, evidence of an unwelcome amount of 'pilfering' of pipes and tobacco.[556] It was all very unsatisfactory. As a consequence some 1,132 lbs of tobacco and 360,940 cigarettes were purchased to replace them, at much inflated costs of 5/- per pound of tobacco (compared with 1/9 to 2/6 per pound in 1914), and 12/- per thousand cigarettes (compared with 8/- to 11/- in 1914).[557] These were supplied in one ounce packets of tobacco and packs of twenty cigarettes – but in wrappers that were not of the standard and distinctive yellow format – meaning that the gifts many received may have been more of a miscellany that would have been preferred.[558]

GIFTS FOR WIDOWS AND PARENTS

With the war raging hard at Sea and on Land in those first few months of the war, it was inevitable that there would be fatalities, men who lost their lives alongside comrades who survived and lived to fight again. Conscious no doubt of the meaning placed upon Queen Victoria's Chocolate Box by the widows and parents of men who had fallen in the Boer War, it was deemed essential that those who had lost their lives in this modern conflict should also be remembered.

Though it may well have been the intention from the start, it was not until early December – after it was known that the subscription call had been a success – that the Executive Committee made any mention of the provision of gifts to the families of the fallen. Nevertheless the intention was announced in late November with a letter from the Duke of Devonshire published a letter in the press seeking further subscriptions and ending with the sentence: 'The box will be sent to the widows or mothers of those who have fallen.'[559] Nevertheless, the matter first appeared in the minutes of 8 December 1914, when Rowland Berkeley reported that he had made arrangements for an index to be made of the names and addresses of the widows and parents of the men who had been killed, in order that they should receive a gift. Though in the end it was agreed that making such a list was properly the responsibility of the of the War Office – and that it should 'be abandoned' – it was an important step.[560]

The form of the gift that families should receive was discussed at the next meeting, when it was 'decided that the widows or parents of Officers should receive the brass box and a suitable card, and the widows or parents of Men should receive a brass box, chocolate and a card.'[561] The suggestion that chocolate be added to the gift for the families of Other Ranks appears to have been dropped. In January, in discussing the gifts to be given to the Navy, it was determined that widows would 'receive the same as the army, namely the box and the card.'[562] This would become the standard gift given to the families of those who had died in the fateful campaigns of 1914. In January 1915, the press started to carry advice for those who had lost their loved ones. For example, the *Sheffield Evening Telegraph* advised that 'widows or mothers of men who have fallen in the war should to the Record Office of the deceased sailor or soldier'.[563]

Letters accompanying these gifts, which were sent out in close-fitting cardboard boxes with lids (half the depth of the standard ones, perfectly fitting the brass box), were stark, particularly those received from the Infantry Records Office: 'In accordance with instructions received from the Secretary, War Office, I beg to forward you herewith Princess Mary's Christmas Gift, which in the case of the Next-of-kin contains neither cigarettes, tobacco or sweets.'[564] In some cases, however, the advice on what relatives would actually receive was contradictory, particularly when posted in the local newspapers:

The General in command of the Scottish District has received a communication

A SAD REMEMBRANCE OF A LIFT LOST The gift received by the family of Gunner Elkinton, who died of wounds received in France

from the War Office with regard to have been killed and Princess Mary's Christmas gift – the brass box containing pipe, tobacco, and cigarettes. It is an intimation that the next of kin of those who have fallen have right to the gift, and should make claim for it through the record offices. In Scotland, No. 1 record office is at Perth and No. 2 Hamilton.[565]

Nevertheless, as the *Final Report* of the Gift Fund identifies, it was, indeed, just the 'embossed brass box [and] a Christmas card' that were intended for 'Widows or Parents'.[566]

In all cases, such gifts obtained by next of kin remain poignant reminders of the impact of war, though it is surely difficult to judge at this distance how the receipt of these gifts was viewed in the context of the loss of a loved one. Perhaps they were considered insignificant tokens, a reminder of a life lost; or perhaps they provided comfort, in the knowledge that their sailor, or soldier, was not forgotten.

Those at Home and in the Colonies, 1915–18

By April 1915, Rowland Berkeley was able to assert that the majority of the gifts to be given to those men and women under the Command of Sir John French and Lord Jellicoe had been delivered. A total of 426,724 had been issued to the Expeditionary Force in France, including 1,329 to nurses, 4,600 to the French Mission who supported the BEF, and 66,168 who had returned home wounded, or who had been on leave.[563] For the Royal Navy, 'the whole of the gifts including the cartridge pencil case' had been handed over to the Admiralty for distribution to its far-flung outposts and ships at sea, and amounted to some 255,271 gifts – far in excess of what had been original 160,000 proposed.[568] It had been an immense undertaking, and was a great success. The Committee charged with delivering the gift had done its job.

But the task was far from over. The decision to extend the scheme taken in November was in response to the flow of subscriptions from the public and small organisations alike. Though the scale of donations would fall following the passing of Christmas, with donations still arriving – and as these funds had been made with the express purpose of providing a gift to sailors and soldiers at Christmas – the Committee had little choice in their actions.[569] It is not surprising, then, that the extension to the scheme proposed by the Executive Committee was formally ratified by the General Committee.[570]

There can be little doubt that the extent of the new distribution had been influenced by concerns similar to those expressed by Sir David Graaff that troops in more remote theatres of war were being ignored, forgotten even; perhaps none so evident than the conflict in the German colonies in East Africa and the Cameroons.[571] With this war seeming so remote,

Authority/Dominion	Number	'Class'
War Office		
New Army, Territorials and Dominion Contingent at Home	1,337,889	C
Troops under War Office in various parts of the world other than the Expeditionary Force (of whom 37,000 were British)	100,000	B
India Office		
Territorials and Indian Volunteer Corps	112,000	B
Indian Troops	155,000	A, B
Indian Marine	5,000	B
Canada (Approximately)	38,000	B
New Zealand		
In Egypt	10,453	B
Samoa	1,196	B
New Zealand	3,609	B
South Africa	40,000	B
Total (excluding Australia*)	1,803,147	
*Men of the Australian Imperial Force (AIF) were also be eligible for Princess Mary's Gift, added to this list later. India's contribution also included men at the Front in 1914		

Identified groups for extension of the scheme, as of January 1915

it was all too easily overshadowed by the events in France and Flanders in 1914:

> Naturally, the vast struggle in France has monopolised public attention. There have been no 'Princess Mary's Gifts' for these fighters on the outposts of the Empire; no letters for lonely soldiers with socks, mittens, and mufflers. These have been reserved for the heroes of Mons, the Aisne, Ypres, and Neuve Chapelle.[572]

These concerns were such that the Colonial Office sent Lord Islington, Under-Secretary of State for the Colonies, to attend the Executive Committee on 1 December 1914 in order to express the opinion that 'it would be desirable to give the present to Home and Native troops in East and West Africa without distinction'.[573] This was an important steer, and the Chairman gave his undertaking that these matters would be 'fully considered'.

Naturally, the success of the fund-raising effort meant that this was a consideration that could now be entertained. And as sufficient funds were now available, the Committee turned its immediate attention away from France and Flanders to all those of the Empire who wore the King's uniform on Christmas Day 1914 – beyond those who had already been overseas under Field Marshal French's command – no matter whether they were operating in a theatre of war or at home. With the navy already fully catered for, the new distribution was to be for the army alone (other than the Royal Indian Marine, who had not been covered by the first distribution), but finding out just out how many extra gifts would need to be produced required assistance. To this end, the Secretary reported in the last meeting before Christmas, that he had 'communicated with the High Commissioners of Canada, South Africa, New Zealand and Australia, the India Office and the Colonial Office' in order to determine just how many men would be eligible to receive the gift. 'A reply by cable' was requested – the matter was urgent.[574]

The scale of the distribution, based on the Secretary's findings, was considered in the first meeting of the Committee in January 1915.[575] It was to cover all of troops of the Empire serving in the 'King's Uniform' at home and abroad,

'KITCHENER'S MOB' Volunteers who had joined the army after Kitchener's 'call to Arms' in August 1914, and who were in training at home by Christmas

including the volunteers who had joined the army since the beginning of the war, and the efforts of those who were serving at home, ready to 'do their bit'.[576] It was a huge expansion way beyond the initial expectations for the Gift.

The extended distribution also now included all those who had answered Lord Kitchener's 'Call to Arms' of 8 August 1914 – a call for 500,000 men to form the 'New Army' – men who became known affectionately as 'Kitchener's Mob'.[577] That this Call was necessary had been identified by the newly appointed and revered Secretary of State for War, Field Marshal Horatio Herbert

Kitchener. The Field Marshal had expressed his view from the outset that the war as likely to last for three years at least, with a consequent need to field an army of millions before the war was over.[578]

Recruitment had been steady in the early days of the appeal, but soon grew to a crush at the recruiting offices in the wake of Mons and Le Cateau, and the idea that the army – and the country – was in peril. These men, from all walks of life, were added to the roster of 'Service Battalions' that were formed as part of the British regimental structure. Those who joined voluntarily in 1914 were in training up and down the country, and their makeshift uniforms of 'Kitchener Blue' became a distinctive sight. But they were not the only men in army uniform at home in 1914. The strength of the Territorial Force at the commencement of the war was 268,777, and recruitment had bolstered that number – just as it had done in the raising of Kitchener's Army.[579]

While the Territorials in France would be eligible for the full gift, many thousands of men, both at Home and on Imperial duties, and none of them serving 'under the command of Sir John French', would not. Though originally considered as Home Defence troops, most 'Terriers' had signed the Imperial Service Obligation, which meant that they would serve overseas when obliged to do so.[580] In 1914, this took Territorial battalions to the corners of Empire in order to release Regular battalions for the Front, but it would also see some

TERRITORIALS IN TRAINING The Honourable Artillery Company was a venerable unit but was a volunteer battalion of the all-Territorial London Regiment. Though some battalions had moved to Flanders by Christmas, most were at home, and otherwise ineligible for Princess Mary's Gift

H.A.C. Fargo Camp. 1914.

twenty-two Territorial battalions deployed to France and Flanders before the end the year, in order to bolster the BEF – amongst them, distinguished battalions of the London Regiment, such as the London Rifle Brigade, the Honourable Artillery Company and the London Scottish.[581]

The remainder of the Territorial battalions and Yeomanry regiments, many of them slated for service overseas, were either in training or deployed to the coast of England, for fear of invasion.[582] Not for them, at first, the promise of a gift from the young Princess; instead they would be be reliant on local citizens to provide some level of Christmas cheer, often to supply the ubiquitous puddings. One such scheme was that of the Mayor of Birkenhead, who proposed to 'give a good share of Christmas pudding to all the troops at present stationed within the Mersey defence area' and who 'opened a fund for this purpose' to supply at least 2,000 lbs of pudding at a cost of between £150-200.[583] And for the Talley brothers, serving with the City of London Yeomanry, Christmas meant manning trenches on the cliff tops of East Anglia; they were grateful for any comforts their family could send:

25 December 1914. The Parcel was simply grand. The only thing was we were warned that evening that we should have to rise at 3 o'clock in the morning, as we were expecting the Germans to raid the East Coast. So we were warned we might not return to our billet, so the result was I had one quarter of the pudding, and gave the other piece and cake and grapes away, but I kept the dates, raisins, etc., to myself.[584]

Even though most would not set foot in the battle-zone in 1914, now, under the extension to the gift, all men of the Terriers and Kitchener's Mob would be eligible for the new Princess Mary gift of box, card, and pencil. Nevertheless, under the 'class system' they would be last in line for a gift, behind those volunteers of the Empire, all of whom were now destined to receive the gift, so long as they had been in uniform on Christmas Day 1914.

India and the Imperial Dominions were deemed to be automatically at war with Germany when Great Britain, the 'mother country', declared war on 4 August 1914. These Dominions

CANADIAN RECRUITS IN TRAINING AT CAMP VALCARTIER, QUEBEC, IN 1914

– Australia, Canada, New Zealand and South Africa – maintained small permanent military forces with a militia for home defence, and therefore sending an army to serve overseas meant raising a larger volunteer force.[585] In Canada alone, the militia had grown from 36,000 in 1904 to 55,000 in 1913, and by 1914 this had risen to 77,323, men who were required to present themselves for annual training, similar to the Territorials at home in the United Kingdom. The Militia was the basis for the huge expansion in the army that would follow mobilisation, and would be followed with an order on 10 August 1914 for the raising of a first contingent of men to

serve overseas that would number 25,000.[586] The first contingent of the Canadian Expeditionary Force who arrived at Camp Valcartier, Quebec, in August numbered 32,665, and these men would be the first to make the trip across the Atlantic.[587] Some few would be in France by Christmas 1914 and they would get the 'full' gift; those in training on Salisbury Plain and those volunteers now in uniform in Canada would now be eligible for the new, simplified gift. Canada's example is typical; the other Dominions had also committed troops to the war effort derived, initially, from their militias, but ultimately involving new volunteers.[588] And while

Authority/Dominion	Number	'Class'
Regular Army, Territorial Force & Dominion Troops at home	1,337,889	C
India [Including men at the Front in 1914]	294,900	A, B, C
Canada	70,000	B
Australia	53,300	B
South Africa	42,647	B
New Zealand	19,915	B
Colonies, Protectorates & Protected Ports	72,086	B
Total	1,890,737	

Final distribution of Princess Mary's Gift to those at Home ('Class C') and 'in the Dominions' ('Class B') excluding those already catered for ('Class A').[589]

Canadians would be transported to Britain and the Western Front, those from Australia and New Zealand would find their way to Egypt and the Dardanelles. All were eligible for a gift under the increase to the scheme.

With so many men being recruited to support the war across the Empire, there would be challenges in both putting the gift together – and delivering it. And all the while, the inception of an idea from the very earliest part of a long war was receding from the public gaze. But for those challenged to carry out the task, it remained very real indeed.

Meeting the target of supplying gifts to all who were in uniform on Christmas Day was a huge expansion of intent, and given the huge numbers involved, there was an urgent need to simplify the Gift. Not surprisingly, it was decided that 'both officers and men of whatever race should receive just the brass box, card and bullet pencil.'[590] The committee had turned its attention away from the multiplicity of gift items that had marked the first distribution, and now concentrated on a simple, one-gift-fits-all approach. Based principally upon the brass box, it contained simply a 'bullet pencil' held in a cardboard insert designed to fit the box, and a card from the Princess more suited to the new year than Christmas. It simply came down to cost and supply – there would be no additional gifts, and no variants for different groups. This gift was destined to the most commonly distributed of them all – and the most often encountered today.

THE BRASS BOX

The extension of the scheme meant more brass boxes, and as always, brass was the major issue. With supply in such a parlous state, and with the sinking of the *Lusitania* and the consequent loss of so much sheet brass 'at the bottom of the Irish Sea', manufacturing sufficient brass boxes to meet requirements was going to be a stretch. The enormity of the task was highlighted at the meeting of the Executive Committee in March 1915, where the total number of boxes left to be manufactured and distributed was calculated to be 1,886,650; yet, due to supply issues, fewer that ten-percent of these had been manufactured, with just 153,200 supplied, and 421,875 only

THE SIMPLIFIED CHRISTMAS GIFT to be given to all those 'in uniform' at Christmas 1914 – and who had not otherwise been eligible to receive one. The gift now comprised the brass box, the bullet pencil and a New Year's card

partially made. That meant starting from scratch to deliver 1,311,575 boxes meant at least 222 tons of brass, and an additional amount of 23 tons to finish off those under construction.[591]

Though the Executive Committee had planned to bypass the box manufacturers, directly sourcing brass strip and holding it in reserve in a Birmingham depot, the plan was not destined for

A GIFT BOX GIVEN TO THE FAMILY OF A DECEASED SOLDIER The brass seems of a lesser quality than is typical of earlier issues, probably a result of brass shortages

success. In reality, there was little chance of obtaining British brass in a hurry. There were heavy demands being made on the alloy because of its use as a component of many munitions, and beyond that, its constituent materials – copper and zinc – were also in short supply.[592] The question of brass supply was raised at every meeting of the Executive Committee subsequent to the initial distribution; it would be major factor in the delay to the distribution of boxes, and the gift as a whole, and until the needs of the Colonial troops could be met, those serving at home would have to await their gift.[593]

To compound matters further, the costs of producing the boxes was also inevitably on the increase. In his report to the Executive Committee in the first meeting of the New Year, Rowland Berkeley explained that the box manufacturers 'would not undertake any further orders except at an increased price per box', with a projected cost of 7d, compared with the 6 ¼ d previously quoted.[594] To modern eyes, this difference appears miniscule – but with just 10d to play with for each gift, there was little room for manoeuvre, as the remaining amount would be needed to complete the gift, and to get it packed. This alone explains the simplification of the gift.

THE NEW YEAR CARD

With the original gift including a card that presented the Princess's Christmas wishes, it made sense

MEN OF THE ARMY SERVICE CORPS RECEIVE THEIR GIFT BOXES WHILE AT CAMP IN ENGLAND While this image is captioned Christmas 1914, this is unlikely; no army unit at home received a gift on Christmas Day. These men hold the boxes and have no pipes or other items, and there are no cardboard outers. This is an image of soldiers of 'class C' who received their gifts much later

that the newly extended scheme should also include a card. But with Christmas fast receding into memory, it would obviously be necessary to amend the text, and a new version was designed by De La Rue to replace it. The new card retained the folding form and layout of the earlier one, and its red monogram, but this time with carried the date •1915•. The message inside expressed a fervent hope for the future outcome of the war, 'With Best Wishes for a Victorious New Year from The

Princess Mary and Friends at Home'.[595] With cost an issue, the new card was now produced without the distinctive envelope of the 1914 version – this was retained for the original recipients of the gifts.[596] On that basis, all 1915 gifts simply have the card placed in the box with the bullet pencil. The cards were reported as having been printed and stored by De La Rue, ready for distribution by early April 1915.[597] It was also the case that the Princess's 'Cigarette Photograph', produced for the standard gift and

THE BULLET PENCIL

The 'bullet pencil', often known and referred to as a 'bullet pencil case' at the time, is an interesting object. While 'bullet pencils' would later become common items in mid-century America, essentially give-aways to host advertising, they were hardly a common item at the time. A precedent had been set, however, with the manufacture of an earlier fund-raising item, a relic of the Battle of Omdurman, in 1898.[599] In this case, MK IV .303 brass cartridge cases, originally fitted with hollow point bullets and used by the British from Lee-Metford rifles at the Mahdi's forces with such devastating effect, had been harvested from the battlefield itself.[600] The battle had been fought to put down the Mahdi's insurrection in the Sudan,

INSCRIBED GIFT BOX TO PTE PARKINSON OF THE 17TH WEST YORKSHIRE REGIMENT, the 2nd Leeds Pals, a Kitchener's Army unit raised by the Mayor of Leeds in 1914. The New Year Card is outwardly similar to the earlier Christmas card, though it is dated 1915, and there is no containing envelope.

enclosed within the cigarette packet, did not form part of this gift set, reserved as it was for, original, 'Class A' recipients.[598]

INTERIOR OF THE NEW YEAR CARD 'With Best Wishes for a Victorious New Year'

With Best Wishes for a Victorious New Year.

From The Princess Mary and Friends at Home.

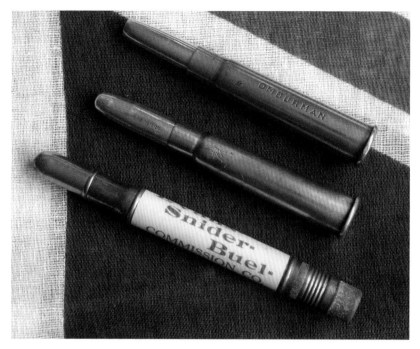

BULLET PENCILS FROM THREE ERAS
American advertising pencil from the 1940s *(bottom)*; Princess Mary's pencil
(centre); and the Omdurman pencil from 1898 *(top)*

an event that led to the death of General Gordon at Khartoum, over a decade earlier. As part of a charitable endeavour Mappin Bros of Cheapside, London, took the cartridges and engraved them in block letters 'OMDURMAN', the reverse carrying the inscription in cursive script 'Remember Gordon'. This early bullet pencil is actually quite a complex propelling pencil, its silver 'bullet', stamped 'MAPPIN BROTHERS' extending such that the whole is 14 cm long, set in a Woolwich-manufactured spent cartridge case. Each was sold, in a presentation box, with a slip of paper that bore the title 'A Souvenir of GORDON', and with the following statement: 'This Pencil is guaranteed to be an actual cartridge case from the Battle of Omdurman... Ten percent of the value is dedicated to the Funds of The Gordon Memorial College of Khartoum', an institution that was set up to provide education to the people of Sudan, and

THE OMDURMAN PENCIL
showing the engraving of the battle
name, and the maker's mark of 'Mappin
Brothers'. The slogan 'Remember
Gordon' is inscribed upon the reverse
of the cartridge, which was reputedly
recovered from the Omdurman
battlefield

either silver (marked in small block letters 'STERLING SILVER') – to be distributed in the first instance to the men of the Royal Navy; or nickel – to be given, initially, to all other recipients. Both held a short pencil (typically coated with red lacquer or plain polished wood) that fitted perfectly, and which were hidden when the 'bullet' was married up with the case.

Once more De La Rue had been called upon to supply the bullet pencils for the much simplified, and now universal gift. De La Rue acted as agents in supplying 750,000 bullet pencils with silver bullet pencil covers at a cost of 3¼d; and a further 1,000,000 with nickel bullet pencil covers at 1¾d or a maximum of 2¼d.[602] This meant that the silver bullet pencils were no longer to be the preserve of the Royal Navy, though it seems that the distribution of the remainder of the silver versions was not to any specific group. All were reportedly manufactured 'well within the contracted time', with the order ready for delivery by the end of April 1915, to be stored and distributed by De La Rue, in the company name.[603] In total, some 1,990,000 were made.[604]

which opened in 1902. It is now the University of Khartoum.[601]

While this might have set a precedent, the bullet pencil case to be used with Princess Mary's Gift in 1914–15 took an altogether simpler form. Although outwardly similar to the Omdurman pencil, the main part of the case was made from a spent brass cartridge, with the Princess's distinctive coronet and M monogram stamped into it. Given Lady Jellicoe's original wishes, the pencil holder itself was made from

Each pencil was housed in

a distinctive cardboard insert, designed to prevent it from rolling around within the brass box. When first supplied, each pencil was wrapped in a twist of white paper to protect it, and then inserted between the diagonal cuts within the cardboard insert, holding it firmly in place.[605] It is to be assumed that De La Rue supplied, or at least sourced, the holders.

The suggestion that the spent cases had been collected from 'the battlefield' – commonly referred to in the press at the time – undoubtedly came from the background to its forebear, the Omdurman pencil. While this is a romantic notion, there is no real evidence to support what was, in reality, an unrealistic expectation. Perhaps it was expressed through a perceived need to connect their recipients at home with the battlefield at the Front, giving greater worth and validity to the

THE CARDBOARD CARTRIDGE HOLDER, designed to hold the pencil in place in the otherwise empty (apart from the 1915 card) box

Comparison of the Omdurman bullet propelling pencil *(top)*, and the simple wooden pencil used by the Princess Mary Gift Fund *(bottom)* Princess Mary's distinctive monogram is stamped on each cartridge given with the Gift

use of such a mundane military object? Or perhaps the story was just a journalistic flourish; in either case, it probable that these spent cartridge cases were more likely to have been harvested from firing ranges in full use by the expanding armies at home, rather than from the actions of the BEF in the battlefields of France and Flanders. Nevertheless, it was the Committee itself that sourced the spent cartridges, finding that it was 'more economical', and ensuring 'punctual delivery' to do so, with a 'saving to the Fund of £255 15s.'[606]

What is interesting is that, in examining the stampings on the base of surviving cartridges, there is some variation in type and date. There are Mark VI and Mark VII cartridges; the Mark VI was used with earlier pattern 'Long Lee' rifles which were still in use at home in some Territorial battalions; while the Mark VII was the bullet used throughout the war in a frontline role. In addition, the stampings show a range of pre-war dates, 1907–1911 (Mk VI) and 1910–1912 (Mk VII), consistent with the army using up its issue

Head Stamp	Manufacturer	Date/Cartridge type
B 10 ↑VII↑	Birmingham Metal & Munitions Co Ltd.	1910 Mark VII
CAC C VI	Colonial Ammunition Co., Auckland	Mark VI
R↑L 09 VI	Royal Laboratory, Woolwich Arsenal	1909, Mark VI
R↑L 10 VI	Royal Laboratory, Woolwich Arsenal	1910, Mark VI
R↑L 11 VI	Royal Laboratory, Woolwich Arsenal	1911, Mark VI
R↑L 12 VII	Royal Laboratory, Woolwich Arsenal	1912, Mark VII
KN 07 VI	Kings Norton Metal Co, Birmingham	1907, Mark VI
KN 14 VII	Kings Norton Metal Co, Birmingham	1914, Mark VII
KN 14↑ VII	Kings Norton Metal Co, Birmingham	1914, Mark VII
K14 VII	Kynoch & Co, Witton, Birmingham	1914, Mark VII

Typical Bullet Pencil cartridge 'head stamps'[607]

ammunition in the early part of the war, at least suggesting that these early examples may line up with the first issue of the bullet pencil cases to the navy, and to the army in lieu of the tinder lighter. It also follows that those with a 1914 date stamp could be representative of the cartridges used to make up the large number of bullet pencils that were the principal content of the gift issued in 1915 onwards.

As a side note, it is interesting that in King George's collection of war artefacts, there is an Ottoman Mauser cartridge and bullet, picked up on X Beach at Gallipoli by Lt C.T.H. White RN, who served on HMS *Irresistible* and later, HMS *Arcadian*. It was given to Col. Sir Malcolm Murray of the Seaforth Highlanders – who had served as Equerry to the Duke of Connaught – and who, in May 1915, made an offer to Princess Mary herself to exchange the bullet for an example

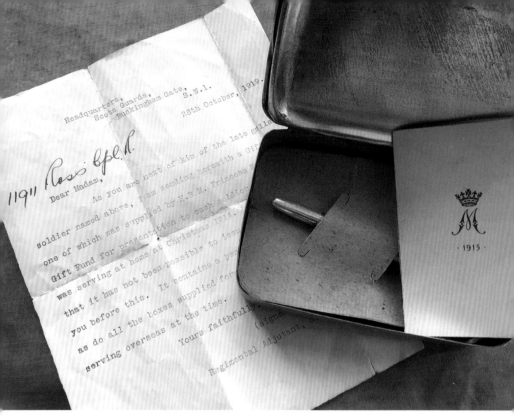

The letter reads:

Headquarters,
Scots Guards,
Buckingham Gate,
S.W.1.

28th October, 1919.

1191 *Ross, Cpl. R.*

Dear Madam,

As you are next of kin of the late
soldier named above, I am sending herewith a Gift,
one of which was supplied by H.R.H. Princess [...]
Gift Fund for presentation to each soldier [...]
was serving at home at Christmas 1914. [...]
that it has not been possible to issue [...]
you before this. It contains a pen [...]
as do all the boxes supplied for [...]
serving overseas at the time.

Yours faithfully,

(signed) [...]

Regimental Adjutant, S[...]

· 1915 ·

THE GIFT RECEIVED BY THE FAMILY OF CORPORAL ROSS OF THE
SCOTS GUARDS, WHO DIED OF HIS WOUNDS IN 1916, BEFORE HE
COULD RECEIVE HIS GIFT Ross had been serving at home at Christmas 1914;
as is typical, his gift was held by local depots before it could be claimed. None were
sent to France

of her own bullet pencil. It is to be presumed that the trade was acceptable to the Princess, and the Turkish bullet landed in the King's collection.[608]

GIFTS FOR WIDOWS AND PARENTS

As already discussed, families of those men who were killed or who had died on active service at Sea or in France in 1914 were entitled to a gift, but could expect to receive just the brass box and Christmas card supplied in a close-fitting cardboard box with lid, which was sufficient to hold the brass box alone.[609] But now the families of those men who would have been recipients of the simplified gift – at home and across the Empire – would actually receive the brass box, card, and bullet pencil.

For instance, take the case of

Corporal Robert Ross of the Scots Guards, who died of wounds at No. 24 General Hospital in Etaples on 24 May 1916. Ross had been serving at home with the Second Battalion on Christmas Day 1914, and he had landed in France almost exactly a year before his death. Entitled to the simplified gift of the box, bullet pencil and New Year card, he was unable to claim the gift, as he landed in France before it was distributed. Following his death, his gift was sent on to his family in 1919, its accompanying message from the Regimental Adjutant carefully and sensitively phrased:

Dear Madam
As you are next of kin of the late gallant soldier named above, I am sending herewith a Gift Box, one of which was supplied by HRH Princess Mary's Gift Fund for presentation to each soldier who was serving at home at Christmas 1914. It is regretted that it has not been possible to issue the box to you before this. It contains a pencil case and a card, as do all the boxes supplied for those who were not serving overseas at this time.[610]

So many other bereaved families would receive the gift, each with similar expressions of sympathy; many would be left untouched, packed away with other memories of a life lost.

DISTRIBUTING THE GIFT ACROSS THE EMPIRE

While the distribution of the gifts on Christmas Day 1914 had been complex and taxing, it was nothing in comparison with the efforts that that the Executive Committee had to face in sending the distinctive embossed boxes (and their bullet pencil and card) across the Empire. This was to go to all those who had served in uniform at Christmas, and was a huge task.[611]

The complexities of despatching so many gifts to so many far-flung destinations were enormous, and the packing responsibilities and the challenges of ensuring that they arrived intact considerable. The method of packing of gifts for men scattered across the Empire ('Class B'), and those at home ('Class C') varied, associated with the distance to be travelled and the journey to be taken. In neither case did the gifts have their own, individual, cardboard box such as had been used for the initial distribution of

'Class A' gifts, but instead were packed together in bulk boxes for distribution.[612]

With a long sea journey ahead, the 'Class B' gifts, packed in multiples for individual distribution, were carried in some 1,360 tin-lined wooden cases, designed to protect them from the rigours of transit, and made to 'Admiralty and War Office specification.'[613] This specification would cause some problems, however, and finding the right labour to make the cases, and sourcing the timber required, were matters of concern.[614] The tin-lined nature of the packing cases, and the heavy wooden structure were heavy on resources, just at a time when they were in greatest demand. In addition, the use of cases that contained multiple individual gifts ultimately caused problems in their distribution. The cases were designed to hold in excess of 1000 individual gifts, yet the numbers required at their destinations 'varied considerably.'[615] All these matters built additional delays into the process.

No tin-lined packing cases were required for 'Class C gifts', given to men at home. Instead, they were packed in large cardboard containers, each one containing smaller boxes, these with multiples of the simple gift of brass box, pencil and card. These were closely packed and devoid of additional wrapping paper. Some 17,526 of the largest boxes were sourced, and these were held together with 1,603 lbs of string, and 18,500 specially marked lead seals to secure the fastening and deter casual theft.[616] The lead seal is an interesting detail, and care was needed to fasten each one correctly. The fact that special attention was needed to crimp the seals is illustrated

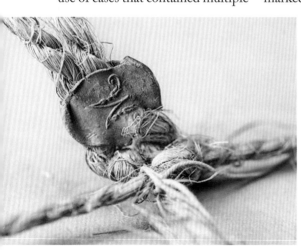

LEAD SEAL USED ON THE STRING BINDING OF CARDBOARD CASES CONTAINING MULTIPLES OF THE BRASS GIFT BOXES The seal bears the Princess's monogram

by a letter addressed to Lady Kathleen Lindsay (presumably from Rowland Berkeley), who was in charge of packing at the SRD Depot, in August 1915:

The Lead Seal Manufacturing Company write to us with regard to the impression of the letter 'M' a very good impression was obtained from pincers before they left, and probably the men who us the pincers will find after a little more experience they will get a better result.[617]

In order to distribute the gifts, whether at home or across the Empire, the Executive Committee would have to rely upon its partners. In April 1915, Rowland Berkeley wrote a report on the complexities of this distribution for the use of the Executive Committee.[618] Though at this stage the full extent of the task was unknown, Berkeley recognised that the commitment would be a big one. Storing large numbers of gift boxes at Deptford SRD would not be possible given competing demands, so some degree of organisation was required in order to despatch packing boxes to various ports for distribution to the Dominions, Protectorates and other locations across the Empire where there were eligible recipients. To achieve this, Berkeley was in negotiation with the High Commissions, and as South Africa and New Zealand had already agreed that they would be responsible for distribution, it was hoped that Canada and Australia would follow suit.[619]

Ultimately, the manner by which the distribution was made was summarised in the Final Report of the Executive Committee in 1920:

The system under which the distribution was made was devised by the War Office, and adopted by the Admiralty, India Office, Colonial Office and the High Commissioners of the Self-Governing Colonies. Under this system each of the above-mentioned authorities became responsible for the distribution in bulk to every ship or regiment under its jurisdiction or control, the individual distribution then being made by the ship or regiment concerned.[620]

The idea was that, once the number of gifts was agreed upon

and requested, they would be packed at Deptford and then sent to nominated addresses within the Dominions for distribution – regimental depots, regional centres and the like. It was to these addresses that the Fund despatched the gifts, with the 'largest consignment containing 294,000 gifts, and the smallest seven gifts' which were 'carried in twenty-four different ships without loss or damage'.[621]

By August 1915, the Secretary was able to report that his work had been focussed primarily upon 'the distribution of the gift to every man wearing the King's Uniform on Christmas Day in India and in the Colonies, Protectorates and Protected Ports of Empire,' and any creases that appeared had been ironed out.[622] The absolute numbers of gifts in packing had been adjusted; packing methods improved; the methods of shipping and numbers of ships needed, had been arranged; and, insurance had been paid. It was not surprising, then, that Mr Berkeley would need some help, and Sir Ernest F. Goodhart was appointed (with permission of Princess Mary) as assistant honorary secretary, supported by Lady Goodhart, and with his father, the noted surgeon

LADY GOODHART, wife of the new honorary secretary of the Gift Fund, Sir Ernest Goodhart. Lady Goodhart assisted her husband in his work on the fund.

Sir James Goodhart, providing the Fund with premises at 25 Portland Place. Recognising the significance of the commitment of the various Colonial administrators, almost the first act of Goodhart's tenure was to write letters of thanks and appreciation to them.[623]

REACTIONS FROM DOMINION TROOPS

That the gifts were well received is evident from the number of reports that were published in local newspapers across the Empire following their distribution. For example, though Australians would

PRINCESS MARY'S GIFT TO ALL THOSE IN UNIFORM ON
CHRISTMAS DAY, 1914

have to wait for their gifts following their long journey to the Southern Hemisphere from Deptford, on arrival they were much appreciated, and were regularly celebrated in the Australian press.

The Australian Imperial Force (AIF) had been raised and despatched to Egypt before there was any chance that the new gift could be manufactured; and it was the case that many who served on the ill-fated shores of Gallipoli would have to wait until they returned home to Australia to receive it. Nevertheless, it appears that some at least made their way to the Island of Lemnos, and were used to send home artefacts from the war in the Dardanelles – just as the brass box would be used in later years, to contain medals, souvenirs and assorted 'nick-nacks':

From her son, Pte Thos. Sayers, who is on active service at Lemnos, Mrs Sayers has received several mementos, including Princess Mary's gifts of silver mounted cartridge pencil case, and New Year greeting cards a heart and a cross carved from a light reddish wood, a clip of Turkish cartridges, showing that blunt-nosed bullets are being used by the enemy. The whole were neatly packed in a tin which had contained Princess Mary's gift of chocolate [*sic*] to the soldiers. Pte. Sayers reports all well with him and with other Wonthaggi boys sends season greetings to home and friends.[624]

In addition to the gifts given to front-line soldiers, naturally there were those distributed to men who had served at home. In some cases, such gifts were presented at special ceremonies designed to mark the occasion, such as at Unley, South Australia, in 1916:

A pleasing ceremony was performed by His Excellency the Governor…when gifts from Princess Mary were presented to members of the 74th Infantry. The presents, which took the form of a message and a pencil made from a cartridge and silver bullet, all contained in an excellently wrought metal box, are intended for all members of His Majesty's forces who were on military duty on Christmas Day, 1914, as mementoes of services rendered…His Excellency, who is Honorary

Colonel of the regiment, said a battalion like the 74th which did not go to the war as a body had no opportunity of making traditions, but in a conflict such as this they could yet perform services of great value. No matter where they were on duty their work was valuable to the cause, and although such men might not have the good fortune to offer their services in the firing line, they could, nevertheless, rest assured that they were very useful in the sphere in which they had worked. He agreed…that it was a happy inspiration which had prompted Princess Mary to make the gifts, which the men would value as mementoes of this critical time in the history of the Empire.[625]

Similar ceremonies continued into 1917, by which time many of the soldiers who had been serving at home had been deployed to other theatres, like Pte Otto Watson of South Australia, who reported the receipt of his gift as a reward in June of that year:

The Princess Mary gift for good conduct has been

received by Private Otto Charles Watson, of Millicent, now in the A.I.F. in France. When the gifts were made available in 1914 Private Watson was on garrison duty at Torrens Island. He qualified for the honor, but it was only this week that the gift reached the young man's father, Mr John Watson, of Millicent North.[626]

In some cases, distribution of the gift to men who had never set foot in a battlezone was a point of concern, and letters in the press played on the distinction between those who had experienced the challenges of the frontline in Gallipoli, and those who had not left Australia:

A mother who lost her son at Gallipoli [has] received the Princess Mary Gift which was intended only for men who were in the battle on Christmas 1914. Of course no Australian Unit was actually in battle on that date. The real condition of this gift was that it should go to soldiers on active service in 1914. You will be surprised to learn that men at Victoria

Barracks in home service have received this gift. They state that men who were at Headquarters here in Christmas 1914 were considered to be with the colours. The gift, therefore, is not prized at all by some genuine soldiers who were abroad in 1914.[627]

Nevertheless, reports of the distribution of the gifts continued to flood in, so much so that Australian newspapers were awash with news of its distribution by the end of 1917, coinciding with yet another Christmas:

Sergeant A.E. Taylor, of Grafton, has received a somewhat belated present rom her Royal Highness Princess Mary. The gift was intended for Christmas, 1915, and in the letter accompanying it was stated that similar gifts were to be made to all soldiers who were serving at Christmas, 1914. In a neat box, which in itself is a magnificent souvenir, a pencil inserted in a bullet shell and enclosed in the cartridge, is contained.[628]

Often there was added poignancy, as the families of deceased soldiers received the brass box as a memory of their husbands, fathers or sons:

> Many parents in Brisbane are just receiving, in the name of their sons, the souvenir gift which Her Royal Highness Princess Mary donated to every British soldier who was serving with the colours at Christmas, 1914... Mr C. F. Murphy, of Sundgato road, has received one of these souvenirs, and a letter of sympathy sent in respect of his son, Timothy Anthony Murphy, in the 4th Battalion, who was killed at the first landing on Gallipoli. He was only 21 years of age. Mr. Murphy is anxious to hear from any soldier who can give him information concerning the young fellow's death.[629]

Inevitably, such memorials of a soldier's life were valued intensely by their families, a treasured memory, tangible evidence of military service and of shared loss:

> A very nice Xmas box has just come into the possession of Mr and Mrs. R. Ross of this town. In the Xmas of 1914 Princess Mary presented each soldier of the AIF abroad with a present, and it fell to the lot of their son Peter (killed in action at Gallipoli) to be one of the many to receive a gift. The present was sent to Queensland where it has been in the hands of the military authorities for some time, and it was only recently that the box was sent to Mrs. Ross. It is a very handsome box, artistically finished in many designs, a cartridge turned into a pencil case, and a Xmas card. Needless to say, Mr. and Mrs. Ross highly prize Princess Mary's gift which has so strangely come into their possession at this Christmas time, and is now become one of their treasured possessions to be kept in memory of the brave sacrifice of their son.[630]

In New Zealand, the press expressed suitable enthusiasm for the gift, and with such a great distance to travel from Britain and the SRD Depot at Deptford, there was a similar lag time for the recipients, especially as the NZEF was deployed to Egypt, Gallipoli and ultimately the Western Front. Perhaps for this reason the eligibility of receiving the gift was extended, in what was presumably a local decision:

Gifts for members of the New Zealand Expeditionary Force and local forces serving or mobilised on Christmas Day, 1914, have come to hand, and will be distributed to those entitled to them... The above applies to District Staffs, Permanent Staff and Territorials by units of those mobilised for duty and serving on Christmas Day, 1914, at forts, railways, wireless stations, magazines and as prisoners-of-war guards or other duties, and to those members of the Expeditionary Force that have returned to this district from the front. Distribution will at once be made in the above cases, provided the men are still in New Zealand. Those members of the Expeditionary Force who have returned to New Zealand from Egypt will be notified to claim for gifts. It is the intention that everyone in New Zealand serving with the Expeditionary Force who is entitled to the gift should receive it. It was originally intended to send the gift only to those who were actually serving on Christmas Day, but as there would be a difficulty in carrying this out it was agreed by HRH Princess Mary's Fund to take in those who had joined the forces for active service up till April 12 [1915].[631]

In Canada, recipients of the gift displayed similar reactions to those from the other Dominions, and the initiative was reported widely in the Canadian press. Though people at home could send their soldiers boxes of chocolate manufactured by Cowans, in brightly coloured patriotic tins bearing the crest of the Dominion and the phrase 'Chocolate for our Soldiers' – yet another echo of Victoria's initiative in 1900 – they would also share in Princess Mary's gift.[632]

While those Canadians who had already arrived in France in 1914 to serve under Lord French as part of the British Expeditionary Force could expect to receive the standard, 'full' gift, this would be a small minority. Not every Canadian in uniform was a frontline soldier in 1914, and with the Canadian

Canada was typical of the Dominions; it maintained a Militia, pre-war, but needed to grow an army of volunteers if it was to take its place in the war

military machine being built into the formidable fighting force it would become, there were a significant number of men at home, as well as in training on Salisbury Plain. And under the extension to Princess Mary's scheme, they would be included, and packing crates of the distinctive brass boxes were sent for distribution to Canada for all those 'wearing the King's Uniform' at Christmas 1914:

Members of the guard employed watching the post office, armories, tunnel and other possible points of fanatical attacks received the Christmas gifts Princess Mary presented to soldiers in Europe... The present is a little brass box containing writing materials and a souvenir pencil. The pencil case is made from German rifle cartridges, which were picked up on a Belgian battlefield.[633]

Having crossed the Atlantic, it was reported that the gifts arrived in the major cities for distribution in September 1915; and were taken to express more than just a teenage Princess's desire to send a gift to all those serving in the King's uniform at Christmas; it had more to say about unity, and the Empire at a time of peril:

The gifts from Her Royal Highness Princess Mary to all soldiers serving the empire at Christmas time 1914, have arrived in this city [Ottawa] for distribution. For Canadians, the gift will mean a new realisation of the Empire and its bonds.[634]

DISTRIBUTION TO THOSE AT HOME

Distribution of the gift to men in uniform on Christmas Day 1914 was not just an issue for the half-million Dominion troops spread across the Empire; there were also almost three times this number of men, from Britain and the Empire,

serving at home.[635] Though sending the gift to the Dominions in tin-lined packing cases may have represented the greatest logistical challenge, once they had been despatched from Deptford, it was then up to the administrators in those countries to ensure they reached their destinations.

But for those serving at home this challenge was passed on to local authorities, for the most part, those regimental depots scattered across Britain. This idea had been suggested by General Long, military member on the Executive Committee, and was devised to provide hubs that would permit onwards distribution. This system was reportedly based, in turn, on the pattern of distribution of Queen Victoria's Chocolate box, in 1900:

Under the system of distribution by regiment the number of gifts asked for were sent to the regiment and so far as the fund was concerned the distribution now in progress the War Office had ascertained from various depots the number of gifts required and the Fund was reliably informed of the total number the distribution

LADY KITCHENER, great grand-daughter of the Field Marshal, presides over the opening of a box of Princess Mary gifts from 1915, in 2014

The system mentioned in the last report (of the 18th May [1915]) that was authorised for Colonial distribution will, with the approval of General Long be adopted here and that gifts will be sent to the various depots either for immediate distribution or, for those who are at the front to be reserved until their return, and in the case of those who have fallen to be sent to their next of kin.[637]

To achieve this, the gifts were sent out en masse to the regimental depots within the bulk, sealed, cardboard boxes – and, miraculously, some of these sealed boxes have been known to survive intact. In 2014, on the eve of the Centenary of the Great War, auctioneers Onslows arranged for the great-grand-niece of Lord Kitchener, the architect of the New Armies, to open a box of gifts that had been 'found in Ireland' some years before.[638] These were 'Class C' gifts, for those serving at home at Christmas 1914. No doubt this brown cardboard box, tied up as it was with coarse string and sealed with its simple lead seal bearing the characteristic cipher 'M', was one that had sat in a regimental depot, abandoned and forgotten, until it

to the depots being carried out from Deptford entirely under War Office direction.[636]

In essence, it was a smaller scale version of the Colonial distribution, again having the benefit of allowing the depots to handle the distribution themselves – thus committing them to an ongoing process that would not be fully resolved until 1920 or so:

was disposed of. [639]

As the string was cut on the box, and the carboard folded back, a label was revealed, a notice careful to emphasise the significance of its contents through the capital letter of the word 'Gift'. The label, dated June 1915, got to the root of the distribution of the gift to those who had been serving at home at Christmas 1914:

The Gift is to be retained for those who have left the United Kingdom since 25th December, 1914, on active service or special mission, until their return. In the case of those who have died since the 25th December, 1914, the Gifts should be distributed to their next of kin. Officers and men are not to participate in this distribution if they had already joined the Expeditionary Force on the 25th December, 1914, whether they had returned to the United Kingdom or not by that date, neither are the next of kin of those who died previous to that date. [640]

H.R.H. THE PRINCESS MARY'S SAILORS' & SOLDIERS' CHRISTMAS FUND

The Gifts herewith are for distribution to Officers and Men who were wearing the King's Uniform on Christmas Day, 1914, whether of the Regular Army, the New Army, or the Territorials. The Gift is to be retained for those who have left the United Kingdom since the 25th December, 1914, on active service or special mission, until their return. In the case of those who have died since the 25th December, 1914, the Gifts should be distributed to their next of kin. Officers and men are not to participate in this distribution if they had already joined the Expeditionary Force on the 25th December, 1914, whether they had returned to the United Kingdom or not by that date, neither are the next of kin of those who died previous to that date. Officers and Men on duty in Gibraltar, Malta, Egypt, India, or in any of the other Colonies, Protectorates, or Protected Ports have already received the Gift, and are therefore not to be included in this distribution.

(4040.) W. P806. 19,500. 6/15. C. P., Ltd.

THIS LABEL HAD BEEN HIDDEN FROM VIEW FOR A HUNDRED YEARS

It is also instructive to note that the label appears to have had a print run of at least 19,500, that also represents 19,500 containers – which, if one does the arithmetic, amounts to some 1,404,000 gift boxes, in line with the requirements for all those serving at home in 1914. As ever, the distribution of the gifts was proving to be a mammoth task.

Digging down deeper, the box, clean and well-kept, contained six shoe-box sized cardboard boxes and lids, each of which, in turn, contained the twelve, bright and shining gilt 'treasure boxes,' otherwise not wrapped. This event, filmed for posterity, recorded the gasp as the audience perceived each one, like so many gold bullion bars; and the palpable disappointment when Lady Kitchener found they contained the bullet pencil in its card-holder, and the simple New Year card. 'I thought they contained all manner of things,' one observer was heard to say.[641]

Here was clear evidence of the actual contents of those stripped-back gifts to be issued to all those who had not been at sea or at the front at Christmas 1914; gifts that would be sent across the world, to the Dominions of Empire, and which were reported from Saskatoon to Bundaberg. There were no envelopes to the New Year cards; no photograph of the young Princess, just the pencil retained in its card-holder each one wrapped in a twist of white protective paper.

In line with General Long's suggestion, each regiment applied its own approach to their distribution, and surviving regimental ephemera in some preserved boxes give clues to the methods used. For example,

a card was included with long-delayed boxes delivered to the 11th (S) battalion, Royal Fusiliers, and dated August 1917:

HRH Princess Mary's Gift. Her Royal Highness Princess Mary made a gift of Brass boxes to every man in the Army and Navy at Christmas 1914, but owing to difficulties of manufacture it was impossible to distribute them all at that time, and those for this battalion have only recently come into our hands, hence the delay.[642]

In another example, gift boxes were distributed to the City Battalion Comforts Fund in Liverpool in February 1916.[643] This fund had originally been set up to support the Liverpool Pals from their raising in August 1914, and was run by Mrs Stanley, the sister-in-law of Lord Derby, and wife of the Brigade Commander F.C. Stanley, a lady who had 'taken such an interest in the comforts for the men.'[644] A card was included with the gift, designed to be inserted within the box itself, with specially rounded corners to fit it: 'These Gift Boxes

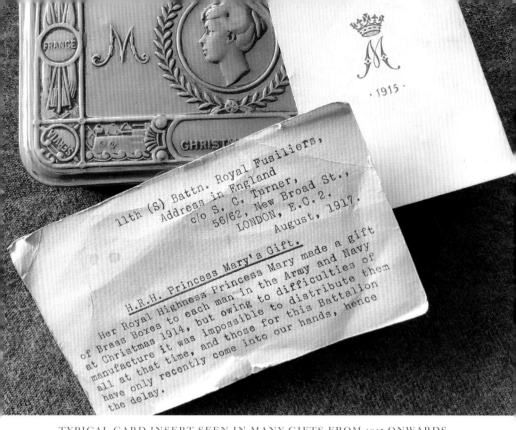

The card insert reads:

11th (S) Battn. Royal Fusiliers,
Address in England
c/o S. C. Turner,
56/62, New Broad St.,
LONDON, E.C.2.
August, 1917.

H.R.H. Princess Mary's Gift.

Her Royal Highness Princess Mary made a gift of Brass Boxes to each man in the Army and Navy at Christmas 1914, but owing to difficulties of manufacture it was impossible to distribute them all at that time, and those for this Battalion have only recently come into our hands, hence the delay.

TYPICAL CARD INSERT SEEN IN MANY GIFTS FROM 1915 ONWARDS
The distribution of these gifts would be the responsibility of the regimental depots

were consigned to the care at the Committee of the Comforts Fund in February, 1916, with instructions to store them until further notice'. The instructions on this card were in line with the direction of General Long, and with those at home being last in line to receive the boxes, they had not been distributed in time to at least some of the original pals. The card went on: 'Permission has now been given to distribute the boxes to the next-of-kin of the men who

were in the City Battalions when they went to France.'

Clearly the idea was that though the men were serving overseas, by 1916 the delay in the distribution of the cards was such that they would be distributed to their families. The card went on: 'The Gift Boxes are in *no case* to be sent overseas, but are to be kept by the next-of-kin until the man to whom the box is destined returns on leave or from Germany'. However, there was recognition that some men

SERGEANT HERBERT MASON WAS A KITCHENER'S VOLUNTEER IN
THE 6TH OXFORDSHIRE & BUCKINGHAMSHIRE LIGHT INFANTRY
He served through the war and was mentioned in despatches; his Gift box was used
to contain his mementoes of service

would not return, nevertheless. 'The sad event of the man having been killed in action or died of wounds or missing, the box may be retained by his next-of-kin.'

There can be little doubt that the distribution of gift boxes to almost a million and a half soldiers who were serving at home at Christmas 1914 became burdensome to the regimental depots and those who administered them. The extent of the problem facing regimental commanders at the end of the war and into the post-war period was huge. Relatives were keen to understand what had happened to their loved ones and bombarded the depots with requests for information. With huge numbers of men still missing, it was no surprise that this was so, and many families continued to search for their lost soldiers well into the new decade.[645]

On top of this considerable burden came an additional responsibility; once again the issue of Princess Mary's gifts to all those who had served in uniform on Christmas Day, 1914. However, the extended distribution devised in November 1914 included men who were at home in Territorial battalions, or who had formed up in Kitchener's Mob in expectation of serving King and country. Many of these men would have to wait for their gift until the war's end. Newspapers up and down the country placed advertisements in their Personal or Notices columns inviting men and the families of those who had died to come forwards and claim their gift. Typical was a notice that appeared in the *Mid Sussex Times* in 1916:

7th ROYAL SUSSEX REGIMENT. PRINCESS MARY'S GIFT

All officers, warrant officers, N.C.O.'s and men who were serving in the 7th Royal Sussex Regiment on 25th December, 1914, and who have not yet received H.R.H. Princess Mary's gift, can have this by applying to the President. Regimental Institute, 3rd Battalion Royal Sussex Regiment, Newhaven. In cases where tine soldier is deceased, the gift may be claimed by the next of-kin.[646]

The problem of unclaimed gifts became a problem for the Regimental Associations and Depots at a time when there were many pressures on them to supply information to grieving families on the last whereabouts of their loved ones.

By 1919, the days of holding events to mark the award of a gift that had been designed to be given out five years previously became an anachronism, a burden, and perhaps an embarrassment. Now messages appeared in the Public Notices columns that made a last appeal for former soldiers to come forwards and claim their gifts. And to support this, the War Office would make good a promise to pay for the postage of gifts, where it was not possible for old soldiers or their families to gather the precious brass box from the local depot. Very few claims were actually made, however.[647] The following examples are typical of Public Notices that appeared in the local press, in 1919–20:

RUGELEY TERRITORIALS.
UNCLAIMED GIFTS FROM PRINCESS MARY.
There are a number of the

above Gifts at the Drill Hall, Burton-on-Trent. Members who were serving with 1/6th Battalion – North Staffordshire Regiment on 25th December. 1914. and who have not yet received the gift should apply in writing to the Officer Commanding at the Drill Hall. Burton-on-Trent, stating Regimental No., and present address, when the Gift will be forwarded those eligible.[648]

4th BATT. THE BLACK WATCH (R.H.). H.R.H. PRINCESS MARY'S SAILORS' AND SOLDIERS' CHRISTMAS FUND, 1914.

A number of the Gifts provided by the abpove Fund are still unclaimed by Officers, N.C.O.s, and Men of the Black Watch. The Gifts can be obtained by those entitled to them at the 4th Black Watch Depot, Drill Hall, Bell Street, Dundee, any

SAPPER E.W. SMITH WAS A ROYAL ENGINEER WITH THE RAILWAY OPERATING DIVISION (ROD); HE DID NOT GET TO FRANCE UNTIL 1915

Week Day between the Hours 9 a.m. and 5 p.m. and between 6 p.m. and 7 p.m.; on Saturdays between 9 a.m. and 1 p.m.[649]

1/5TH SHERWOOD FORESTERS: PRINCESS MARY'S GIFTS

All N.C.O.s and Men who went out with above Battalion in February, 1915, and who have not yet received Princess Mary's Gift for Christmas, 1914 are requested to apply for same at the Drill Hall, Derby, on or before Sept. 27, 1919.[650]

Nevertheless, some 54,800 gifts were claimed, but 197,750 gifts of varying types still remained; forgotten, overlooked, and belonging, it seems, to an age long past.[651] They were called in for disposal, a sad end to a gallant gesture.

It had been a long haul; and the winding up of the Scheme in 1919, there were still a large number of items left at Deptford: 1,546 cases of the 'Smokers' Gift (Full gift)', amounting to: 184,000 brass boxes; 43,000 pipes; 157,000 bullet pencils, 43,000 packets each of tobacco and cigarettes; 200,000 cards; 70,000 photographs, and 2,000 stationery wallets.[652] It was a significant inventory – and testimony to the hard work and dedication of the Executive Committee in meeting the needs of all the sailors and soldiers it had fought so long to serve in the name of Her Royal Highness Princess Mary. Left with so much to dispose of there was the inevitable question, what could be done with it? Museums would be a good port of call, but could only take so many examples, with 'a specimen of the gift from this fund consisting of a brass box, Christmas card, bullet pencil case and photograph of Her Royal Highness Princess Mary' being offered to 'various War Museums in the country.'[653] In other cases, materials could be scrapped and sold, bringing a residue of monies that could be used in a charitable endeavour that would be in line with the Princess's own sense of duty and dedication: Queen Mary's Maternity Home, a Home set up from 'surplus funds of the Queen Mary's Needlework Guild'[654]

And there was no doubt that the legacy of the Princess's big idea would live on a century later, and would never be forgotten.

A BOX OF
MEMORIES

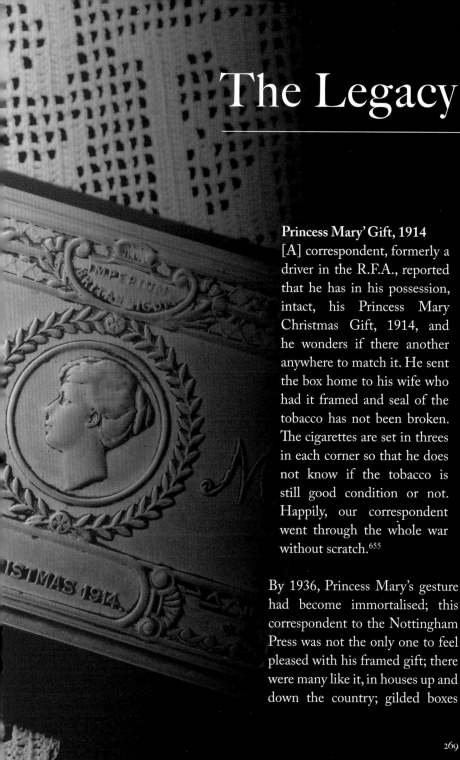

The Legacy

Princess Mary' Gift, 1914
[A] correspondent, formerly a driver in the R.F.A., reported that he has in his possession, intact, his Princess Mary Christmas Gift, 1914, and he wonders if there another anywhere to match it. He sent the box home to his wife who had it framed and seal of the tobacco has not been broken. The cigarettes are set in threes in each corner so that he does not know if the tobacco is still good condition or not. Happily, our correspondent went through the whole war without scratch.[655]

By 1936, Princess Mary's gesture had become immortalised; this correspondent to the Nottingham Press was not the only one to feel pleased with his framed gift; there were many like it, in houses up and down the country; gilded boxes a snapshot of remembrance of the early years of the war. Others were polished, mounted on plinths or even encased in precious metals. Memories, cherished memories were captured there; perhaps with reflections of hard times, of heavy seas and of even heavier soils in the fields of Flanders that conspired against men to make this war one of personal fights against the elements, as much as any other enemy. Such memories are surely difficult to erase.

H. R. H. PRINCESS MARY.
LATEST PORTRAIT

PHOTO
ERNEST BROOKS.

126.V.
BEAGLES POSTCARDS

PRINCESS MARY, A SEVENTEEN-
YEAR OLD WHO MADE A
DIFFERENCE

Perhaps it is difficult today to perceive what it must have been like to serve under the banner of King and Country in such a terrible conflict, and this phraseology has been shaped into motifs that have arguably become devalued through association and juxtaposition to images of the staggering casualty figures of two world wars. But enough evidence is there to suggest that these phrases were not empty to all men and women who served in the Great War. The oath that all soldiers took was a solemn one, and simply represented a personal bond to serve one's country.

Princess Mary was just seventeen in 1914. She was the daughter of a serious King and a dedicated Queen who instilled a sense of duty – with varying success – in their children. Alongside the future King George VI, the Princess dedicated her life to service; and arguably that service commenced with the simple desire to make a difference, a child's view of the meaning of Christmas that even transcended war. No doubt the Princess observed what was going on around her, in 1914; seeing her mother's determination, her father's drawn face, her older brother's engagement, albeit as a figurehead, with the National

Relief scheme. It is not hard to understand how, with encouragement, a suggestion was soon made into a reality, an idea to make a difference made concrete. And it is staggering to reflect on what was accomplished through the leadership of the General and Executive Committees and the many workers that made Princess Mary's Gift a reality.

THE GIFT BOX SHINES EVEN TODAY

That this gift was respected and valued was never in doubt; at a cost of £193,667 4s 10d, some 2,620,019 gifts of varying types had been prepared for delivery across the Empire to men and women who wore the King's uniform on Christmas Day, 1914.[656]

Princess Mary's service continued throughout her life; as her most recent biographer had emphasised, 'her pre-eminent devotion to duty set a standard for the modern era.'[657] In 1918, with Britain still at war, Princess Mary reached the age of twenty-one, and she gained permission to train as a paediatric nurse and carried out her duties in earnest at Great Ormond Street Hospital. She was not one to shrink from challenges. Her subsequent achievements were many and varied, and the rhythm of her devotion to duty did not skip a beat.[658] And still, the physical expression of that desire to make a difference, her brass Gift Box and all it contained, and all that it meant to its recipients, remain as an icon of the days of peril and the brief pause at the end of a year that had seen a global conflict erupt.

With the signing of the Armistice in November 1918, Princess Mary was the first member of the Royal Family to see for herself the aftermath of the dramatic impact of war. Her brother David, the future Edward VIII, had served in various

THE BOX TRANSFORMED, BUT STILL PRINCESS
MARY IS CENTRAL TO THE DESIGN

capacities in France and elsewhere as an officer in the Grenadier Guards, while her father had been a frequent visitor to the Western Front, suffering injury when thrown from his horse in October 1915, fracturing his pelvis.[659] But when Princess Mary went to France, it was an entirely new experience, a chance, in some way at least, to see with her own eyes the places, sights and sounds the men and women of the British and Indian Expeditionary Forces had experienced back in 1914. She was honoured with a march past of the 17th Royal Scots in the devastated and hallowed city of Ypres. This was a battalion of Kitchener's Army, perhaps some of them men who received the Princess's gift as part of the expansion of the scheme in November 1914. Nevertheless, it was symbolic, as Ypres was a city that had only just emerged from the terrible conflict, and was standing in ruins. This beleaguered city had stood in Allied hands for the whole of the war, defended in that First Battle in the winter of 1914, a battle that died away as the winter deepened with awful conditions to be endured. The defenders of the city from the battle, British, Indian and Canadian combatants, were all recipients of the Princess's treasured gift. It must have been a special moment for the Princess, and for those who marched past:

The battalion arrived within the hour, and had the signal honour of marching past Her Royal Highness in the Grand Place. It was most inspiring and appropriate that the march past should take place in the famous old city which typifies the ruin and desolation scattered abroad by the enemy , and in the drizzle of a November afternoon, with the ruins of the Cathedral and the Cloth Hall looking down

on the scene, it provided a never-to-be-forgotten memory to all who were present.[660]

Beyond the brief respite of the Christmas Truce felt in scattered groups along the Western Front 1914, the war began in earnest almost from the first day of the New Year; the sinking of the *Formidable* had seen to that. The continuation of the war in 1915 brought new fronts, new commitments, and always the Royal Navy was on active service; British and Empire troops were distributed on three continents, from India to Europe, East Africa to Gallipoli. It is not surprising, then, that the huge effort expended by the Princess Mary Gift Fund to supply gifts for Christmas 1915 was not to be repeated. With the war deepening and expanding, and

68. YPRES AFTER TWO YEARS OF WAR.

YPRES: 'MANY A WEARY HOUR DID I SPEND IN THIS PLACE OF HELL.' A wounded soldier sends a card home

with the distribution of the original gifts extended across the Empire, there was little hope that a national fund to supply Christmas Gifts would re-surface. The logistics were just too difficult, the commitments too challenging, and not once did the Executive Committee of the Princess Mary entertain the idea; they had just too much to do in wrapping up the affairs of 1914. The giving of the gift would remain a special event:

A year ago, Princess Mary sent a Christmas gift to each our soldiers in the fighting line. It consisted of an engraved brass box containing pipe, tobacco and cigarettes, and in thousands of homes to-day the Royal souvenirs are cherished as mementoes, not merely the Princess's kindly thought, but also of loved ones who have fallen in their country's cause. This year the numbers of men on active service are of such vastly increased proportions that a project similar to that of a year ago and embracing all the men, was scarcely conceivable.[661]

Not only that, the King and Queen's own gesture to supply a personal Christmas card to members of their armed forces overseas was also not to be repeated – the war had, indeed, moved into its new phase:

The King and Queen have been compelled…to abandon their intention of presenting Christmas cards to the troops on active service, as they did [in 1914]. Their Majesties felt that this year it would be impossible to adhere to this restriction, and that if any cards were sent it would be necessary to give them to our soldiers fighting in almost all quarters of the globe, to our sailors at sea, and to the men sick and wounded in hospitals. The matter was referred to the military authorities in this country and at the front, and they came to the conclusion that, having regard to the exigencies of the military situation, it would be impossible to undertake the transport and distribution of the cards. Every bit of available space on board ship is required for hospital necessaries, ammunition, and other military supplies. In deference, therefore, to the representations made by the authorities the King and

'THE OVERSEAS CLUB' - RAISING MONEY TO SEND GIFTS OF
TOBACCO TO SAILORS AND SOLDIERS, 1915

Queen have found it necessary to relinquish their intention, which they have done with the greatest possible reluctance.[662]

Christmas in subsequent years would not be forgotten, however, though whether the intensity of the early years was repeated in all subsequent years is a moot point. Wounded soldiers still received attention, of course, with cigarettes from Queen Alexandra, and 'a dainty box of chocolate, presented by Cadbury Bros' received by them in 1915 and 1916 at least.[663] For everyone else, newspaper tobacco funds continued to follow the lead of the *Weekly Dispatch*, and then there was The Overseas Club, set up in 1910 to 'promote the unity of British subjects the world over.' The Club established its 'pennies scheme' in order to gather money from 'the school Children of the Empire', rewarding them with certificates for their efforts.[664] The scheme was established to provide Christmas Day Gifts of tobacco from 1915, and the children alone raised some £54,604.[665] If tobacco continued to be favoured through the war, so did the ubiquitous and humble Christmas pudding.

Supported by *The Daily News* donations from the scheme had delivered one million puddings in 1914, one-and-a-half million 1915, in concert with *The Daily Telegraph*, three million for 1916. With a logistical nightmare looming, the Army Council was keen to reduce any impact on its postal services, and the scheme received official support by the Commander-in-Chief of the British Expeditionary Force himself, Field Marshal Sir Douglas Haig; 'leave the supply of puddings entirely to the Pudding Fund. Send us some pudding money, and send the soldiers some other seasonable gift.' Sixpence would buy 'one ration' for a single man; twenty-one pounds, a battalion. [666]

For those who could afford them, commercially packaged comforts were also available to supplement the centrally organised comforts funds, with the London department stores such as Harrods Ltd providing a specialist service and a suitably named 'War Comforts Room' that was 'stocked with just those things which have proved to be most useful and acceptable to men on Active Service'.[667] An innovation in 1915 was 'Rowntree's Service Box', a handsome offset-printed tin box produced by the company that had supplied the City of York's own box in 1914:

Rowntree's Service Gift Box is a fine present for soldiers and sailors and for everyone. The Box contains a large cake of Elect Chocolate…highly valued for its nourishing and sustaining qualities as food, well as for its exquisite flavour. In addition to this high-quality chocolate there are six postcards, printed in colours, and lead pencil in fluted metal case. A special feature of this "Service" Box is the base which is fitted with detachable slide and match striker. This forms a separate and handy receptable for cigarettes, matches, etc.[668]

The box was obtained in 1915 (and 1916) by collecting tokens given away with purchases of 'Elect' Chocolate; thirty tokens would deliver one of the boxes post free.[669] It was a nice gift; but it did not carry the meaning of the Princess's brass box.

Alongside these endeavours, national and personal alike, there was the continuing and the selfless commitment of local communities

THE ROWNTREE'S 'SERVICE BOX', which contained chocolate and a sliding compartment holding postcards. It could be obtained by collecting coupons given away with Rowntree's chocolate, in 1915 and 1916

to provide 'comforts' for those on Active Service, continuing in the vein of the Comforts Funds set up so long ago, in former wars. With their personnel far away from home, these funds were especially important to the Dominions. As an example of success, the Australian Comforts Fund was established in August 1916 to send 'care parcels to Australians serving overseas, including letters, periodicals, extra clothing, food, tobacco and other comforts', with great aplomb.[670]

Closer to home, each borough contributed its own, with that Coventry, a Mediaeval city that had grown to be an industrial giant and a significant manufacturer of vehicles and munitions, typical. Sending out some 10,000 parcels, nine inches by six, the boxes contained the usual diversity of useful items: Oxo cubes, two ounces of pipe tobacco and a briar pipe, forty cigarettes, Cadbury's chocolate,

THE AUSTRALIAN
COMFORTS FUND WAS
HIGHLY SUCCESSFUL
IN CATERING FOR
THE COMFORTS OF
AUSTRALIAN SERVICE
PERSONNEL IN THE
GREAT WAR

'Old Joe's toffee', peppermints, foot salve, shaving and washing soaps, and a copy of the local paper. Costing as much as half a sovereign, demanding postage costs, each one was sent with admiration in November, 1915: 'On behalf of the citizens of Coventry, we ask your acceptance of this parcel. It is just a little remembrance show have not forgotten you and that your splendid efforts on behalf of the British Empire are appreciated behind in the old city.'[671]

That such tokens were appreciated cannot be doubted, and comforts schemes were supported throughout the war, from cities like Coventry, to small towns like Stokesley in North Yorkshire. Even if the flurry of 'comforts' activity that seemed to highlight the early years of the war were waning, the engagement of local initiatives seem to have held sway. For example, though Stokesley's population of some few thousands was small, the country town contributed its fair share of servicemen, forty-three of whom would not return. To support the living, the Stokesley and District Parcel Fund raised funds through whist drives, craft sales and concerts, and sent parcels of varying types throughout the war.[672] Letters home were full of warmth at the recognition they received: 'I can assure you gentlemen that I was greatly delighted to find such useful and serviceable items... The parcel I can assure you greatly remind[s] the lads in the trenches of the good spirit and feeling that is felt for them by the people of Stokesley.'[673]

A hundred years later, and the concept of comforts funds for those on Active Service, and the idea behind them, has not diminished. Since the early 1990s, British servicemen and women have served in a number of conflicts, primarily in the Middle East and the Balkans. Far from home, and separated from loved ones, it is perhaps not surprising that the concept of the Comforts Fund was revived. Since 2005, 'Operation Christmas Box' and its forerunner UK4U has acted as a charity that provides 'Christmas Boxes full of presents (affectionately known as the 'Square Stocking') as a gift from the nation to all those serving overseas in the UK Armed Forces away from their families and loved ones on Christmas Day.'[674] These boxes contain an assortment of small gifts – an

OPERATION CHRISTMAS BOX – sending Christmas Gifts to all those on Operational Deployment since 2005 – inspired by the example of Princess Mary

echo of past 'comforts' – with some 200,000 distributed since the scheme was started, invoking the historical legacy of 'comforts funds', and in particular, that set by the Princess Mary Gift Fund in 1914.[675] The modern gifts, packaged in a tin 'the same size as the 24-hour operational ration box', are designed to 'include a variety of items that are gender free, good fun, that will not cause offence on grounds of religion or race and that will not perish whilst *en route*.'[676] As presented, this is a logical extension of the principles that evolved from the original meeting of the General Committee of HRH The Princess Mary's Gift Fund on 14 October 1914, and the link is strongly made by the charity, who draw directly upon its predecessor: 'The initiative was inspired by the 1914

Christmas Gift Fund, established by Princess Mary, the daughter of King George V.'[677] And with the Centenary of the Great War looming in 2014, the Ministry of Defence announced that it would send '8,500 Christmas boxes to all those deployed on operations this Christmas', from 'Sierra Leone to the Falkland Islands'.[678] Naturally, they were well received.

David Currant, a sergeant in the Royal Air Force RAF was deployed to Qatar in support of 51 Squadron at Christmas 2014. Here, receiving mail was a bit hit-and-miss, and often the squadron went weeks without it, or would receive bags'

full when the old 'kits plane' arrived. The Centenary of the Great War had already been commemorated, with a parade and Remembrance Service at the Compound, and personnel were eagerly awaiting the arrival of the old BAe146. 'When the old 'kits plane' arrived in time for Christmas we were relieved. We received a Christmas gift box filled with nice bits and pieces from different companies, in the shape of an ammo box, and we were very grateful for that.'[679] The square box was suitably brass coloured, and part of it was a packet of playing cards in a smaller tin that was designed to mimic the

REPLICA TIN AND SPECIAL PLAYING CARDS produced to mark the Centenary of Princess Mary's Gift

Princess's totemic brass box of 1914. It was a nice idea. But it would not be the only tin made to commemorate the Princess's achievement in that year.[680]

This was not the only time in 2014 that serving personnel would be exposed to the work of Princess Mary's Gift Fund, in supplying a gift for those on Operational Service overseas a hundred years before. Fortnum & Mason is a central London company that has occupied the same site since the eighteenth century, and is a brand that is synonymous with quality, recognised for its fine foods. According to company archivist Andrea Turner: 'In many ways, the expansion of Fortnum & Masons coincided with the Great War, as the company grew to meet the need of the armed forces as they fought on many fronts. Officers would request hampers of food and other items to be sent to the front – and Fortnum's worked had to meet these needs.'[681]

In view of the significance of the Centenary, to the company and to the nation, and as a Royal Warrant holder, Fortnum & Mason's decided that it needed to mark the occasion with something suitable and effective:

Soundings were taken amongst the staff, and a discussion document was prepared for the WW1 Committee, which met in January 2014. Amongst the suggestions were special biscuits, a themed afternoon tea, discounts for serving men and women, and exhibitions at Piccadilly and St Pancras. As [Fortnum's] had had a great success with the Active Service Gift Tin that had been sent out to 17,000 men and women on active service in the British Armed Forces in celebration of Her Majesty's Diamond Jubilee in 2012, it was decided that a filled tin would be an appropriate product to donate to service personnel as a mark of commemoration, and to sell to the public.[682]

There was no doubt that this 'filled tin' should honour the legacy of Princess Mary's own 'brass box':

It was finally decided to approach Harewood House for permission to reproduce a tin in the style of Princess Mary's WW1 tins, which was graciously given, and the archivist there kindly lent us

FORTNUM & MASON'S 'TOMMY'S TIN' 2014

materials for a small exhibition in the store. The tin was made for us by the Bermondsey-based William Say & Co., the only tin maker left in Britain. The contents of the tin were settled as two bars of chocolate in F&M's WW1 livery, and a pack of playing cards, designed by Anna Perchal. Britannia featured on the front, and the face cards were portrayed by George V, Queen Mary and the Prince of Wales. The Ace of Spades was a British bulldog, and the Jokers were Mr Fortnum & Mr Mason. Initial discussions with the Royal British Legion as our chosen charity to receive a donation from the products failed, owing to that charity's rules regarding amounts pledged and monies received from the sale of product. The tin was packed by Enham El Alamein Trust (who pack our teas), and a percentage of the profits went to that charity.[683]

The production of the tin by a company that was a contemporary of (and near neighbour to) one of the principal manufacturers of Princess Mary's Gift Box, Barclay & Fry of Southwark, was especially fitting. Great care was taken to reference Professor Adshead's iconic design, though with some inevitable logistical requirements:

Unfortunately to mimic the original Tommy's Tin structure would have meant having a bespoke custom-made shape which required a substantial tooling investment being made. We looked at the various shapes and sizes they already produced. Although the chosen structure was slimmer height wise and also longer, we adjusted & redrew all the elements to fit. On the lid, we replaced Princess Mary with

THE DESIGN OF FORTNUM & MASON'S TIN ECHOED
THAT OF PRINCESS MARY'S ORIGINAL

THE BOX WAS A GREAT SUCCESS WITH SERVICE PERSONNEL,
AND WAS A COMPLETE SURPRISE IN 2014

Britannia and used the British Armed Forces logos in three of the embossed cartouches. We replaced the M & M initials on either side of the central laurel wreath with our F & M initials in a similar script to the original and embossed 'Tommy's Tin 1914 – 2014' in the bottom central lozenge cartouche.[684]

Fortnum & Mason's tin, carefully designed and containing chocolate that was intended to keep in widely varying climate, from the Middle East to the Falkland Islands, was distributed wherever there were service personnel on operational deployment at Christmas 2014:

10,000 tins were sent to serving men and women in the British armed forces. Tins were also sent to Her Majesty the Queen and senior members of the royal family with military connections, to the heads of the branches of the armed services, the

Prime Minister, the Defence Secretary, the Consuls General of Commonwealth countries who fought in the Great War, and to the ambassadors in London of our allies, and also of Austria, Germany, Hungary and Turkey. 10,000 tins were offered for sale in the stores and online, once it was ascertained that all the gifted tins had been safely received.[685]

Fortnum's tin represented just two percent of the number of brass boxes given at Christmas 1914, and a third of a percent of those final sent out. Though in no way directly comparable with Princess Mary's gift, it represented a reflection of the past, and an earnest and respectful one at that:

When the 'Tommy's tin' arrived it was a complete surprise, to be honest. I love history, and I knew what it was as soon as I saw it, a replica of the Princess Mary tin from 1914. My great uncle has his father's tin, as well as a pipe that was carved with his service in Suvla Bay. There were people at the compound who had no idea what it was,

but I was able to explain to them what it meant and what it represented. I think that they must have sent out a few thousand of these at least, to all who were deployed. Its contents were some chocolate and a small pack of cards, as well as a card from Fortnum & Masons. I held on to the Chocolate for as long as I could, but mail was scarce. [686]

Squadron Leader Stuart Roxburgh was on a six-month deployment as an RAF Liaison Officer at the US Naval Support Facility in Bahrain when he received his:

I was aware of the Princess Mary tin, sent to those deployed in the British Expeditionary Force at Christmas 1914, although I'd never seen one. It was surprising and quite nice to receive a facsimile copy of the tin whilst deployed on operations over Christmas 2014 – complete with Fortnum & Mason's playing cards and chocolate. I kept it intact; I thought it looked good and it seemed a shame to break it up.[687]

'KNICK-KNACKS', a box on memories – then and now – an enduring legacy

Queen Victoria's New Year's tin, Princess Mary's brass box, and Fortnum & Mason's 'Tommy's Tin' – lineal descendants of the same principle, a simple recognition of the universal needs of service personnel – to be considered, to be remembered, and, in some ways to be honoured.

> I kept the box, the cards and the little card explaining what it was. I have my tin now, and I keep knick-knacks in it. [688]

And so it is, for all three boxes today, as it was a hundred years' past. A legacy of care and of respect for those who serve, separated from their families and loved ones at Christmas. A seventeen-year-old Princess understood that over a hundred years ago, and decided to make a difference. She achieved her aim, and the act, and her kindness, has never been forgotten.

Acknowledgements

Written during the global pandemic of 2020-21, I am indebted to the dedicated archivists and librarians of several institutions who have made this book possible. In the depth of the crisis, it was uplifting to see just how much importance they placed on helping me carry out my research, and to dig into obscure corners in order to get to the root of some the most hoary of myths. I commend Jane Rosen and Sarah Patterson of the Imperial War Museum Library for setting me on the right path and giving me access to the amazing Women's War Work collection, which is the start point of any serious research into the Princess Mary Gift Fund. I could not have embarked on this journey without their assistance. Rebecca Burton, Assistant Curator and Archivist at Harewood House provided me with much valuable material, and access to key parts of Princess Mary's personal diary, which is quoted here by kind permission of the Earl and Countess of Harewood and the Harewood House Trust. Reproduction of the image of the Princess's gift box case is by the kind permission of the Trustees of the 7th Earl of Harewood Will Trust and Harewood House Trust. I am grateful to Agata Rutkowska of the Royal Collection Trust for giving permission to reproduce the image of the battle-damaged Princess Mary Box that was part of King George V's personal war relics collection (© Her Majesty Queen Elizabeth II). Princess Mary's most recent biographer, Elisabeth Basford is thanked for her kindness in guiding me and providing her impressions on the Princess, in advance of the publication, in 2021, of her own biography, *Princess Mary, The First Modern Princess*. I am grateful also to Alex Churchill, author of *In the Eye of the Storm. George V and the Great War*, for her knowledge and energy, and for assisting me with specific points. It is always a pleasure working with Taff Gillingham, and I am grateful for access to his extensive collection of artefacts (between 'lockdowns'), and for his detailed insights. Ben Hodges kindly shared with me the diary of PO Samuel George Hobbs RN, HMS *Glasgow*, which give an interesting insight into life at sea. Richard Archer, Rich Smith, and Paul Laidlaw are all thanked for their interest, enthusiasm and access to interesting and important items that have enriched my story; thank you gentlemen. Matt Dixon shared with me some of his large collection of charity and commemorative items from the war, and Dr Irfan Malik kindly gave me his insight into the meaning of the Gift Box to descendants of soldiers from India and Pakistan. Mitch Peeke is thanked for details of the *Lusitania* loading manifest. Thanks are due in equal measure to my friends Rob Schäfer for his insight into the German *Liebesgaben*, and to Chris Foster for his advice and encouragement. Tim Kurvers is thanked for details of Crown Prince Wilhelm's gifts to his troops in 1914 and 1915. I am grateful to Patrick Bogue of Onslows Auctioneers for kindly supplying images of the opening of a sealed box of gifts in June 2014. The National Army Museum assisted me with images, and particularly Kate Swann, so came to me rescue when I had lost some images. Those images appear Courtesy of the Council of the National Army Museum, London. Dr Andrea Tanner of Fortnum & Mason has been breathtakingly helpful in giving her time to express the meaning of their centenary tin and how it came about. I cannot thank her generosity, and those of Anna Perchal the designer of the tin (and Bimal Turner, digital designer) – enough. Sally Little and Charles Wookey of Operation Christmas Box (operationchristmasbox.org) have been similarly outstanding in their help and support, and I am so grateful for their engagement, and for supplying me with information, images and examples of the outputs from their wonderful charity – which provides Christmas gifts to all those of the armed forces on operational deployment at Christmas. Thanks also to Andy Currant and Stuart Roxburgh for their recollections of the receiving gifts in 2014. Sofie Vanhoutte and Marc Dewilde of the Flanders Heritage Agency have been generous in providing details of the Indian soldiers recovered in 2014, soldiers still in possession of their gifts from 1914. The late Franky Wyffels took the photographs of the artefacts recovered, and thanks are due to my friend Simon Verdegem for alerting me to the discovery. I'm grateful for Felicity Price-Smith's

careful design skills and patience. Ryan Gearing's belief in the project (and patience) has kept me going – thanks Ryan! My mother-in-law, Elisabeth Simpson, has, as ever, proven to be a valuable sounding board for me to test my ideas. As ever, I could not have got this far without the support and guidance of those most close to me: Julie and James.

Thank you all.

Bibliography

ARCHIVE RESOURCES
Harewood House
Princess Mary's Diary, 1914. Princess Mary's Archive, Courtesy of the Earl and Countess of Harewood and Harewood House Trust

Newspaper archives
British Newspaper Archive
Canadian Newspaper Archives
Library of Congress
National Library of Australia
National Library of New Zealand
The Times Archive
US Newspaper Archives

Women's War Work Special Collection, IWM:
B.O.2 1–815 HRH The Princess Mary's Sailors' and Soldiers' Christmas Fund, Payments and Receipts Account to 20 June 1919
BO 2 1/4 Letter from Rowland Berkeley to Agnes Conway, NWM, 9 April 1920,
BO 2 1/7 Minutes of the Committee Meetings of the General Committee of the Princess Mary Gift Fund [MGC]; Minutes of the Committee Meetings of the Executive Committee of the Princess Mary Gift Fund, [MEC]
BO 2 1/9 HRH The Princess Mary's Sailors' and Soldiers' Christmas Fund, Report, May 1920, IWM
BO 2 1/22 Letter from Rowland Berkeley, 17 December 1918
BO2 1/491 Letter to Lady Kathleen Lindsay, 23 August [1915]

Other Documents, IWM
1552, Manuscript Diary & typescript of soldier in 1/11th London Regiment, 1914-1915
7813, Field Marshal Sir John French's diaries, 1891-1921
8631, Typescript diary of soldier in 2nd Border Regiment
8674, Manuscript Pocket Diary 1914-1915
12327, private papers of Brigadier Mortimer, Indian Army

The National Archives
Reports on various Army nursing services in France
1914-1918. The work of the Nursing Services
with British Ambulance Trains and Station Units
in France, 1914 TNA WO222/2134
War Diary, Headquarters Branches and Services,
Matron-in-Chief, TNA WO 95/3988/2

Other Archive Collections
Peter Doyle
Taff Gillingham/Great War Huts
Ben Hodges
Rich Smith

MEMOIRS
Anonymous [attributed to Kate Luard], *Diary of
a Nursing Sister on the Western Front, 1914-15*.
London: William Blackwood, 1915
Anonymous [attributed to D.H. Bell] *A Soldier's
Diary of the Great War*. London: Faber & Gwyer,
1929
An Exchanged Officer [Malcolm Vivian Hay],
Wounded and a Prisoner of War, Edinburgh:
William Blackwood, 1916
Benn, Capt. W. *In the Side Shows*, London: Hodder
& Stoughton, 1919
Brookes, Sgt B. *A Signaller's War. Notes Compiled
from My Diary 1914-1918*. The Editor (Una
Barrie), 2012
Burgoyne, G.A, *The Burgoyne Diaries*. London:
Thomas Harmsworth, 1985
Congreve, B. (Terry Norman ed.) *Armageddon
Road. A VC's Diary, 1914-16*. London: William
Kimber, 1982
Craster J.M. (ed.) *'Fifteen Rounds a Minute' The
Grenadiers at War 1914. Edited from the Diaries
of Major 'Ma' Jeffreys and Others*. London:
Macmillan, 1976
French of Ypres, Field Marshal Viscount, *1914*,
London: Constable & Co, 1919
Grimshaw, Capt. R. *Indian Cavalry
Officer,1914-15*. Tunbridge Wells: Costello, 1986
Herbert, A. *Mons, Anzac & Kut*. London:
Hutchinson, 1919
Kennedy, Rev. E.J. *With the Immortal Seventh
Division*. London: Hodder & Stoughton, 1916
Lucy, J.F. *There's a Devil in the Drum*, Naval &
Military Press, 1993.

Orex [Major H.F. Bidder] *Three Chevrons*. London:
John Lane, The Bodley Head, 1919
Richards, Pte. F. *Old Soldiers Never Die*. Naval &
Military Press, 2009
Roynon G. (ed.) *Ypres Diary 1914-1915. The
Memoirs of Sir Morgan Crofton*. Stroud: The
History Press, 2010
Scrimgeour, A. *The Complete Scrimgeour, From
Dartmouth to Jutland: 1913-16*. London: Conway
Bloomsbury, 2016
Terraine, J. (ed.) *General Jack's Diary 1914-1918*.
London: Eyre & Spottiswoode, 1964
Walker, A.L. *Experiences at a Base Hospital in
France, 1914-15*, http://www.scarletfinders.
co.uk/156.html
Walkinton, M.L. *Twice in a Lifetime*. London:
Samson, 1980

BOOKS
Anon. *Princess Mary's Gift Book*, London: Hodder
& Stoughton, 1914
Anon. *The Prince of Wales' National Relief Fund*,
https://wellcomelibrary.org/item/b22445912
Aitken, Sir Max *Canada in Flanders*, London:
Hodder and Stoughton, 1916
Anderson, R. *The Chocolate Letters. York Men and the
Great War*, The Author, 2019
Atkins, A., *Rock Valley and Oddicroft Recollections*,
Bradford: Moorfield Press, 2015
Baker, C. *The Truce. The Day the War Stopped*.
Stroud: Amberley, 2014
Basford, E. *Princess Mary, The First Modern Princess*,
Stroud: The History Press, 2021
Basu, S. *For King and Another Country. Indian
Soldiers on the Western Front 1914-18*. London,
Bloomsbury, 2016
Bean, C.E.W. *The Official History of Australia in the
War of 1914–18. Volume 1. The Story of Anzac: The
First Phase*. Angus & Robertson, Sydney, 1921
Berridge, V. *Demons. Our Changing Attitudes
to Alcohol, Tobacco & Drugs*. Oxford: Oxford
University Press, 2013
Bostridge, M. *The Fateful Year, England 1914*.
London: Penguin, 2014
Broom, J. *A History of Cigarette and Trade Cards: The
Magic Inside the Packet*. Barnsley: Pen & Sword,
2018
Brown, M. *Tommy Goes to War*. London: Dent,
1978

Brown, M. *1914. The Men Who Went to War.* London: Sidgwick & Jackson, 2004

Brown M. & Seaton, S., *The Christmas Truce: The Western Front December 1914*, London: Leo Cooper & Secker & Warburg, 1984

Carey, M.C. *Princess Mary.* London: Nisbet & Co, 1922

Churchill, A. *In the Eye of the Storm. George V and the Great War,* Helion, Warwick, 2018

Colville, Q. *The British Sailor of the First World War*, Oxford: Shire, 2015

Committee of Imperial Defence, *History of the Great War Based on Official Documents. Principal Events 1914-1918.* London: HMSO, 1922

Corbett, Sir J. C. *History of the Great War Based on Official Documents. Naval Operations, Volume 1* Second Edition, London: Longmans, Green & Co, 1938

Corrigan, G. *Sepoys in the Trenches. The Indian Corps on the Western Front 1914-15.* Staplehurst: Spellmount, 1999

Doyle, P. *Rough Riders. Two Brothers and the Last Stand at Gallipoli.* Stroud: The History Press, 2015

Doyle P. & Foster C., *Kitchener's Mob, The New Army to the Somme, 1916.* Stroud, History Press, 2016

Dunn, Capt. J.C. *The War the Infantry Knew.* London: Janes Publishing, 1987

Edmonds, Brig.-Gen. J.E. *Official History of the Great War. Military Operations, France & Belgium 1914*, Volume 1. London: Macmillan, 1922

Edmonds, Brig.-Gen. J.E. *Official History of the Great War. Military Operations, France & Belgium 1914*, Volume 2, London: Macmillan, 1922

Elliot, R.E. *'Destructive but Sweet': Cigarette Smoking Among Women, 1890-1990,* PhD Thesis, University of Glasgow, 2001

Evans T. *The Christmas Tin,* The Author, 2014

Ferro, M., Brown, M., Cazals, R. & Mueller, O. *Meetings in No Man's Land. Christmas 1914 and Fraternization in the Great War.* London: Constable & Robinson, 2005

Flook, R. *British and Commonwealth Military Knives,* Charlottesville: Howell Press, 1999

Gosling, L. *Knitting for Tommy. Keeping the Great War Soldier Warm.* Stroud: The History Press, 2014

Graham, E. [Netley Lucas], *Princess Mary, Viscountess Lascelles,* London: Hutchinson, 1929

Grant, P. *Philanthropy and Voluntary Action in the First World War: Mobilizing Charity,* London: Routledge, 2014

Hammerton Sir J. (ed.) *The Great War...'I Was There!'* London: Amalgamated Press, 1938

Harewood, Lord *The Tongs and the Bones. The Memoirs of Lord Harewood.* London: Wiedenfield & Nicholson, 1981

Hayavadana Rao, C. (ed.) *The Indian Biographical Dictionary,* Madras: Pillar & Co, 1915

Hilton, M. *Smoking in British Popular Culture 1800–2000,* Manchester: Manchester University Press, 2000

Hubbard E. & Shippobottom, M. *A Guide to Port Sunlight Village,* Liverpool: Liverpool University Press, 2016

Illustrated War News, Vols 1-III, London, 1914

Johnson, S.C. *Chats on Military Curios,* London: Fisher Unwin, 1915

Keatley Moore, Alderman H (ed.) *Croydon and the Great War,* Croydon, 1920

Kebar, L. *The Story of the Queen's Chocolate Tin.* Durban: Privately Published, 1997

Kruger, R. *Good-bye Dolly Gray. The Story of the Boer War.* London: Cassell, 1964

Le Bas Sir H. (ed.) *The Lord Kitchener Memorial Book,* London: Hodder & Stoughton, 1916

Lloyd, M. *The London Scottish in the Great War,* Barnsley: Leo Cooper, 2001

Lever, W.H. *Viscount Leverhulme, by His Son,* London: George Allen & Unwin, 1928

Mazansky, C. *The First World War on Cigarette and Trade Cards: An Illustrated and Descriptive History.* Schiffer, 2015

McCance, Capt. S. *History of the Royal Munster Fusiliers 1861–1922,* Aldershot: Gale & Polden (For Private Circulation), 1927

Merewether, W.B. & Smith, F. *The Indian Corps in France,* London: John Murray, 1917

Messenger, C. *Call To Arms, The British Army 1914-18.* London: Wiedenfield & Nicholson, 2005

Mitchinson, K.W. *England's Last Hope. The Territorial Force, 1908-14.* Basingstoke: Palgrave Macmillan, 2008

Nicholson, G.W.L. *Canadian Expeditionary Force 1914-1919,* Montreal: McGill-Queens University Press, 2015

Nicholson, H. *King George The Fifth. His Life and Reign,* London: Constable & Co, 1952

Neillands, R. *The Old Contemptibles. The British Expeditionary Force, 1914*. London: John Murray, 2004

Opie, R. *The 1910s Scrapbook. The Decade of the Great War*. London: New Cavendish, 2003

Page W. & Willis-Bund J.W. (ed.) *A History of the County of Worcester: Volume 4*, London, 1924

Pakenham, T. *The Boer War*. London: Wiedenfield and Nicolson, 1979

Parkhouse, V.B. *Memorializing the Anglo–Boer War of 1899–1902*, London: Matador, 2015

Pollendine, C. *Campaign 1914*, London: Military Mode, 2013

Pollendine, C. *Campaign 1915*, Military Mode Publishing, 2015

Pope-Hennessy, J. *Queen Mary. The Official Biography*, London: Hodder & Stoughton, 2019

Reader, W.J. *Metal Box. A History*. London: Heinemann, 1976

Robinson A. & Hamilton Stubber, T. *Princess Mary. The Princess Royal, Countess of Harewood*. Harewood [nd]

Rickards, M & Moody, M. *The First World War: Ephemera, Mementoes and Documents*. London: Jupiter, 1975

Scott, P.T. *Home for Christmas. Cards, Messages and Legends of the Great War*. London: Tom Donovan, 1993.

Shawcross, W. *Queen Elizabeth The Queen Mother. The Official Biography*. London: Macmillan, 2009

Simpson, C. *The Lusitania*, Boston: Little, Brown & Company, 1972

Stanley, Brig-Gen. F.C. *The History of the 89th Brigade 1914-1918*. Liverpool: Daily Post, 1919, p. 27

The War Budget, Vol. II. London: Daily Chronicle, 1914

Van Emden, R. *Missing*. Pen & Sword, Barnsley, 2020

Verhey, J. *The Spirit of 1914, Militarism, Myth and Mobilisation in Germany*, Cambridge: CUP, 2000

Wakefield, A., *Christmas in the Trenches*, Stroud: Sutton, 2006

Weintraub, S. *Silent Night. The Remarkable Christmas Truce of 1914*. London: Simon & Schuster, 2014

Willcocks, Sir J. *With the Indians in France*, London: Constable & Co, 1920

Williamson, H. *A Fox Under My Cloak*, London: Faber & Faber, 2010

Williamson, H. *The Great War Medal Collector's Companion*, The Author, 2011

Ziegler, P. *King Edward VIII*, London: Harper Press, 2012

War Office, *Our Indian Empire. A Short Review and Some Hints for the Use of Soldiers Proceeding to India*, London: HMSO, 1913

War Office, *Statistics of the Military Effort of the British Empire During the Great War 1914-1920*. London: HMSO, 1922

ARTICLES

Austral Wright Metals - ferrous, non-ferrous and high-performance alloys. *Metal Alloys - Properties and Applications of Brass and Brass Alloys*. https://www.azom.com/article.aspx?ArticleID=4387

Basford, E.A. Quiet Devotion to Duty, *Majesty Magazine*, August 2020

Collins, M.P. The development of town planning education at University College London 1914–1969: the contributions of professors S.D. Adshead, L.P. Abercrombie and W.G. Holford. *Planning Perspectives*, v. 31, p. 284, 2016

Condell, D. 1989. A gift for Christmas: the story of Princess Mary's Gift Fund, 1914. *Imperial War Museum Review*, n. 4, pp. 69-78

Daniels, H. When the smoke cleared: tobacco supply and consumption by the British Expeditionary Force, 1914-1918. *Revue Française de Civilisation Britannique*, v. XX-1, 2015, https://doi.org/10.4000/rfcb.218

Hentz Jr F.C. & Long, G.G. Lighter flint chemistry. *Journal of Chemical Education*, v. 53(10), p. 651

Hiley, N. 'Sir Hedley Le Bas and the origins of domestic propaganda in Britain 1914-1917'. *European Journal of Marketing*, v.21, 1987, p. 31

Kumar, V. Seven spices of India–from kitchen to clinic, *Journal of Ethnic Foods*, v. 7, (23), 2020, doi.org/10.1186/s42779-020-00058-0

O'Connell, Sean review of Matthew Hilton, *Smoking in British Popular Culture 1800–2000*, Manchester: Manchester University Press, 2000; *Reviews in History*, https://reviews.history.ac.uk

Prior, K. H., Sir John Prescott (1854–1941) *Oxford Dictionary of National Biography*, https://doi.org/10.1093/ref:odnb/33847

Reeve, M. Special Needs, Cheerful Habits: Smoking and the Great war in Britain, 1914-18. *Cultural and Social History*, 13, 483-501, 2016

Reeve, M. Smoking and cigarette consumption, in *1914-1918-online, International Encyclopedia of the First World War*, Freie Universität Berlin, 2014

Tout-Smith, D. Australian Comforts Fund, World War I in Museums Victoria Collections https://collections.museumsvictoria.com.au/articles/1848, 2003, accessed 07 March 2021

Williamson, H. The Christmas Truce, *History of the First World War*, (1969) edited by Barry Pitt, v.2 (4), pp. 552-559

OBITUARIES

Victor Christian William Cavendish, The Duke of Devonshire, 1868-1938. *Biographical Memoirs of Fellows of the Royal Society, 2(7)*, January 1939, pp.557–559

Sir James Goodhart, *British Medical Journal*, 1916 (3), pp. 803-4

REPORTS

Dewilde, M. Márquez-Grant N. & Wyffels F. *een onvolledig geruimd militair Kerkhof in de Ypres Salient. Een toevalsvondst in de Briekestraat te Ieper.* Onderzoeksrapporten Agentschap Onroerend Erfgoed, Brussel, 2015; thanks to Marc Dewilde and Sofie Vanhoutte

Pype, P. Cattrysse, A. De Smaele, B. Pieters H. & Crug, C. *Archeologisch onderzoek van Wereldoorlog I-erfgoed lands de Briekestraat te Ieper (prov. West-Vlaanderen). II. Opgraving.* Gent: ADEDE Arheologisch Rapport, 54, Gent

WEBSITES

www.auer-von-welsbach-museum.at/en/cer-en

www.bbc.co.uk/news/uk-england-wiltshire-28224808

www.british-history.ac.uk/vch/worcs/vol4

www.dailymail.co.uk/news/article-2688267/Treasures-trenches-They-symbols-generations-awesome-sense-duty-Kings-shilling-given-new-recruits-royal-Christmas-Box-sent-Front-Now-Mail-giving-away-glorious-replicas.html

www.encyclopedia.com/social-sciences-and-law/economics-business-and-labor/businesses-and-occupations/de-la-rue-plc

www.fairestforce.co.uk/14.html

glamarchives.wordpress.com/2016/12/12/puddings-and-parcels-christmas-fundraising-in-the-first-world-war/

www.gov.uk/government/news/uk4u-thanks-christmas-box-campaign-launched

www.gracesguide.co.uk/1914_Who's_Who_in_Business

harewood.org/about/blog/in-focus/reviving-the-art-of-letter-writing/

harewood.org/about/blog/notes/a-christmas-legacy-continues/

www.iwm.org.uk/history/boy-1st-class-john-jack-travers-cornwell-vc

managingbusinessarchives.co.uk/news/2015/01/tommys-tin/

www.lustania.net/deadlycargo.htm

operationchristmasbox.org/what-we-do/why-was-the-charity-formed/

www.rct.uk/collection/themes/trails/king-george-vs-war-museum/

www.rosl.org.uk/ww1/the-war-that-made-rosl

www.royal.uk/first-world-war-royal-archives

sammlungen.ulb.uni-muenster.de/hd/content/pageview/247256

www.telegraph.co.uk/food-and-drink/cadbury-heritage/ww1-angels/

www.trenchartofww1.co.uk/xmas_1914_tin_21.html

vintagepens.com/Omdurman_pencil.shtml

www.yorkmuseumstrust.org.uk/news-media/latest-news/1914-when-the-world-changed-forever-star-objects

Endnotes

CHAPTER 1

1 Prince Maurice of Battenberg, Princess Mary's cousin, was killed in action on 27 October 1914. The Prince's family was eligible to receive one of the Princess's gift boxes, in memoriam. The King made seven visits, one in each year and three in 1918; see https://www.royal.uk/first-world-war-royal-archives, accessed 13 February 2021.

2 Anna Robinson & Tara Hamilton Stubber *Princess Mary. The Princess Royal, Countess of Harewood.* Harewood [nd], p. 5. Despite taking many significant roles in the early part of her life, Mary has had few biographers, with M.C. Carey, *Princess Mary.* London: Nisbet & Co, 1922 (and the derivative Evelyn Graham, actually written by notorious confidence trickster Netley Lucas, *Princess Mary, Viscountess Lascelles,* London: Hutchinson, 1929) and Elisabeth Basford *Princess Mary, The First Modern Princess,* Stroud: The History Press, 2021 being the most important.

3 Carey, *Princess Mary,* p11-12.

4 Alexandra Churchill, *In the Eye of the Storm. George V and the Great War,* Helion, Warwick, 2018, pp. 52, 53

5 Princess Mary to the Duchess of York (later Queen Mary), 1901. Rebecca Burton, *Reviving the Art of Letter Writing* blog post https://harewood.org/about/blog/in-focus/reviving-the-art-of-letter-writing/, accessed 6 July 2020.

6 Philip Ziegler, *King Edward VIII,* London: Harper Press, 2012, p. 8.

7 Royal Archives, quoted in *In the Eye of the Storm,* p. 54.

8 *Princess Mary, The First Modern Princess,* p. 48

9 David was destined to be King Edward VIII, who abdicated in 1936 in order to marry divorceé Mrs Simpson; the shy Bertie would become King George VI. Both served; David in the Grenadier Guards, Bertie in the Royal navy.

10 *The Star* [New Zealand], 27 February, 1915

11 Biographies of King George V and Queen Mary are consistent in expressing the patriotism and sense of duty of the royal couple, and defending the serious faces they presented to the public: e.g. *In the Eye of the Storm;* James Pope-Hennessy, *Queen Mary. The Official Biography,* London: Hodder & Stoughton, 2019 [first published in 1959].

12 *Queen Mary. The Official Biography,* p. 490.

13 Elisabeth Basford, email communication, September 2020

14 Elisabeth Basford, A Quiet Devotion to Duty, *Majesty Magazine,* August 2020

15 Carey, *Princess Mary,* p. 14.

16 *In the Eye of the Storm,* p. 54.

17 Official photographs & postcards, c. 1931

18 A Quiet Devotion to Duty, August 2020.

19 Carey, *Princess Mary,* p. 18

20 Carey, *Princess Mary,* p. 21

21 Basford, *Princess Mary, The First Modern Princess,* p. 46

22 *The Star* [New Zealand], 27 February, 1915

23 Lord Harewood, *The Tongs and the Bones. The Memoirs of Lord Harewood.* London: Wiedenfield & Nicholson, 1981, pp. 26–28.

24 *Princess Mary. The Princess Royal, Countess of Harewood.* Harewood [nd] illustrate some of the collections of Mary and her husband, Viscount Lascelles.

25 *Princess Mary, Viscountess Lascelles,* p. 58

26 *Princess Mary, Viscountess Lascelles,* p. 57

27 Princess Mary's Diary, 1914. Princess Mary's Archive, Harewood House Trust. Extracts reproduced by courtesy of the Earl and Countess of Harewood and Harewood House Trust, with thanks to Rebecca Burton

28 Carey, *Princess Mary,* p. 72

29 *Edmonton Journal* [Edmonton, Alberta], 2 January 1915

30 Carey, *Princess Mary*, p. 44

31 *Princess Mary, Viscountess Lascelles*, p. 68

32 *Princess Mary, Viscountess Lascelles*, p. 16.

33 Elisabeth Basford, A Quiet Devotion to Duty, *Majesty Magazine*, August 2020

34 Letter from Queen Mary to Prince Albert, 10 August 1918, https://www.royal.uk/first-world-war-royal-archives, accessed 13 February 2021

35 *The Daily Mirror*, 16 October 1914

36 Example letter in private archive

37 For example, *Dublin Daily Express*, 16 October 1914

38 *The Daily Mirror*, 16 October 1914

39 Dates in sequence from *History of the Great War Based on Official Documents. Principal Events 1914-1918*. HMSO, 1922, p. 6 *et seq.*

40 *The Daily Mirror*, 19 October 1914

41 Sir James Willcocks, *With the Indians in France*, London: Constable & Co, 1920, p.48

42 Queen Mary's diary, quoted in *Queen Mary*, p. 490

43 *In the Eye of the Storm. George V and the Great War*, p. 54: A Quite Devotion to Duty, *Majesty Magazine*, August 2020; *Princess Mary, The First Modern Princess*, 2021

44 Minutes of the Committee Meetings of the General Committee of the Princess Mary Gift Fund [MGC] and Minutes of the Committee Meetings of the Executive Committee of the Princess Mary Gift Fund, [MEC]; IWM BO2 1/7 HRH The Princess Mary's Sailors' and Soldiers' Christmas Fund, Report, May 1920, IWM BO2 1/9

45 MGC, 14 October 1914; Wallington would eventually chair the Committee

46 MGC 14 October 1914; Lady Coke's duties entailed assisting with the Queen's correspondence and other administrative matters, *Queen Mary*, p. 293.

47 A photograph in the National Portrait Gallery (x136892) illustrates a family occasion and the closeness of all of Queen Mary's personal staff with the Royal Family, including Lady Coke

48 Princess Mary's Diary, 1914. Princess Mary's Archive, Harewood House Trust.

49 Obituary Notice, Victor Christian William Cavendish, The Duke of Devonshire, 1868-

1938. *Biographical Memoirs of Fellows of the Royal Society, 2(7)*, January 1939, pp.557–559.

50 Obituary, *Dundee Evening Telegraph*, 8 May 1938

51 MEC, 28 July 1916, note 1

52 https://www.baringarchive.org.uk/history/biographies/john_baring_2nd_lord_revelstoke accessed 19 September 2020

53 MGC, 14 October 1914; very little is known of Rowland Comyns Berkeley (1865-1925), who became lord of the manor at Cotheridge in 1885; *A History of the County of Worcester: Volume 4*, ed. William Page & J W Willis-Bund (London, 1924), British History Online http://www.british-history.ac.uk/vch/worcs/vol4, pp. 255-260, accessed 19 September 2020].

54 MGC, 14 October 1914

55 *The Daily Mirror*, 16 October 1914

CHAPTER 2

56 *The Prince of Wales' National Relief Fund*, York House, St James Palace, SW, p. 1. https://wellcomelibrary.org/item/b22445912

57 *Queen Mary*, p. 489

58 Princess Mary's Diary, 1914. Princess Mary's Archive, Harewood House Trust.

59 *Queen Mary*, p. 491

60 *Mobilizing Charity*, p. 26.

61 Peter Grant, *Philanthropy and Voluntary Action in the First World War: Mobilizing Charity*, London: Routledge, 2014, p. 23.

62 *In the Eye of the Storm*, p.58.

63 *King Edward VIII*, p. 52

64 *King Edward VIII*, p. 27; Sir Walter Peacock, Obituary, *Cornish Guardian*, 1 March 1956.

65 Captain Wedgwood Benn, *In the Side Shows*, London: Hodder & Stoughton, 1919, p. 1.

66 *In the Eye of the Storm*, p. 59.

67 See, for example, the London Needlework Guild, http://qmcg.org.uk/history/ accessed 6 July 2020; similar efforts were carried out by the *Bund deutscher Frauen* in 1914, see Jeffrey Verhey, *The Spirit of 1914, Militarism, Myth and Mobilisation in Germany*, Cambridge: CUP, 2000, p. 106.

68 Valerie B. Parkhouse, *Memorializing the Anglo–Boer War of 1899–1902*, London: Matador, 2015, p. 76

69 *The Scotsman* 10 August 1914

70 *Western Daily Press*, 22 August 1914

71 Carey, *Princess Mary*, p. 45

72 Princess Mary's Diary, 1914. Princess Mary's Archive, Harewood House Trust.

73 Particularly from the inception of the Guild, with records from 11 August onwards, thanks to Rebecca Burton, Princess Mary's Diary, 1914. Princess Mary's Archive, Harewood House Trust; *Princess Mary, Viscountess Lascelles*, p. 67

74 *Daily Mirror*, 19 October 1914

75 Example reproduced in Lucinda Gosling, *Knitting for Tommy. Keeping the Great War Soldier Warm*. Stroud: The History Press, 2014, p. 105

76 War Diary, Matron-in-Chief to the BEF, 2 December 1914, TNA WO95/3988

77 Sample letter in private archive; see, for example, Terence Evans, *The Christmas Tin*, The Author, 2014 (no page numbers); Howard Williamson, *The Great War Medal Collector's Companion*, The Author, 2011, p. 569

78 An example in private collection bears the contemporary annotation: 'Received with a pair of socks which were given to us'

79 *Mobilizing Charity*, p.37; see also *Knitting for Tommy*, p.13.

80 Letter from Captain Arthur Ion Fraser to Commander John Gordon Fraser, HMS *Shannon*, 3 January 1915. (Author's archive)

81 *Queen Mary*, p. 491

82 *Mobilizing Charity*, p.38; *Queen Mary*, p. 492.

83 *Princess Mary's Gift Book*, London: Hodder & Stoughton, 1914; the book was often given to wounded men in hospital; Princess Mary did this herself in 1916, when she gave out 1600 copies as a Christmas Gift at King George Hospital, Waterloo; https://www.royal.uk/first-world-war-royal-archives, accessed 13 February 2021

84 *Philanthropy and Voluntary Action*, p. 47, data relating to the War Charities Act, 1916. The next largest effort was the provision of medical support at 25%.

85 Rev. E.J. Kennedy, *With the Immortal Seventh Division*. London: Hodder & Stoughton, 1916, pp. 134-135

86 For example, *The Express* for 5 December 1855, reported: 'Comforts For The Crimea. Government Care of Our Troops in The East —Large supplies of vegetables have arrived at Balaklava. An order has been transmitted to freight a ship of 250 or 330 tons from Venice to Balaklava, half with potatoes, and half with onions. Another has been lent to Trieste for a cargo of fresh vegetables and fur clothing. Inquiries have been instituted as to the possibility of procuring in Istria a supply of wooden homes fur our soldiers in the Crimea.'

87 *The Newcastle Journal*, 9 December 1854

88 See Michael Reeve, Special Needs, Cheerful Habits: Smoking and the Great War in Britain, 1914-18. *Cultural and Social History*, 13, 483-501, 2016.

89 *Essex Standard*, 9 February 1855

90 A leaflet encouraging young women to help the troops in 1870 is available at https://sammlungen.ulb.uni-muenster.de/hd/content/pageview/247256 accessed 13 February 2021; see also *The Spirit of 1914*, p. 106.

91 *Dundee Evening Telegraph*, 22 March 1900; *East Anglian Daily Times*, 4 March 1901

92 Harold Nicholson, *King George The Fifth. His Life and Reign*, London: Constable & Co, 1952, pp. 4–5.

93 *The Morning Post*, 12 October 1901

94 *The Morning Post*, 14 October 1901

95 *The Morning Post*, 28 December 1901

96 See Lenaid Kebar, *The Story of the Queen's Chocolate Tin*. Durban: Privately Published, 1997.

97 Rayne Kruger, *Good-bye Dolly Gray. The Story of the Boer War*. London: Cassell, 1964, pp. 122-142.

98 *Good-bye Dolly Gray*, p. 139.

99 *Good-bye Dolly Gray*, p. 167

100 Taff Gillingham/Great War Huts Collection

101 *The Irish Times*, 21 November 1899

102 *The Irish Times*, 21 November 1899

103 *Penny Illustrated Paper*, 25 November 1899

104 *The Story of the Queen's Chocolate Tin*, pp.8-9

105 *The Story of the Queen's Chocolate Tin*, pp.6–7.

106 *Mansfield Reporter*, 3 July 1914

107 *Memorializing the Anglo-Boer War of 1899–1902*, p. 77

108 *Good-bye Dolly Gray*, p. 469.

109 'Queen's chocolate box for sale, partly full' *Edinburgh Evening News*, 11 April 1900; 'A Queen's chocolate box for sale, complete with chocolate; best offer' *Bucks Herald*, 23 June 1900

110 *Strathearn Herald*, 10 March 1900; a 'guinea' was one pound and one shilling

111 *Reading Mercury*, 19 May 1900
112 *Dundee Evening Telegraph*, 16 April 1900; *South Wales Daily News*, 13 July 1900.
113 *Falkirk Herald*, 23 June 1900.
114 *The Daily Mirror*, 20 October 1914
115 Stanley C. Johnson, *Chats on Military Curios*, London: Fisher Unwin, 1915, p. 309

CHAPTER 3
116 Princess Mary's Diary, 1914. Princess Mary's Archive, Harewood House Trust.
117 *Princess Mary, Viscountess Lascelles*, p. 69
118 'The Queen commands me to inform you of her anxiety to make some personal present as soon as possible to each of her soldiers serving in South Africa.' *Penny Illustrated Paper*, 25 November 1899.
119 MEC, 15 October 1914
120 MEC, 15 October 1914, note 7
121 It is interesting that two early biographies of Princess Mary, including one that was claimed to have been 'published by approval of Her Royal Highness', both get the date of inauguration wrong. Carey (*Princess Mary*, 1922, p. 78) cites it as 16 November 1914; Graham, (*Princess Mary, Viscountess Lascelles*, 1929, p. 69), as 16 November *1915*.
122 *The Daily Mirror*, 16 October 1914
123 MEC 27 October 1914 note 5
124 *The Daily Mirror*, 16 October 1914
125 *The Daily Mirror*, 16 October 1914
126 Many newspapers across the USA, including, for example, *The Harrisburg Independent* [Pennsylvania, USA], under the title 'Princess Mary Asks Gifts for Every Man at Front', 16 October 1914.
127 *Vancouver Daily World* [Canada], 16 October 1914.
128 *Auckland Star* [New Zealand], 17 October 1914
129 *The Windsor Star* [Windsor, Ontario, Canada], 26 November 1914
130 MEC, 20 October 1914, note 1
131 *The Daily Mirror*, 20 October 1914
132 *Liverpool Echo*, 30 October 1914.
133 *Yorkshire Evening Post*, 11 November 1914
134 'No2 Drawing Account'; MEC, 20 October 1914, note 5
135 MEC 15 October 1914, note 9
136 MEC 27 October 1914, note 2

137 Nicholas Hiley, 'Sir Hedley Le Bas and the origins of domestic propaganda in Britain 1914-1917'. *European Journal of Marketing*, v.21, 1987, p. 31.
138 Hiley, p. 31
139 Sir Hedley Le Bas, Advertising for an Army, In: Sir Hedley Le Bas (ed.) *The Lord Kitchener Memorial Book*, London: Hodder & Stoughton [1916, no page numbers]; Hiley, pp 34–36.
140 *Perthshire Constitutional & Journal*, 30 November 1914
141 *Mobilizing Charity*, p.47
142 Alderman H. Keatley Moore (ed.) *Croydon and the Great War*, Croydon, 1920, Appendix VIII.
143 MEC 20 October 1914, note 3
144 *Stirling Observer*, 1 December 1914
145 A single sheet of foolscap paper, one-sided, and folded to fit a standard envelope. (Example in private collection)
146 MEC 20 October 1914, note 5
147 MEC 27 October 1914, note 3
148 *Westminster Gazette*, 30 November 1914
149 MEC 22 December 1914, note 8; Princess Mary described it as 'a very good matinée' in her diary entry for 4 December 1914 (Princess Mary's Diary, 1914. Princess Mary's Archive, Harewood House Trust)
150 The receipt was a simple pro-forma, again with Buckingham Palace header, with spaces for the date, the amount donated and the signature of Queen Mary's Private Secretary, E.W. Wallington. (Author's collection)
151 MEC 20 October 1914, note 6
152 Author's archive
153 MEC 27 October 1914, note 2
154 *Montrose Standard*, 30 October 1914
155 *Liverpool Daily Post*, 16 November 1914
156 Final Report, *Receipts and Payments to 30th June 1919*
157 Glamorgan Archives, ELL26/2; reported in https://glamarchives.wordpress.com/ 2016/12/12/puddings-and-parcels-christmas-fundraising-in-the-first-world-war/ accessed 13 September 2020
158 *Montrose Standard*, 20 November 1914
159 *Manchester Evening News*, 25 November 1914
160 *North Devon Gazette* 5 November 1914
161 *The Windsor Star* [Windsor, Ontario, Canada] 18 December 1914

162 *Birkenhead News*, 24 October 1914

163 *Whitstable Times and Herne Bay Herald*, 14 November 1914

164 *Sheffield Daily Telegraph*, 19 October 1914

165 *Burnley News*, 28 November 1914

166 *HRH The Princess Mary's Sailors' and Soldiers' Christmas Fund, Payments and Receipts Account to 20 June 1919* IWM B.O.2 1–815

167 G.W.L. Nicholson, *Canadian Expeditionary Force 1914-1919*, Montreal: McGill-Queens University Press, 2015 [originally published in 1962], p. 31

168 *Canadian Expeditionary Force 1914-1919*, p. 40

169 *The Winnipeg Tribune* [Canada], 4 December 1914

170 *Dublin Daily Express*, 26 November 1914

CHAPTER 4

171 *Thanet Advertiser*, 14 November 1914

172 Nicholson, *King George V*, p. 35

173 MEC, 15 October 1914, note 4

174 Obituary, *Birmingham Daily Gazette*, 22 November 1928

175 MEC, 3 November 1914, note 4

176 MEC, 10 November 1914, note 4

177 MEC, 17 November 1914, note 4

178 MGC, 24 November 1914, note 1

179 *Report of the HRH the Princess Mary Christmas Fund, May 1920* IWM B.O.2 1/9. Most authors writing about the Gift make use of this *post facto* classification

180 For example: Condell, D. 1989. A gift for Christmas: the story of Princess Mary's Gift Fund, 1914. *Imperial War Museum Review*, n. 4, p.75

181 *Report of the HRH the Princess Mary Christmas Fund, May 1920*, pp.2-4

182 *Daily Mirror*, 16 October 1914

183 *Atlanta Constitution* [GA, USA], 25 October 1914

184 *Liverpool Daily Post and Mercury*, 2 November 1914

185 *The Scotsman*, 18 January 1915

186 *Surrey Mirror*, 4 December 1914

187 Glamorgan Archives, EM10/11, *ibid*.

188 MEC, 15 October 1914, notes 5, 6

189 Gerald Achilles Burgoyne, *The Burgoyne Diaries*. London: Thomas Harmsworth, 1985, p. 23.

190 *Sheffield Daily Telegraph*, 18 December 1914

191 *Warwick and Warwickshire Advertiser*, 5 December 1914

192 Letter from General Rawlinson to Clive Wigram (Secretary to George V), 26 December 1914; Royal Archives, https://www.royal.uk/first-world-war-royal-archives, accessed 13 February 2021; also referred to by Condell, p. 75

193 Author's archive

194 *The Burgoyne Diaries*, p. 27.

195 *The Burgoyne Diaries*, p. 44.

196 Michael Reeve, Smoking and cigarette consumption, in *1914-1918-online, International Encyclopedia of the First World War*, Freie Universität Berlin, 2014; accessed 8 September 2020

197 Reeve, Smoking and cigarette consumption

198 *Buckingham Advertiser and Free Press*, 19 December 1914

199 *Penrith Observer*, 15 December 1914

200 Sir John Hammerton, *The Great War... 'I Was There!' Undying Memories of 1914-1918*. London: Amalgamated Press, Vol 2, 1938, p. 271.

201 *The Birmingham Age-Herald* [Birmingham, Alabama], 13 December 1914

202 *The People*, 8 November 1914

203 *The Financial Times*, 27 November 2015

204 *Nottinghamshire Evening Post*, 24 December 1914; 'Formeloids' were throat lozenges

205 Christmas Card from the Nottingham Christmas Presents Fund Committee, 1914 (author's archive)

206 *Berwick Advertiser*, 4 November 1914; pandrops are a type of Scottish mint confectionary

207 *Western Daily Press*, 30 November 1914

208 *Western Daily Press*, 30 November 1914

209 Example examined in York Castle Museum, https://www.yorkmuseumtrust.org.uk/news-media/latest-news/1914-when-the-world-changed-forever-star-objects/, accessed 24 October 2020

210 *York Press*, 8 November 2019; Rosemary Anderson, *The Chocolate Letters. York Men and the Great War*, The Author, 2019, p. 3.

211 *Daily Express for Middlesborough*, 16 December 1914

212 Example from Sawyers Stores Ltd, Notting Hill, London, IWM EPH9387

213 Framed example in private collection

214 *The Times* reported (forgetting the Royal Navy) on 7 December 1915 that the 'distribution of the cards was confined…to the troops serving in France and Flanders'

215 *Sheffield Independent*, 26 December 1914

216 Charles Messenger, *Call To Arms, The British Army 1914-18*. London: Wiedenfield & Nicholson, 2005, p. 469

217 https://www.royal.uk/first-world-war-royal-archives, accessed 13 February 2021

218 Author's archive; Sgt Bernard Brookes, a participant in the Christmas Truce, kept both the card and its envelope in his memoirs: Sgt Bernard Brookes, *A Signaller's War. Notes Compiled from My Diary 1914-1918*. The Editor (Una Barrie), 2012, p.52

219 Anonymous [attributed to Kate Luard], *Diary of a Nursing Sister on the Western Front, 1914-15*. London: William Blackwood, 1915

220 Gavin Roynon (ed.) *Ypres Diary 1914-1915. The Memoirs of Sir Morgan Crofton*. Stroud: The History Press, 2010, p.116; see also M.L. Walkinton, *Twice in a Lifetime*, London: Samson, p. 45.

221 *The Week* [Brisbane, Australia], 1 January 1915

222 Billy Congreve (Terry Norman ed.) *Armageddon Road. A VC's Diary, 1914-16*. London: William Kimber, 1982, p. 96

223 *Leeds Mercury*, 30 December 1914

224 Great War Huts/Taff Gillingham Collection; the only other example seen was also owned by a sailor

225 Author's archive

226 *The Daily Mirror*, 18 December 1914

227 Letter from F.T. Clayton, quoted in *Princess Mary: The First Modern Princess*, p. 55

228 *The Daily Mirror*, 18 December 1914

229 *Nottingham Evening Post*, 30 December 1914

230 *Nottingham Evening Post*, 30 December 1914

231 J.M. Craster (ed.) *Fifteen Rounds a Minute. Edited from the Diaries of Major 'Ma' Jeffreys and Others*. London: Macmillan, 1976, p. 164

CHAPTER 5

232 Alexander Scrimgeour *The Complete Scrimgeour, From Dartmouth to Jutland: 1913-16*. London: Conway Bloomsbury, 2016, p. 194

233 Anon [D.H. Bell] *A Soldier's Diary of the Great War*. London: Faber & Gwyer, 1929, p. 67

234 J.F. Lucy, *There's a Devil in the Drum*, Naval & Military Press, 1993, p. 288.

235 Field Marshal Viscount French of Ypres, *1914*, London: Constable & Co, 1919, pp. 288-290.

236 *Final Report*, p. 3, BO 2.1-9

237 https://www.dailymail.co.uk/news/article-2688267/Treasures-trenches-They-symbols-generations-awesome-sense-duty-Kings-shilling-given-new-recruits-royal-Christmas-Box-sent-Front-Now-Mail-giving-away-glorious-replicas.html, accessed 23 February 2021

238 *The Leader* [Melbourne, Australia], 27 February 1915

239 *Daily Record* 29 October 1914; the story also made the front page of *The Tatler*, 4 November 1914.

240 *The Times*, 11 December 1914

241 *Final Report*, p. 4

242 *Gloucestershire Echo*, 4 November 1914

243 Michael P. Collins, The development of town planning education at University College London 1914–1969: the contributions of professors S.D. Adshead, L.P. Abercrombie and W.G. Holford. *Planning Perspectives*, v. 31, p. 284, 2016.

244 *The Times*, 13 April 1946

245 See Edward Hubbard & Michael Shippobottom, *A Guide to Port Sunlight Village*, Liverpool: Liverpool University Press, 2016

246 William Hulme Lever, *Viscount Leverhulme, by His Son*, London: George Allen & Unwin, 1928, p. 188

247 *Viscount Leverhulme, by His Son*, p. 189

248 *The Times*, 13 April 1946

249 *Stirling Observer*, 1 December 1914

250 W.J. Reader, *Metal Box. A History*. London: Heinemann, 1976

251 *Mansfield Reporter*, 18 December 1914

252 MEC, 17 November 1914, note 3

253 'Several firms produced as elaborate box…' *Metal Box. A History*, p. 35; Condell (p. 72) suggests the firm of O.T. Banks as a manufacturer, but this firm is mentioned as a supplier of brass in the minutes of the Executive Committee. Collectors have identified that there are six separate box 'types' based on minor differences in lid stamping details.

254 *Mansfield Reporter*, 26 November 1915

255 *Illustrated London News*, 19 December 1914

256 Alan Atkins, *Rock Valley and Oddicroft Recollections*, Bradford: Moorfield Press, 2015, p. 87; *Metal Box, A History*, p. 35.

257 *Metal Box, A History*, p. 34 *et seq.*

258 *The Northern Whig*, 22 September 1914

259 *Mansfield Reporter*, 26 November 1915

260 *Final Report*, p, 4

261 *Mansfield Reporter*, 18 December 1914

262 IWM BO 2 1/4, letter from Rowland Berkeley to Agnes Conway, NWM, 9 April 1920.

263 *Receipts & Payments Account*, to 30 June 1919

264 See for example, Evans, *The Christmas Tin* (no page numbers)

265 Austral Wright Metals - ferrous, non-ferrous and high-performance alloys. *Metal Alloys - Properties and Applications of Brass and Brass Alloys*. https://www.azom.com/article.aspx?ArticleID=4387, accessed 29 November 2020.

266 Author's collection

267 *Metal Box, A History*, p. 35

268 MEC, 8 December 1914, note 3

269 MEC 15 December 1914, note 7

270 *Final Report*, p. 5

271 *Final Report*, p. 4

272 MEC, 19 February 1915, note 3

273 MEC, 19 February 1915, note 3

274 MEC, 19 February 1915, note 3

275 *Final Report*, p. 5

276 MEC 19 February 1915, note 3

277 MEC 2 March 1915, note 2

278 MEC 2 March 1915, note 1

279 MEC 16 March 1915, note 2

280 Rowland Berkeley, Report to MEC, 18 May 1915

281 Rowland Berkeley, Report to MEC, 18 May 1915

282 Colin Simpson, *The Lusitania*, Boston: Little, Brown & Company, 1972, p. 105.

283 *New York Times*, 8 May 1915; the official manifest contained in the *Franklin D Roosevelt Presidential Archive* (available online at http://www.lusitania.net/deadlycargo.htm accessed 21 November 2020) is more difficult to interpret. Thanks to Mitch Peeke for his assistance.

284 Rowland Berkeley, Report to MEC, 18 May 1915

285 *Final Report*, p. 5

286 Rowland Berkeley, Report to MEC, 18 May 1915

287 *Final Report*, pp 4–5; though sale of brass strip at the end of the scheme helped offset some of the risk, there Fund made a loss on this transaction of £2980 7s 3d. It was deemed to be worth the risk.

288 *Final Report*, p. 6; the sale of surplus brass netted £3,187 19s 6d, *Receipts and Payments Account*, 30 June 1919.

289 MEC, 26 January 1915, note 1; this was retained by the Princess as a significant part of the collections at Harewood House, where it sits today. The gilt version is now housed in a fine brown kid case, and its fine blue leather case is also present, blocked in gold. Thanks to Rebecca Burton, Curator, HHT.

CHAPTER 6

290 As described in the next chapter, Indian 'Camp Followers' were the only recipients not to be given the brass gift box

291 See for example, Stanley Weintraub *Silent Night. The Remarkable Christmas Truce of 1914*. London: Simon & Schuster, 2014, p. 11.

292 *Gloucestershire Echo*, 4 November 1914

293 *Minutes of the General Committee* [MGC], 14 October 1914

294 *Minutes of the Executive Committee* [MEC], 15 October 1914, note 8.

295 *Manchester Evening News*, 26 November 1914

296 MEC 22 December 1914, note 5

297 See Malcolm Brown & Shirley Seaton, *The Christmas Truce: The Western Front December 1914*, London: Leo Cooper & Secker & Warburg, 1984

298 National Army Museum, 134564; reproduced in many illustrated papers at the time, including, for example, the *Aberdeen Weekly Journal*, 8 January 1915.

299 Measured from an original specimen from the Great War Huts/Taff Gillingham collection. This box has an unused packing label attached, presumably added by the soldier to send his gift back.

300 These dimensions relate to the original boxes, designed to contain the whole gift; those destined for returning prisoners of war were less deep, see Chapter 9.

301 Private collection, http://www.trenchartofww1.co.uk/xmas_1914_tin_21.html accessed 4 December 2020

302 https://www.gracesguide.co.uk/1914_Who's_Who_in_Business:_Company_J, accessed 7 November 2020

303 MEC 17 November 1914, note 3

304 MEC 3 November 1914, note 6

305 *Call To Arms, The British Army 1914-18*, p. 469 (quoting TNA WO 293/1)

306 MEC 1 December 1914, note 3; the total number was actually 14,263, containing 903,328 cardboard boxes, *Final Report*, p. 8

307 Official Photograph series of men of the Army Veterinary Corps receiving their gifts; published in Sir John Hammerton (ed.) *The Great War...'I Was There!'*, vol. 1. London: Amalgamated Press [1938] p. 270

308 For example, see *Daily Record*, 19 December 1914, and *Aberdeen Weekly Journal*, 18 January 1915

309 Lady Kathleen Lindsay, Liddle Collection, University of Leeds Liddle/WW1/DF/076, https://explore.library.leeds.ac.uk/special-collections-explore/30736

310 The total number of items was 11,805,900; *Final Report*, p. 8

311 *Final Report*, p. 8

312 MEC 15 December 1914, note 1; Letter from The Gift Fund to SRD, and reply, 3 February 1916, IWM BO2 1/485

313 MEC [final minutes] 21 May 1919, note 4

314 MEC 12 January 1916, note 8

315 Princess Mary's Diary, 1914. Princess Mary's Archive, Harewood House Trust.

316 *The Sydney Stock and Station Journal* [Sydney, Australia], 12 March 1915

317 Captain S. McCance, *History of the Royal Munster Fusiliers 1861–1922*, Aldershot: Gale & Polden (For Private Circulation), 1927, p. 123

318 *History of the Royal Munster Fusiliers*, p. 126

319 *History of the Royal Munster Fusiliers*, p. 1113 et seq; 24-year-old Pte Meaney, killed in action on 27 August 1914, lies in Etreux British Cemetery.

320 *The Telegraph* [Brisbane, Australia], 14 April 1915; Duffy's regimental number, from his Medal Index Card at TNA, is actually 3567, and he landed in France on 8 September 1914.

321 One specimen in the author's collection, given to Sergeant James Parsons of the Coldstream Guards, was probably modified to have a lighter attached and no doubt contained tobacco

322 MEC 3 November 1914, note 7

323 MEC 17 November 1914, note 3

324 MEC, 17 November 1914, note 3

325 MEC 19 February 1915, note 2

326 MEC 24 November 1914, note 6

327 MEC, 22 December 1914, note 5

328 *Final Report*, p. 6

329 MEC 20 October 1914, note 1 'The secretary reported that...100 pipes and some tobacco had been presented'. MEC, 3 November 1914, note 1, 'Mr Lewis Coen had presented 100 pipes and 10,000 cigarettes...'. This pattern would continue.

330 MEC 20 October 1914, note 9

331 MEC 22 December 1914, note 2

332 MEC 19 February 1915, note 2

333 A rare, unopened, pack of cigarettes is illustrated in Evans, *The Christmas Tin*

334 John Broom, *A History of Cigarette and Trade Cards: The Magic Inside the Packet*. Barnsley: Pen & Sword, 2018

335 *Ibid*; Cyril Mazansky, *The First World War on Cigarette and Trade Cards: An Illustrated and Descriptive History*. Schiffer, 2015.

336 Example in Rich Smith collection

337 MEC, 22 December 1914, note 5

338 Henry Williamson, *A Fox Under My Cloak*, London: Faber & Faber, 2010 [first published 1955], p. 48.

339 *Ypres Diary*, p. 117

340 Chris Pollendine, *Campaign 1914*, London: Military Mode, 2013, p. 161, Pollendine speculates that these frames may have been 'one of the extra gifts provided to make up for the shortfall of tinder lighters', though there is no contemporary documentary evidence of this.

341 *Final Report*, p. 7.

342 MEC 27 October 1914, note 11

343 https://www.encyclopedia.com/social-sciences-and-law/economics-business-and-labor/businesses-and-occupations/de-la-rue-plc, accessed 6 November 2020

344 https://www.encyclopedia.com/social-sciences-and-law/economics-business-and-labor/businesses-and-occupations/de-la-rue-plc, accessed 6 November 2020

345 https://www.gracesguide.co.uk/1914_Who's_Who_in_Business:_Company_D, accessed 6 November 2020

346 MEC 3 November 1914, note 3

347 MEC 22 December 1914, note 5

348 Author's collection

349 *Final Report*, p. 7

350 *The People*, 8 November 1914

351 *Final Report*, p. 6

352 *Who's Who in Business* 1914, available at https://www.gracesguide.co.uk/1914_Who's_Who_in_Business:_Company_A, consulted 31 October 2020

353 Author's collection

354 F.C. Hentz Jr & G.G. Long, Lighter flint chemistry. *Journal of Chemical Education*, v. 53(10), p. 651.

355 There is a museum dedicated to Von Welsbach and his work; see http://www.auer-von-welsbach-museum.at/en/cer-en, accessed 31 October 2020

356 *Final Report*, p. 6

357 MEC, 1 December 1914, note 4

358 MEC, 1 December 1914, note 4

359 MEC, 1 December 1914, note 5

360 MEC, 15 December 1914, note 3

361 *Final Report*, p. 6

362 MEC, 15 December 1914, note 3

363 MEC, 22 December 1914, note 6

364 *The People*, 8 November 1914

365 MEC 15 December 1914, note 8, 'Gifts in substitution for tinder lighters'

366 MEC 22 December 1914, note 6, 'Assorted gifts'

367 MEC, 22 December 1914, note 6; the *Final Report*, p. 6, also indicates that 'purses' were also given, though these do not appear in Berkeley's original report to the Executive Committee.

368 Ron Flook, *British and Commonwealth Military Knives*, Charlottesville: Howell Press, 1999, p. 136; thanks to Paul Laidlaw.

369 On this authority, a specimen has been accessioned into the IWM collection, as an example of a gift fund knife despite not having any reliable provenance (IWM EPH 5448)

370 Author's collection

371 Obituary, *The Times*, 1 March 1928,

372 MEC 15 October 1914, note 3

373 MEC 25 November 1914, note 6; see also *Final Report*, p. 2

374 See https://www.iwm.org.uk/history/boy-1st-class-john-jack-travers-cornwell-vc, accessed 3 January 2021

375 MEC, 24 November 1914, note 3

376 MEC 26 January 1915, note 4

377 MEC 15 December 1914, note 8

378 MEC 22 December 1914, note 7.

379 *Illustrated War News*, 14 April 1915, p. 46

380 See http://www.trenchartofww1.co.uk/xmas_1914_tin_21.html accessed 4 December 2020; thanks to Steven Booth

381 MEC 26 January 1915, note 4

382 MEC 21 May 1919, note 2

383 See, for example, Terence J. Evans. *The Christmas Tin*

384 MEC, 27 October 1914, note 6.

385 MEC, 17 November 1914, note 3

386 The existence of marked pipes has entered 'collector's mythology', but no examples have been encountered; see Terence Evans, *The Christmas Tin*

3873 MEC 22 December 1914, note 6

388 MEC, 17 November 1914, note 3

389 MEC, 22 December 1914, note 6

390 For pipe styles, see bespokeunit.com/pipes/shapes/ accessed 26 June2020.

391 MEC, 20 October 1914, Note 2.

392 Rich Smith archive

CHAPTER 7

393 *Western Daily Press*, 15 February 1915

394 MEC, Report of the Secretary, 8 April 1915

395 Sir Julian C. Corbett, *History of the Great War Based on Official Documents. Naval Operations, Volume 1* Second Edition, London: Longmans, Green & Co, 1938.

396 MEC, Report of the Secretary, 8 April 1915

397 Letter from Seaman William Hartnell, HMS *Argyll*, 19 December 1914, author's archive

398 Author's collection

399 *The Complete Scrimgeour*, p.225

400 Quintin Colville, *The British Sailor of the First World War*, Oxford: Shire, 2015, p. 25.

401 Manuscript diary of PO Samuel George Hobbs RN, HMS *Glasgow*; courtesy of Ben Hodges, December 25, 1914

402 Manuscript diary of PO Samuel George Hobbs RN, HMS *Glasgow*; courtesy of Ben Hodges, June 8th, 1915

403 *Harrogate Herald*, 24 February 1915

404 *Portsmouth Evening News*, 11 January 1915

405 *Portsmouth Evening News*, 11 January 1915

406 Pte Frank Richards, *Old Soldiers Never Die*. Naval & Military Press, 2009, p. 65; see also Dunn, Capt. J.C. *The War the Infantry Knew*. London: Janes Publishing, 1987, p. 101 *et seq*.

407 J.M. Craster (ed.) *'Fifteen Rounds a Minute' The Grenadiers at War 1914*. London: Macmillan, 1976, p. 167

408 John Terraine (ed.) *General Jack's Diary 1914-1918*. London: Eyre & Spottiswoode, 1964, p. 88

409 Figures from *Statistics of the Military Effort of the British Empire*, p. 64 (i, ii); see also Chris Baker, *The Truce. The Day the War Stopped*. Stroud: Amberley, 2014, p. 27.

410 Author's Archive; Cutting pasted in contemporary scrapbook; account from 'EyeWitness', 28 December 1914, probably from the *Daily Telegraph*

411 *The Daily Express*, 4 January 1915; see also https://www.henrywilliamson.co.uk/hw-and-the-first-world-war/57-uncategorised/158-henry-williamson-and-the-christmas-truce, accessed 6 February 2021. Williamson also described the Truce in an article in the part-work *History of the First World War*, (1969) edited by Barry Pitt, v.2 (4), pp. 552-559.

412 Letter to Clive Wigram from General Rawlinson, Royal Archives https://www.royal.uk/first-world-war-royal-archives, accessed 13 February 2021, also quoted in Condell, p. 75; Field Marshal Sir John French's diary, in the IWM Archives, makes no mention of the gift, though he would have been eligible to receive one.

413 *Bedfordshire Times and Independent*, 8 January 1915

414 *Saturday Mail* [South Australia], 20 February 1915

415 *Western Chronicle*, 8 January 1915

416 https://harewood.org/about/blog/notes/a-christmas-legacy-continues/, accessed 16 January 2021

417 *Evening Despatch*, 8 January 1915; Letter from Pte W. Chambers (8680) "B" Coy, Worcesters, to his wife, Mrs. W. Chambers, 102 Tudor-street, Winson Green

418 Service Records, Pte William Chambers

419 *Bath and Weekly Gazette*, 14 August 1915

420 *Yorkshire Evening Post*, 23 January 1915

421 *Belfast News-letter*, 16 January 1915

422 *Northampton Mercury*, 12 March 1915

423 https://harewood.org/about/blog/notes/a-christmas-legacy-continues/, accessed 16 January 2021

424 *Shields Daily News*, 28 June 1915; *Illustrated Police News*, 1 July 1915. Confusingly, there are two Michael Brabstons who served with the 1st Irish Guards (regimental numbers 4693 and 4751), both of whom landed in France on 23 November 1914.

425 *Bendigo Advertiser* [Victoria, Australia], 29 June 1915

426 https://www.rct.uk/collection/themes/trails/king-george-vs-war-museum accessed 28 September 2020

427 Royal Collections Trust, Accession Number RCIN 69472

428 *Derbyshire Courier*, 21 August 1915 Pte Anselm George Hallam served with the 2nd Y&L Regiment and had landed in France on 9 September 1914; his older brother, Pte Thomas Edwin Hallam, of the 1st Y&L Regiment died of wounds on 9 May 1915. TNA, Medial Index Cards.

429 *The Burgoyne Diaries*, p. 38, entry for 30 December 1914

430 *Lincolnshire Chronicle*, 20 March 1915

CHAPTER 8

431 P.Pype, A. Cattrysse, B. De Smaele, H. Pieters & C. Crug, *Archeologisch onderzoek van Wereldoorlog I-erfgoed lands de Briekestraat te Ieper (prov. West-Vlaanderen). II. Opgraving*. Gent: ADEDE Arheologisch Rapport, 54, Gent.

432 M. Dewilde, N. Márquez-Grant & F. Wyffels *een onvolledig geruimd militair Kerkhof in de Ypres Salient. Een toevalsvondst in de Briekestraat te Ieper*. Onderzoeksrapporten Agentschap Onroerend Erfgoed, Brussel, 2015; thanks to Marc Dewilde and Sofie Vanhoutte

433 1903 pattern infantry equipment, and an experimental Mills-Burrowes entrenching tool holder; neither were in common usage by infantry of the period, though widespread in the Indian Army.

434 *Archeologisch onderzoek van Wereldoorlog I-erfgoed lands de Briekestraat te Ieper*, p. 76 *et seq*.; thanks to Simon Verdegem

435 'This 'tin' is filled with memories', *The Hindu*, 7 May 2016

436 *The Hindu*, 7 May 2016

437 Dr Irfan Malik, personal correspondence, 30 December 2020; the museum is run by Dr Malik's uncle, Riaz Malik.

438 J.W.B. Merewether & F. Smith, *The Indian Corps in France*, London: John Murray, 1917, p. viii.

439 *The Indian Corps in France*, p. ix

440 *The Indian Corps in France*, p. 10; Sir James *With the Indians in France*, p. 18 *et seq.*

441 *The Indian Corps in France*, pp. 10–11.

442 *The Indian Corps in France*, p. 26.

443 Letter from Captain Arthur Ion Fraser to Commander John Gordon Fraser, HMS *Shannon*, 3 January 1915. (Author's archive)

444 Private papers of Brigadier P. Mortimer, 25th December, half lb plum pudding from Daily News issued to every man – also King's and Queen Mary's Christmas Card', (IWM Documents 8674)

445 *The Daily Mirror*, 19 October 1914

446 War Office, *Our Indian Empire. A Short Review and Some Hints for the Use of Soldiers Proceeding to* India, London: HMSO, 1913, p. 33 *et seq*; *The Indian Corps in France*, p. 482 *et seq.*; *With the Indians in France*, pp. 56–59.

447 *The Indian Corps in France*, p. 482

448 *Our Indian Empire*, p. 52

449 MEC, 15 October 1914, note 8

450 Katherine Prior, Hewett, Sir John Prescott (1854–1941) *Oxford Dictionary of National Biography*, https://doi.org/10.1093/ref:odnb/33847 accessed 18 December 2020

451 Gordon Corrigan, *Sepoys in the Trenches. The Indian Corps on the Western Front 1914-15*. Staplehurst: Spellmount, 1999, p. 8

452 *Bismarck Daily Tribune* [Bismarck, North Dakota], 7 November 1914

453 *The Indian Corps in France*, p. 500

454 *The Indian Corps in France*, p. 503

455 *Birkenhead News*, 28 November 1914

456 MEC 20 October 1914, note 10

457 Sir Ratan Tata, London: *Encyclopedia Britannica*, 1922; the Tata Group was built by his father Jamsetji Tata, with steel being its principal concern.

458 MEC 27 October 1914, note 10

459 MEC 3 November 1914, note 5; MEC 10 November 1914, note 3; *Final Report*, p. 7, listed General Gaslee together with Col C.S. Wheeler [*sic*], Col. Ridgeway; Lt-Col. O.C. Bradford and Brevet-Col. N.A.K. Burn; C. Hayavadana Rao (ed.) *The Indian Biographical Dictionary*, Madras: Pillar & Co, 1915, pp. 154–55, 336, 362.

460 MEC 10 November 1914, note 3

461 *Bismarck Daily Tribune* [Bismarck, North Dakota], 7 November 1914; also *The Sunday Star* [Washington D.C.], 15 November 1914

462 MEC 24 November 1914, note 3

463 *Final Report*, p. 3

464 *Our Indian Empire*, pp. 84–87; In France alone, for the whole period of the war, i.e., not just 1914, there were 49,273 non-combatants, compared to 138,608 Indian combatant soldiers: *Statistics of the Military Effort of the British Empire*, p.777.

465 *Final Report*, p. 7; MEC 22 December 1914, note 5, gives the total as 39,400.

466 MEC, Report by Rowland Berkeley, 18 May 1915

467 Specimen in private collection

468 *Final Report*, p. 7

469 See Vinod Kumar, Seven spices of India–from kitchen to clinic, *Journal of Ethnic Foods*, v. 7, (23), 2020, doi.org/10.1186/s42779-020-00058-0

470 MEC 22 December 1914, note 5

471 *Final Report*, p. 7

472 MEC 22 December 1914, note 5; no surviving examples have been observed; *Final Report*, p. 7

473 *Final Report*, p. 7; the brass box certainly contains four ounces when packed alone.

474 Specimen in private collection

475 Unpublished Archaeological records, thanks to Marc Dewilde and Sofie Vanhoutte

476 *Sepoys in the Trenches*, p. 127.

477 Author's Archive; Cutting pasted in contemporary scrapbook; account from 'EyeWitness', 28 December 1914, probably from the *Daily Telegraph*

CHAPTER 9

478 Princess Mary's Diary, 1914. Princess Mary's Archive, Harewood House Trust.

479 Reeve, Smoking and cigarette consumption, https://encyclopedia.1914-1918-online.net/article/smoking_and_cigarette_consumption, accessed 27 December 2020; Henry Daniels, When the smoke cleared: tobacco supply and consumption by the British Expeditionary Force, 1914-1918. *Revue Française de Civilisation Britannique*, v. XX-1, 2015, https://doi.org/10.4000/rfcb.218

480 *The Sporting Times* dedicated a whole piece to the topic of smoking in railway carriages on 23 May 1914, stating that smokers outnumbered non-smokers by six to one.

481 Quoted in Reeve, Special Needs and Cheerful habits, *Journal of Social History Society*, v. 13, 2016

482 Sean O'Connell, review of Matthew Hilton, *Smoking in British Popular Culture 1800–2000*, Manchester: Manchester University Press, 2000; *Reviews in History,* https://reviews.history.ac.uk, accessed 29 December 2020;

483 Virginia Berridge, *Demons. Our Changing Attitudes to Alcohol, Tobacco & Drugs*. Oxford: Oxford University Press, 2013, pp. 53–4.

484 MEC 20 October 1914, note 2

485 MEC 27 October 1914, note 9

486 http://www.fairestforce.co.uk/14.html, accessed 25 October 2020

487 MEC 15 October 1914, note 4

488 A.L. Walker, *Experiences at a Base Hospital in France, 1914-15*, http://www.scarletfinders.co.uk/156.html, accessed 28 December 2020

489 A.L. Walker, *ibid*

490 Reports on various Army nursing services in France 1914-1918. The work of the Nursing Services with British Ambulance Trains and Station Units in France, 1914 TNA WO222/2134

491 MEC 27 October 1915, note 4

492 MEC, 15 October 1914, note 7

493 MEC, 24 November 1914, note 4

494 MEC, 24 November 1914, note 5

495 *Sheffield Daily Telegraph*, 28 December 1914

496 *Ypres Diary 1914-1915. The Memoirs of Sir Morgan Crofton,* p. 117.

497 MEC, 22 December 1914, p. 5; the total cost was £862 10s.

498 This is in line with the identified proportion of 'two non-smokers to every fifty-six smokers'; MEC, 24 November 1914, note 4.

499 *Final Report*, p. 6; this report itemised the total number obtained as 18,048.

500 The Eagle Pencil Company was established in New York in 1859, and opened its London Branch in 1864. The Company was 'the largest of its kind in the world' by 1922, and was a contractor to HM Stationery Office. https://www.gracesguide.co.uk/Eagle_Pencil_Co, accessed 29 December 2020

501 Taff Gillingham/Great War Huts Collection

502 *Ypres Diary 1914-1915. The Memoirs of Sir Morgan Crofton*, p.117.

503 *Final Report*, p. 7

504 *Ypres Diary 1914-1915, Ibid*

505 Private Collection, thanks to Ben Sandford, who estimates that this may have amounted to something like 48 individual tablets if 'polo mint sized' and stacked two deep; e-mail correspondence 29 August 2020; see also the example in the National Army Museum (NAM 1998-06-131-1)

506 Anonymous [attributed to Kate Luard], *Diary of a Nursing Sister on the Western Front, 1914-15*. London; William Blackwood, 1915, entry 23rd December 1914; these may not have been acid drops as supplied by the Gift Fund given the date.

507 R.E. Elliot, '*Destructive but Sweet': Cigarette Smoking Among Women, 1890-1990*, Unpublished PhD Thesis, University of Glasgow, 2001, pp 52, 153 *et seq.*

508 *Final Report*, p. 3

509 *Statistics of the Military Effort of the British Empire During the Great War, 1914-1920*, pp. 192-3; 2783 were members of the TFNS

510 MEC, 24 November 1914, note 5

511 War Diary, Headquarters Branches and Services, Matron-in-Chief, TNA WO 95/3988/2

512 *Final Report*, p. 4.

513 MEC 22 December 1914, note 5; *Final Report* specifies 1585 packets (p. 7)

514 https://www.gracesguide.co.uk/James_Pascall, accessed 15 February, 2021

515 *Final Report*, p. 7

516 Example in Great War Huts/Taff Gillingham Collection

517 'With the exception of Havre', War Diary, Headquarters Branches and Services,

Matron-in-Chief, TNA WO 95/3988/2; 23 December 1914.

518 Anonymous [attributed to Kate Luard], *Diary of a Nursing Sister on the Western Front, 1914-15.* London; William Blackwood, 1915, 26th December 1914.

519 War Diary, Headquarters Branches and Services, Matron-in-Chief, TNA WO 95/3988/2

520 MEC 2 March 1915, note 3

521 MEC 16 March 1915, note 4

522 *Princess Mary*, p. 97

523 See Robin Neillands, *The Old Contemptibles. The British Expeditionary Force, 1914.* London: John Murray, 2004

524 *Statistics of the Military Effort of the British Empire 1914-1920*, p. 258

525 Aubrey Herbert, *Mons, Anzac & Kut.* London: Hutchinson, 1919, pp. 72-3, 81

526 An Exchanged Officer [Malcolm Vivian Hay], *Wounded and a Prisoner of War*, Edinburgh: William Blackwood, 1916, p. 64

527 MEC, 17 November 1914, note 4; some 1500 men of the 1st Royal Naval Brigade crossed over into neutral Netherlands in October 1914, and were interned there.

528 MEC, 8 December 1914, note 3

529 *Diary of a Nursing Sister on the Western Front, 1914-15*, 25th December 1914

530 *Final Report*, p. 4

531 *Sheffield Daily Telegraph*, 28 December 1914

532 Author's archive

533 Captain Roly Grimshaw, *Indian Cavalry Officer 1914-15*, Tunbridge Wells: Costello, 1986, p59

534 *Cornishman*, 17 December 1914; *Liverpool Echo*, 21 December 1914

535 Author's collection; see also *Campaign 1914*, p. 162

536 *The Telegraph*, 22 October 2018, https://www.telegraph.co.uk/food-and-drink/cadbury-heritage/ww1-angels/, accessed 1 January 2021

537 *Manchester Guardian*, 24 December 1914

538 War Diary, Headquarters Branches and Services. Matron in Chief WO 95/3988/2, 22 December 1914

539 Letter from Sir Henry Streathfield to Sir Edward Wallington, 4 November 1914, IWM BO2 1/4

540 Chris Pollendine has speculated that this gift was given to serving soldiers of the Household Division, but no contemporary evidence of this has so far been identified, see *Campaign 1914*, p. 165

541 *The Birmingham Daily Post*, 28 December 1914; also reported nationally in *The Scotsman* and the *Aberdeen Press and Journal* on the same day

542 Contemporary press cuttings scrapbook; cutting presumed to be from *The Daily Telegraph*, December 1914

543 *Gloucestershire Echo*, 26 December 1914

544 Author's collection; see Chris Pollendine, *Campaign 1915*, London: Military Mode Publishing, 2015, p. 254.

545 *Campaign, 1915*, p. 254

546 The *Final Report* comments: 'It being impractical to make any distribution to prisoners of war on Christmas Day, 1914…', p. 10

547 MEC, 8 December 1914, note 1

548 *Statistics of the Military Effort of the British Empire*, p.253; *Final Report*, p. 4

549 *Belfast News-Letter*, 24 December 1914

550 *Aberdeen Evening Express*, 23 February 1915

551 MEC, 28 July 1916, note 7

552 *Final Report*, p. 10

553 IWM BO 2 1/22 Letter from Rowland Berkeley, 17 December 1918

554 IWM BO 2 1/11 –328 'Prisoners of War Lists of those qualifying for the Gift, or who are dead'

555 Author's collection; full gift with letter, Lt-Col Lamond to Mr F. Angrave, 24 June 1920

556 MEC, 21 May 1919, note 4

557 MEC, 21 May 1919, note 4

558 *Final Report*, p. 10

559 *Manchester Evening News*, 26 November 1914

560 MEC, 8 December 1914, note 3

561 MEC, 15 December 1914, note 6

562 MEC, 26 January 1915, note 4; also *Final Report*, p. 2

563 *Sheffield Evening Telegraph*, 19 January 1915

564 Example illustrated by Pollendine, *Campaign 1915*, p. 251

565 *Hamilton Advertiser*, 23 January 1915

566 *Final Report*, p. 3

CHAPTER 10

567 MEC, 26 January 1915, note 5

568 MEC, 26 January 1915, note 4; Report to MEC, 8 April 1915

569 MEC, 26 January 1915, note 2 'receipts had gradually fallen to £15 to £20 per day'

570 MGC, 24 November 1914, note 1

571 MEC, 10 November 1914, note 4

572 *The Mercury* [Hobart, Tasmania], 5 June 1915

573 MEC, 1 December 1914, note 1

574 MEC, 22 December 1914, note 3

575 MEC 5 January, note 3

576 The *Final Report* (p. 2) classified these groups as Class B 'all British and Colonial Troops Serving outside of the British Isles (exclusive of those provided for in Class A)' and Class C 'all troops serving in the British Isles'

577 Peter Doyle & Chris Foster, *Kitchener's Mob, The New Army to the Somme, 1916*. Stroud, History Press, 2016.

578 See Peter Doyle & Chris Foster, *Kitchener's Mob. The New Army to the Somme*, Stroud: The History Press, 2016, p.22 *et seq.*

579 *Statistics of the Military Effort of the British Empire*, p. 30

580 *Call To Arms. The British Army 1914-18*, p. 68 *et seq.*

581 *Call To Arms. The British Army 1914-18*, pp. 72-73; Mark Lloyd, *The London Scottish in the Great War*, Barnsley: Leo Cooper, 2001, p. 29 *et seq.*

582 K.W. Mitchinson, *England's Last Hope. The Territorial Force, 1908-14*.Basingstoke: Palgrave Macmillan, 2008, p. 191 *et seq.*

583 *Liverpool Daily Post*, 12 December 1914

584 Trooper Percy Talley, City of London Yeomanry, 25 December 1914; Author's archive: Peter Doyle, *Rough Riders. Two Brothers and the Last Stand at Gallipoli*. Stroud: The History Press, 2015, p. 49.

585 C.E.W. Bean, *The Official History of Australia in the War of 1914–18. Volume 1. The Story of Anzac: The First Phase*. Angus & Robertson, Sydney, 1921, pp.8-9; G.W.L Nicholson, *Canadian Expeditionary Force 1914-1919. Official History of the Canadian Army in the First World War*. Montreal: McGill-Queen's University Press, 2015 [first published 1962], p. 5 *et seq.*

586 *Canadian Expeditionary Force 1914-1919*, p.7–18

587 *Canadian Expeditionary Force 1914-1919*, p.20; Sir Max Aitken, *Canada in Flanders*, London: Hodder and Stoughton, 1916, p. 2

588 According to Bean, Canada had promised an Expeditionary Force of 20,000, Australia the same; while New Zealand had pledged 8,000 from a much smaller population; *The Official History of Australia in the War of 1914–18*, p. 32.

589 *Final Report*, p. 4

590 MEC 5 January, note 3

591 MEC 16 March 1915, note 2

592 *Final Report*, p.5

593 MEC, Reports by Rowland Berkeley, 8 April 1915 & 30 August 1915

594 MEC, 5 January 1915, note 2

595 Author's Collection; *Final Report*, p. 7

596 MEC 22 December 1914, note 4 indicates that an extension to the original contract to De La Rue for the cards was 'without envelopes', and extrapolated, it makes sense that envelopes were not provided in the wider extension to the gift.

597 MEC, Report by Rowland Berkeley, 8 April 1915

598 *Final Report*, p. 7

599 Little has been written about this pencil; this is taken from surviving examples. There are a number of online resources, e.g. https://vintagepens.com/Omdurman_pencil.shtml. Other examples exist: a specimen survives in the collection of the National Army Museum, London: 'Pencil, 1898, made from a converted brass cartridge case and steel bullet, inscribed, 'THE BATTLE OF OMDURMAN Sept 2nd 1898', contained in a presentation box' Accession number 1971-01-29.

600 An article in the 'Omdurman Bullet' that appeared in the *Dundee Evening Telegraph* on 3 January 1899 demonstrated that the bullet, with a lead point covered in nickel has a hollow centre 2x9 mm, and had a 'stronger effect' than a dum-dum bullet.

601 Specimen in private collection

602 MEC, 5 January 1915, note 2

603 MEC, Report by Rowland Berkeley, 8 April 1915

604 *Final report*, p. 7

605 Original, untouched examples uncovered by Onslows Auctioneers in 2014

606 *Final Report*, p. 7
607 Author's observations from surviving examples
608 https://www.rct.uk/collection/themes/trails/king-george-vs-war-museum/rifle-cartridge, Accession Number RCIN 69490
609 See Pollendine, *Campaign 1915*, p. 251
610 Author's collection
611 *Final Report*, p. 2
612 *Final Report*, p. 8; An Official Photograph shows men of the ASC holding their boxes as distributed at home, fresh out of a bulk box. This is dated December 1914, but this caption is likely to be incorrect.
613 MEC, Report of Rowland Berkeley, 8 April 1915
614 MEC, Report of Rowland Berkeley, 18 May 1915
615 MEC, Report by Rowland Berkeley, 18 May 1915
616 *Final Report*, p. 8
617 Letter to Lady Kathleen Lindsay, IWM BO2 1/491, 23 August [1915]
618 MEC, Report by Rowland Berkeley, 8 April 1915
619 MEC, Report by Rowland Berkeley, 8 April 1915
620 *Final Report*, p. 9
621 *Final Report*, p. 9
622 MEC, Report by Rowland Berkeley, 30 August 1915
623 MEC, 12 January 1916, note 2; Sir James Goodhart was a senior consultant to Guy's Hospital, he died two months later. Obituary, Sir James Goodhart, *British Medical Journal*, 1916 (3), pp. 803-4
624 *Powlett Express and Victorian State Coalfields Advertiser* [Powlett, Vic., Australia], 31 December 1915
625 *The Mail* [Adelaide, South Australia], 18 March 1916
626 *The South-Eastern Times* [Millicent, South Australia], 8 June 1917
627 *Maryborough Chronicle, Wide Bay and Burdett Advertiser* [Qld, Australia] 21 February 1918
628 *Daily Examiner* [Grafton, NSW, Australia], 6 December 1917
629 *The Telegraph* [Brisbane, Qld, Australia], 29 November 1917; Pte Timothy Anthony Murphy, 1341, 4th Battalion AIF, was killed in action on 3 May 1915, and is commemorated on the Lone Pine Memorial at Gallipoli.
630 *The Broadford Courier* [Broadford, Vic., Australia] 21 December 1917
631 *Taranaki Daily News* [NZ], 15 December 1915
632 Example in Canadian War Museum, sent by children from Ontario in 1914, https://www.warmuseum.ca/collections/artifact/1048876/?q=christmas&page_num=2&item_num=12&media_irn=5193469, accessed 23 January 2021
633 *The Windsor Star* [Windsor, Ontario, Canada], 28 September 1915
634 *The Ottawa Citizen* [Ottawa, Ontario, Canada], 30 September 1915; the same message was repeated for Montreal; *The Gazette* [Montreal, Quebec, Canada], 30 September 1915.
635 *Final Report*, p. 4; a total of 552,848 troops across the Empire ('Class B') and 1,337,889 at Home ('Class C')
636 MEC, Report by Rowland Berkeley, 12 January 1916
637 MEC, Report by Rowland Berkeley, 30 August 1915
638 https://www.bbc.co.uk/news/uk-england-wiltshire-28224808 accessed June 2020; thanks also to Patrick Brogue, Onslows Auctioneers
639 Taff Gillingham recalls that such boxes were encountered by him in the basement of the Regimental museum of the Royal Anglian, a successor through amalgamation to regiments of the Great War.
640 Based on an image of the box label, with the printing information in the footer. Quoted with kind permission of Patrick Bogue, Onslows Auctioneers.
641 https://www.youtube.com/watch?v=5k6dMTzwfWo, accessed June 2020
642 Author's archive, card included within the box, dated August 1917.
643 Sample box and card, thanks to Paul Laidlaw, February 2020
644 Brig-Gen. F.C. Stanley, *The History of the 89th Brigade 1914-1918*. Liverpool: Daily Post, 1919, p. 27.
645 Richard Van Emden, *Missing*. Pen & Sword, Barnsley, 2020
646 *Mid Sussex Times*, 5 September 1916

647 MEC, 21 May 1919, note 1

648 *Lichfield Mercury*, 5 September 1919

649 *Dundee Courier*, 11 September 1919

650 *Derby Daily Telegraph*, 22 September 1919

651 *Final Report*, p. 11

652 MEC, 21 May 1919, note 6

653 MEC, 21 May 1919, note 6

654 MEC, 21 May 1919, note 8; *Final Report*, p. 12

CHAPTER 11

655 *Nottingham Journal*, 14 November 1936

656 *Final Report*, p. 4; *Receipts and Payments Account to 30 June 1919*

657 Elisabeth Basford, *A Quiet Devotion to Duty*, p. 14

658 *Princess Mary: The First Modern Princess*, p.260 *et seq.*

659 *King Edward VIII*, p. 48 *et seq*; *In the Eye of the Storm*, p. 131, *et seq*

660 *The Scotsman*, 7 December 1918

661 *Daily Record*, 13 December 1915

662 *The Times*, 7 December 1915

663 *Wigton Advertiser*, 1 January 1916; Pollendine, *Campaign 1915*, p. 254

664 Author's collection

665 https://www.rosl.uk/ww1/the-war-that-made-rosl, accessed 31 January 2021

666 *The Daily Telegraph*, 2 October 1916

667 Harrods Ltd 1915, in Alan Wakefield, *Christmas in the Trenches*, Stroud: Sutton, 2006, p. 39.

668 *Berwickshire News and General Advertiser*, 31 August 1915

669 Pollendine, *Campaign 1915*, pp 252–3

670 Tout-Smith, D. 2003. Australian Comforts Fund, World War I in Museums Victoria Collections https://collections.museumsvictoria.com.au/articles/1848, accessed 07 March 2021

671 *Coventry Evening Telegraph*, 22 November 1915

672 *Whitby Gazette,* 16 November 1917

673 Letter, Coy Sgt-Maj. Gundry to the Gift Fund, 14 January 1918, Author's archive

674 https://operationchristmasbox.org/who-we-are/ accessed 31 January 2021

675 *Operation Christmas Box, 2020*; the included Christmas card in this gift makes a direct link 'The first box was produced in 1914 and was the idea of King George V's daughter, Princess Mary…In 2004 the idea was revived…', thanks to Charles Wookey, Operation Christmas Box.

676 https://operationchristmasbox.org/what-we-do/why-was-the-charity-formed/, accessed 11 January 2021

677 https://operationchristmasbox.org/who-we-are/ accessed 31 January 2021

678 https://www.gov.uk/government/news/uk4u-thanks-christmas-box-campaign-launched, accessed 10 January 2021

679 Interview with Sergeant David Currant, RAF, 17 December 2020

680 In addition to that the *The Daily Mail* produced, which could be applied for through the newspaper.

681 Interview with Dr Andrea Tanner, Fortnum & Mason, 19 January 2021.

682 'Tommy's Tin Overview', manuscript supplied by Dr Andrea Tanner, 19 January 2021.

683 Tommy's Tin Overview', manuscript supplied by Dr Andrea Tanner, 19 January 2021; https://harewood.org/about/blog/notes/a-christmas-legacy-continues/; https://managingbusinessarchives.co.uk/news/2015/01/tommys-tin/, accessed 11 January 2021

684 Anna Perchal, designer of 'Tommy's Tin', text of e-mail to author, 20 January 2021

685 Tommy's Tin Overview', manuscript supplied by Dr Andrea Tanner, 19 January 2021

686 Interview with Sergeant David Currant, RAF, 17 December 2020

687 Communication, Squadron Leader Stuart Roxburgh, RAF, 31 January 2021

688 Interview with Sergeant David Currant, RAF, 17 December 2020

Index

Picture Credits

All images are courtesy of the author, with the following exceptions:
Alex Churchill: **p.21**; Andrea Tanner/ Fortnum & Mason: **pp.283, 285**; Anna Perchal/ Fortnum & Mason: **p.284**; 20020070-90, Canadian War Museum: **p.171**; Ch. Vijaya Bhaskar/*The Hindu*: **p.179** Charles Wookey/Operation Christmas Box: **pp.280, 281**; City of Vancouver Archives: **p.27**; Earl and Countess of Harewood, and the Harewood Trust: **p.115**; Franky Wyffles/Flemish Heritage Agency: **pp.178, 179, 186, 193**; Q053478, Imperial War Museum: **p.241**; Library of Congress: **pp.9, 10, 11, 13, 15, 24, 37, 68, 177, 210, 212, 223, 235, 237, 270**; Meerut Division: **p.181**; 134609, National Army Museum, London: **p.87**; 134564, National Army Museum, London: **p.120**; 92007, National Army Museum, London: **p.206**; NPG x 46548, National Portrait Gallery: **p.55**; Onslows Auctioneers: **pp.250, 260, 261**; Rich Smith Collection: **pp.132, 136**; Roger Fenton/Library of Congress: **p.35**; RCIN69472, Royal Collection Trust/© Her Majesty Queen Elizabeth II 2020: **p.175**; Taff Gillingham/Great War Huts Collection: **pp.43, 84, 89, 121, 130, 135, 138, 150, 155, 168, 203, 204, 208, 271**.

This edition first published in the UK by Uniform
an imprint of Unicorn Publishing Group LLP, 2021
5 Newburgh Street,
London
W1F 7RG

www.unicornpublishing.org

10 9 8 7 6 5 4 3 2

ISBN 978-1-913491-53-6

Design by Felicity Price-Smith and Vivian Head
Cover design by Matt Wilson

Printed in Turkey by Fine Tone Ltd